ETHICS IN THE
CONFUCIAN TRADITION

American Academy of Religion
Academy Series

edited by
Susan Thistlethwaite

Number 70
ETHICS IN THE CONFUCIAN TRADITION
The Thought of Mencius and Wang Yang-ming

by
Philip J. Ivanhoe

Philip J. Ivanhoe

ETHICS IN THE
CONFUCIAN TRADITION
The Thought of Mencius
and Wang Yang-ming

Scholars Press
Atlanta, Georgia

ETHICS IN THE CONFUCIAN TRADITION
The Thought of Mencius and Wang Yang-ming

by
Philip J. Ivanhoe

© 1990
The American Academy of Religion

Library of Congress Cataloging in Publication Data

Ivanhoe, P.J.
    Ethics in the Confucian tradition / by Philip J. Ivanhoe.
    p. cm. -- (American Academy of Religion academy series ; no.
70)
    Includes bibliographical references.
    ISBN 1-55540-450-2. -- ISBN 1-55540-451-0 (pbk.)
    1. Confucian ethics. 2. Mencius--Contributions in Confucian
ethics. 3. Wang, Yang-ming, 1472-1529--Contributions in Confucian
ethics. I. Title. II. Series.
BJ117.I83 1990
170'.92'251--dc20   90-33176
                                                     CIP

Printed in the United States of America
on acid-free paper
∞

In Memory of
Anna Carson
1908-1985

Abbreviations and Conventions

Abbreviations:

1)	*BOAS*	Bulletin of the School of Oriental and African Studies
2)	*HNCSYS*	Ho-nan Ch'eng-shih yi-shu
3)	*HYIS*	Harvard-Yenching Institute Sinological Index Series
4)	*MJHA*	Ming-ju hsüeh-an
5)	*SPPY*	Ssu-pu pei-yao
6)	*SPTK*	Ssu-pu ts'ung-k'an
7)	*TSD*	Taishō Shinshū Daizōkyō
8)	*WWCKCS*	Wang Wen-ch'eng-kung ch'üan-shu
9)	*YMCS*	Yang-ming ch'üan-shu
10)	*YMGTK*	Yōmeigaku taikei
11)	*YMHSCY*	Yang-ming hsien-sheng chi-yao

Conventions

1) CITATIONS FROM THE CH'UAN-HSI LU:

The majority of citations of Wang's writings are from his best known work, the *Ch'uan-hsi lu*. There are two English translations of this work: an early translation of an abridged version of the text by Frederick Goodrich Henke: *The Philosophy of Wang Yang-ming*, (reprint) (New York: Paragon Book Corporation, 1964) and a complete translation by Professor Wing-tsit Chan: *Instructions for Practical Living and other Neo-Confucian Writings by Wang Yang-ming*. (New York: Columbia University Press, 1963). In order to bring out, with greater clarity, the philosophical issues raised in this study I have provided my own translations of all passages from Wang's works. In this effort, I have been aided tremendously by the pioneering work of these two scholars, especially the fine and careful work of Professor Chan. In order to allow the reader to consult Professor Chan's translations, all citations from the *Ch'uan-hsi lu* are keyed to the section numbers he used in his translation.

The third appendix is a finding list which correlates Professor Chan's section numbers with the *Ssu-pu ts'ung-k'an* edition of Wang's complete works: *Wang Wen-ch'eng-kung ch'üan-shu* (Taipei, 1965).

For example, the reference for the first quote of Wang's works in chapter one is:

Chan, *Instructions*, section 276.

This directs the reader to pages 222-223 of Professor Chan's translation. For those who wish to examine the Chinese text, the appendix provides the location of this section in the *WWCKCS* (see below for the format of the Chinese citations).

2) CITATION OF CHINESE SOURCES:

a. In the case of the *WWCKCS*, citations provide:

chüan number / page number of the 1965 Taipei edition / upper (a) or lower (b) section

Example: WWCKCS 26:156a = chüan 26, page 156, upper section

Note: If no chüan number is given, this indicates the passage is included among the prefaces to this work.

b. In all other cases, citations provide:

chüan number / shang (A) or hsia (B) (if such division exists) /
page within the chüan / recto (a) or verso (b)

Examples: MJHA 14:5a = chüan 14, page 5, recto
HNCSYS 2A:4b = chüan 2, shang, page 4 verso

3) MULTIPLE CITATIONS:

After its first citation, further citations of a given work are shortened,
providing the minimum amount of information necessary to identify the
source. These shortened citations always include the author's surname and the
first word of the full title, in order to facilitate easy identification in the
bibliography.

> *Example:* Wing-tsit Chan, (trans.), *Instructions for Practical Living
> and other Neo-Confucian Writings of Wang Yang-ming*,
> (New York: Columbia University Press, 1963.)

> *Becomes:* Chan, *Instructions*

4) CITATIONS OF THE *HYIS*:

Citations of volumes in this series provide the name of the text to which a
concordance has been made, the number of that concordance in the series, the
page(s) in the text, the book and chapter within the text (if the text is subdivided
into chapters) and the section or line(s) (depending on the pagination) within
the text.

> *Example: Mencius (HYIS* #17: 44/6A/7)

This reference is to a passage in the *Mencius (Harvard-Yenching Institute
Sinological Index Series* Supplement no. 17). The passage in question is
section 7, chapter A of book 6, and it is on page 44 of the Harvard-Yenching
text.

5) TRANSLATIONS:

Unless otherwise noted, all translations are my own.

Table of Contents

Chapter V: Sagehood

Appendices

Notes

Works Cited

Index

Introduction

Wang Yang-ming (1472-1529) was a man of many means: a man who repeatedly faced great personal and professional challenges, at times suffered terribly and almost always managed to triumph. He had a successful career as a government official: surviving an unjust public flogging and banishment to Kueichow and eventually rising to become governor of Kiang-hsi province.[1] He was a general who commanded a series of important anti-rebel campaigns in south and central China and played a major role in the suppression of the revolt by Prince Ning in the summer of 1518—an accomplishment for which he never received due credit.[2]

Wang studied many Ways—Buddhist, Confucian and Taoist—and after years of deep introspection and worldly struggle, he came to the conviction that Confucianism was the one true path. He became a teacher of the Confucian way but a teacher who did not want his teachings written down and passed on, a teacher who expressed his thought more often in poetry and parables than in essays, who wanted to counsel individuals not construct philosophical systems. He was the most influential moral teacher of his day.

Wang was the object of great controversy both during his lifetime [3] and after his death.[4] His teaching greatly influenced the development of Confucian thought in Korea and Japan.[5] In Japan, he is still carefully studied and deeply appreciated.[6]

Wang's accomplishments were numerous and diverse; many today would find it difficult to imagine how he could unite them all within a single lifetime: how a man who felt distressed to see plants trampled under foot or tiles wantonly destroyed[7] could—without hesitation or regret—order the immediate decapitation of any soldier under his command who disturbed so much as a blade of grass without the proper authorization.[8] But to see the many facets of Wang's life as tense dichotomies in need of resolution is to see ourselves as Wang. For him there was no tension; all these actions flowed, calmly and in proper measure, from a single source: an innate spring of moral knowledge which lies within all human beings.

To understand how Wang could feel this way, we must understand how he saw himself and his world. We must realize that, being Confucian, he saw both almost exclusively in moral terms. To understand him, we must understand his moral philosophy: his conception of virtue, human nature, self-cultivation and sagehood. But, in order to do this, we must first explore the moral thought of Mencius; for above all else Wang saw himself as a follower and defender of Mencius and his cause.[9] Wang saw himself related to Mencius in much the same way as Mencius saw himself related to Confucius: as a follower and defender—not a revisionist.[10] But understanding Mencius is the beginning—

1

not the end—of understanding Wang; their moral philosophies are related but quite distinct. Both thinkers changed the Confucian tradition fundamentally, but in very different ways.[11]

Mencius saw himself as a follower of Confucius and the defender of Confucianism against its rivals in his day: primarily the followers of Mo Tzu and Yang Chu.[12] In retrospect, we can see, in a way Mencius could not, how dramatically he reshaped Confucianism in the face of the challenges of his age, just as Confucius—despite his claim to the contrary—had created as he transmitted the Way of the ancient sage-kings.[13] In a curious way, by changing Confucian thought as they did, both Mencius and Wang were being true to the tradition begun by Confucius: a tradition that was so wedded to its idealized past that it did not perceive its own evolution. In order to understand Confucius, Mencius or Wang we need to know where they stood and what they faced as well as what they looked back to and how they saw themselves; we need to know their place in history as well as their view of history. When studying their works, we must at times read not only between the lines but behind them, in order to understand these thinkers clearly.

To understand Wang's moral philosophy, we must not only examine his beliefs concerning his intellectual heritage, we must explore the intellectual currents that were in force during his time—currents that moved him without his awareness of being moved. These not only provided challenges to the tradition he followed; they provided many of the categories through which he understood his own tradition. In Wang's case, the major influence—one that shaped his thought and sharply distinguishes it from Mencius'—was the highly sophisticated and widely acclaimed competitor: Buddhism.

Wang did not reject his Confucian heritage and "go over" to Buddhism, but he could not ignore Buddhism or remain untouched by its influence. He borrowed freely and knowingly from Buddhism, and in this respect he was more aware of its influence than most thinkers in the Neo-Confucian period. But Buddhist thought also affected him in ways he did not see, in ways one cannot fault him for not seeing. In Wang's time, Buddhist thought was part of the intellectual landscape in China; it had been a force in Chinese thought for almost 1500 years—at times dominating the intellectual scene—and had fundamentally changed the way Chinese thinkers thought about themselves and their world. Many of these changes had been in place for so long and were so well integrated with accepted historical interpretations, they were seen as fundamental categories in Chinese thought.[14] The notion that, throughout history, China absorbed foreigners and their ideas, sinicizing them in the process, is a half-truth, and the interplay between native Chinese intellectual traditions and Buddhism provides an opportunity to study both halves of the truth.[15] It is true that Buddhism was never the same after coming to China, but it is equally true that China was never the same after Buddhism had arrived.

In this work, I examine the moral philosophy of Wang Yang-ming in light of its relation to the moral philosophy of Mencius by exploring their respective views on a number of issues held in common and central to both thinkers' moral teachings. I pay particular attention to the ways in which Wang recasts Mencian moral teachings in terms characteristic of his time: how he shifts from a distinctively Mencian set of images to characteristically Buddhist images as metaphors for his thought. This shift in images is more than the retelling of an old tale in a new language. The images Wang relied upon came with their own assumptions; they led him in new directions and to different conclusions. Only by examining these images closely can we understand the nature and extent of the differences between Mencius and Wang.

I begin by describing, in the first part of chapter one, some of the ways in which Mencius transformed the teachings of his spiritual mentor, Confucius. Mencius saw himself as the legitimate heir to Confucius' legacy and the champion of the Confucian cause. But he faced new and formidable intellectual competitors, the followers of thinkers like Mo Tzu and Yang Chu. These competitors deeply influenced Mencius' thinking, both by defining the realm of discourse and providing certain key components of the debate. This scene was to be replayed, with a different cast and a new script, in Wang Yang-ming's time.

Wang thought of himself as a follower and defender of Mencius, and a comparison of their moral teachings reveals the breadth of Wang's Mencian heritage. But there is great philosophical as well as temporal distance between Mencius and Wang. Buddhism had entered China about four centuries after Mencius' death, and by Wang's time it had fundamentally changed the way Chinese thinkers thought about themselves and their world. Buddhist thought had challenged Confucian thinkers to answer a set of metaphysical questions that were never a part of Mencius' thinking. This resuled in a dramatic shift, in moral philosophy, from moralities based on claims about human nature to moralities grounded on comprehensive metaphysical theories. In this transition, both the range and form of moral thinking changed.

Wang looked back to the Mencius and other early texts for his inspiration, but he saw these texts differently. He was not fully aware of how much Chinese thought had changed since the time of Mencius, most importantly, how deeply Buddhism had influenced the way in which Chinese thinkers approached certain issues in moral philosophy. Wang saw Mencius through a Buddhist filter, and he transformed Mencius' moral philosophy as he sought to understand it, altered by this filter.

There are three appendices to this work. The first is a study of the historical evolution of the most important collection of Wang's teachings, the *Ch'uan-hsi lu*. In this appendix, I discuss not only the content and format changes the text underwent but the different opinions, regarding the nature and application of the text, professed by those who produced and circulated the various editions. The second appendix is an analysis of the meaning of the term *ch' uan-hsi* in the title *Ch' uan-hsi lu*. It contains a history of the interpretation of the title in Western languages and concludes by offering a new interpretation and translation. The third appendix is a finding list for citations from the *Ch' uan-hsi lu*. It correlates the section numbers in Professor Wing-tsit Chan's translation to the corresponding text in the Wang Wen-ch'eng-kung ch'üan-shu edition of the *Ch' uan-hsi lu*.

Chapter 1

The Nature of Morality:
Mencius

Confucius described the moral life in terms of a harmonious and happy family, a family whose different members contributed to the common welfare, each according to his or her role-specific obligations. These obligations were determined by one's position within the traditional family structure and were the primary and over-riding moral imperatives of life.

The traditional family served as the paradigm for the moral life, but the moral life did not end with family obligations. There were obligations to society as well: obligations modeled on the structure of the family. One had an obligation to king and state that paralleled, but never superseded, one's obligation to one's parents and family. Recognizing these obligations and fulfilling them—motivated by the sense that it is one's proper duty to do so—constituted *yi* (righteousness).

Social obligations exerted a powerful and persistent moral pull on individuals, but they always pulled out—away from the fundamental forces binding the family together.[1] The obligations to one's family were most important because, to Confucius, they were naturally the earliest and strongest bonds human beings form. They were also seen as the source of our social obligations; our obligations to others flowed out from and were modeled on the family. The moral life was a constellation of such obligations—a constellation defined by a set of rituals and social practices known as *li* (rites). These rituals and social practices secured for one a place within one's family and in society. They defined a system that was more than the best possible shape for society; they had transcendent value. They were the discovered structure of the way the world should be.

> Someone asked about the meaning of the Great Sacrifice. The master said, "I do not know. One who knew its meaning could govern the world as easily as looking at this!" (he pointed to his palm)[2]

A society based on *li* would be a peaceful and prosperous society because it followed the grand design laid down by Heaven. It was the right way to live one's life because it accorded with this design—not because of the benefits to be derived by such a life.[3]

But there was much more to the moral life than merely fulfilling certain obligations and following certain practices. Each of these actions had to be performed with sincerity: with the attitude appropriate for each occasion.

When performing a sacrifice, one was to feel reverence for the spirits; when carrying out the rites of mourning, one was to feel grief for the deceased. In serving his lord, a minister was to be respectful; in governing his people, a ruler was to be benevolent. Without this emotional component, according with ritual becomes a hollow performance. One's actions will not elicit the appropriate responses from others, and the social system will collapse.[4]

These internal aspects of the moral life also took the family as their paradigm. Parents are not just providers of food, clothing and lodging for their children, and good children do more than simply maintain their parents in old age.

> Tzu-yu asked about filial piety. The master said, "Nowadays, one who provides for (his parents) is called filial. But even dogs and horses are provided for. If there is no reverence—what is the difference?"[5]

There are attitudes that must accompany these actions, if they are to be considered genuine expressions of parental love and filial piety.

Comprehending any specific example of an appropriate action and accompanying attitude, was a general concern for all people. Just as a proper family member feels concern for each and every member of his family, the morally cultivated person feels a general concern—a feeling of *jen* (benevolence)—for every member of society, and this feeling informs his every action. He treats them as he himself would like to be treated, were they to change positions with each other.[6] To gauge one's obligations to others by measuring one's own feelings is the method of *jen* (benevolence). To fail to feel this concern for others is to fail to be fully human.[7]

The feeling of *jen* extends to all people, but the magnitude of concern diminishes as it moves outward from the family. Just as emanating concentric waves decrease in magnitude as they move further from their point of origin, the intensity of one's love decreases as it moves out beyond the family and down through society. The strongest feelings are originally and forever, those within the family. The virtues of *hsiao* (filial piety) and *ti* (respect for an elder brother) are the most profound examples of the feeling of *jen* and are the source from which one draws in extending this feeling as concern for others.

> Yu Tzu said, "It is rare indeed to find one who is filial to his parents and respectful to his elder brother who likes to disobey his superiors. And there has never been one who, not liking to disobey his superiors, liked to cause rebellion within the state. The gentleman works at the root. When the root is established, the Way flourishes. Filial piety and respect for one's elder brother—are these not the root of benevolence!"[8]

In the well-ordered state, society becomes the family, writ large. The king, as father to his people, must care for them and, as a proper parent, provide for them. The ruler must enrich his people—both materially and spiritually. The enlightened state is an extended family, providing for the needs of all its members while preserving a strict hierarchy in its structure. Most important of all, the enlightened state, like the ideal family, is permeated at every level with a deep concern for each of its members.

The moral life is the life lived cultivating oneself for participation in this enlightened state. But the commitment is never one of *enlightened self-interest*; participation in such a society affords one the unique opportunity of fulfilling one's *destiny* as a human being.[9] The relationships one enters into as a member of such a society are not restrictive; they are liberating and fulfilling.

Confucius believed there was only one way to live—the Way[10]—and that this Way had been discovered and put into practice by certain sage kings in the past. He believed in a mythological, utopian society: a golden age when the Way was practiced and the world prospered in peace. He desired to restore the ancient order, to put the world back together again, in peaceful, prosperous harmony.

Mencius followed Confucius in this general scheme of the moral life. But in Mencius' time, there were many who questioned Confucius' appeal to tradition and his version of the golden age. These competitors offered different versions of the past, and they provided an explicit account of the principles that had enabled society to attain such glory. They argued for their principles and their version of history; they rejected Confucius' picture of the past and demanded to know the rationale behind the Confucian vision.[11] These competitors offered explicit *yen* (doctrines) as standards for morality and, like the Confucians, they supported these with religious sanctions.[12]

Judging from what we know of the period, Confucians were losing ground to well-prepared and articulate competitors. It was Mencius who responded to their challenges and forever changed the face of Confucian thought. He was able to maintain the basic structure of Confucianism, but he reset its foundation. He preserved Confucius' traditionalism but grounded it in a new and persuasive vision of human nature and its relation to society.

Mencius argued that the ancient traditions and values Confucius cherished were not just the remnants of a by-gone age: they were a perfect expression of what we truly are. When we follow the way of the ancients, we are practicing to be what we, at our best, are meant to be. Mencius maintained that anyone can realize this for himself if he is willing to study and cultivate his own innate moral sensibilities. For we are all endowed with nascent moral sense, and if we nurture it, it will lead us to the Confucian Way. If we develop it fully, it serves as an infallible, internal standard—guiding us in the moral life.[13]

For Mencius, the Confucian Way was the one true way, and it was so by virtue of it being the manifestation of our Heavenly-endowed nature. At times Mencius seems to offer consequentialist grounds for his moral scheme. He claims following the Confucian way will result in a strong and wealthy kingdom—that it alone is the way to gain the empire, and that not to follow it will certainly lead to weakness and ruin.[14] He also seems to offer egoistic hedonistic grounds for choosing the Way. He insists that acting morally is one of the highest forms of pleasure, and that our more common types of pleasure can only be truly enjoyed by those who follow the way.[15] But these are only characteristics of the moral life, never his *reasons* for acting morally. A pleasant feeling accompanies moral action— this marks the moral life as natural and makes Mencian self-cultivation possible. And a moral state will become strong and wealthy—this enables morality to survive. These are signs that the universe is not indifferent to the course of human events: that we live in a morally-charged universe which favors those who are moral.[16]

Mencius provided a new rationale for this ideal society. He maintained that the traditional obligations, rituals and social practices were right, because they were the refined expression of what we truly are. They were grounded in our very nature, and to fulfill them was to accord with the design of Heaven. For Confucius, the structure and activities of the ideal society were like terrestrial constellations; they were Heavenly patterns that moved with the stately regularity of stars.[17] Mencius maintained this Heavenly sanction, he but lowered his gaze. He left the stars to Confucius and pointed to human nature as the guide for human action.

Following human nature did not deny individuals the enjoyment of pleasure, power or profit. But these were not to be ends in themselves. Mencius argued such things can only be truly enjoyed when they are shared by every member of society, when they are part of a full and proper human life.[18] This too was Heaven's decree: only by following the Way could one realize these lesser ends of wealth, pleasure and power.

But material benefits had no direct bearing on the issue of morality. Mencius eschewed using any notion of material well-being as a measure of moral value. He, like Confucius before him, often pointed out that the Way is not for the faint-hearted: it may lead to poverty, adversity and even death.[19] But still it must be followed, and it must be followed because it is right—not for some ulterior motive. Following the Way is its own reward. As Confucius once remarked: "If one could hear the Way in the morning, he could die by evening, feeling satisfied."[20]

Mencius drew a sharp distinction between *li* (profit) and *shan* (goodness) or *te* (virtue).[21] In so doing, he was following a precedent established by Confucius himself.[22] But Mencius drew this distinction more often, probably as a reaction to the challenges posed by his philosophical competitors. He drew it most clearly in his attacks on some of his most difficult adversaries: the followers of Yang Chu and Mo Tzu.

Mencius describes the thought of both Yang Chu and Mo Tzu in terms of *li* (benefit or profit). Yang Chu's principle was: "...everyone for himself. If he could *li* (benefit) the world by plucking out a single hair, he would not do so."[23] Mencius clearly was focusing in on Yang Chu's selfishness, but this should not obscure his fundamental point. His more telling criticism lies in his description of Yang Chu's thought as one which take *li* (benefit)—in Yang Chu's case personal benefit—as the measure of morality. This becomes clear when we consider Mencius' description of Mo Tzu, a man who could never justly be accused of selfishness: "Mo Tzu loved all impartially. If grinding off every hair on his body would *li* (benefit) the world, he would do it."[24] Mencius never criticized Mo Tzu for selfishness—it would have been a hard case to make—but he did criticize him together with Yang Chu. In Mencius' mind they had something significant in common.[25]

According to Mencius, one thing they had in common, was they were both popular alternatives to Confucianism. But the *Mencius* contains very few examples of Mencius debating the followers of Yang or Mo; they were not his only adversaries. Perhaps their true significance has been overlooked. They share a deeper and more important feature: a feature revealed when we notice Mencius described the positions of both thinkers in terms of *li* (benefit) and when we keep in mind how often he juxtaposed the notions of *benefit* and *what is right*.[26]

Mencius criticized Yang and Mo together because in his mind they both had made a similar kind of mistake: they had argued for moral judgments based upon calculations of *li* (benefit).[27] Yang and Mo represented the extremes of selfishness and altruism, but neither of these two extremes *per se* were objects of Mencius' criticism.[28] For Mencius, basing moral judgments on any notion of utility, is the worst example of a general type of error: a type he criticized in many forms. This more general objection to Yang and Mo is a theme which runs throughout Mencius' criticisms of his contemporaries, and tracing this theme throws into relief Mencius' notion of morality. It also provides a revealing point for comparison in my later discussion of Wang Yang-ming's notion of morality.

We see this common theme most clearly in Mencius' criticism of the philosopher Kao Tzu.[29] Mencius' long debate with Kao Tzu and his criticism of him earlier in the *Mencius* establish Kao Tzu as Mencius' primary opponent.[30] Mencius accused Kao Tzu of failing to understand *yi* (righteousness). Mencius believed our sense of right is an essential part of what we are—our nature—not something welded onto us from the outside, as Kao Tzu would have it. The obligations described by Confucian society are in no way ad hoc; they are the refined expression of human nature.

In book two,[31] Mencius attacked what we must assume was a well-known teaching of Kao Tzu's:

> What you do not get from *yen* (doctrine) do not seek for in your *hsin* (heart/mind).

Mencius offered this as evidence that Kao Tzu never really understood *yi* (righteousness). He objected to Kao Tzu's seeking to ground morality in a doctrine—something exterior to us—and thereby denying the internal standard of one's *hsin* (heart/mind). But this is a more general form of his argument against Yang and Mo. They tried to ground morality in different notions of *li* (benefit): one egoistic and the other altruistic. All three thinkers sought for moral sanctions outside of human nature, and this is why Mencius objected to their thought.

We see the same argument in Mencius' exchange with the Mohist I-chih.[32] I-chih had softened Mo Tzu's hard line volunterism and admitted that the Mohist goal of *chien ai* (impartial love) is attainable only by extending to all the love one naturally feels for one's parents. Mencius rejects this as an impossible goal—impossible because, by its own admission, it violates the natural order of one's feelings. Morality must follow this natural order if it is to be genuine. Morality flows from a single source—human nature—to seek for it in any other quarter is to search in vain and only leads one further from what one needs most. As Mencius said:

> "Heaven, in creating creatures, caused them to have but one root, but I-chih wants to have two" (i. e., a doctrine—Mohist utility—and the heart/mind).[33]

Mencius's attacks on Mo Tzu and Yang Chu are forms of this general distinction between *internally* and *externally* grounded moralities. Since Mencius maintained the *hsin* (heart/mind) was the source of traditional values and practices—that these values and practices were the outward manifestation of what we, by nature, truly are—any deviation from these values and practices was a denial or distortion of morality's true source. Any social scheme which relied upon a false standard for morality, would itself be false and unacceptable to Mencius. Underlying Mencius' criticisms of his contemporaries is this deeper criticism: all externally-grounded moralities violate the natural order—an order which is revealed by the well-cultivated *hsin* (heart/mind). We see this deeper criticism when we look carefully at Mencius' arguments.

For example, Mencius criticized Mo Tzu for advocating a way of life that is "without a father".[34] But Mo Tzu never advocated doing away with either parent. We must understand Mencius to mean: to live Mo Tzu's way of life is to be without a *father in the true sense*. He criticized Yang Chu, as one who is "without a sovereign." Again, we must understand Mencius to mean a *sovereign in the true sense*.[35] For Mencius, Confucianism was the unique solution; there could be no substantial variation on the classic themes.[36] Other ways of life could not accommodate the full development of our nature; they stunted or warped its natural growth. Following any Way other than the Confucian Way denied human nature the opportunity to develop and fulfill its potential. This violated Heaven's will; it prevented the world from being *as it should be*.

We also see this aspect of Mencius' thinking in his criticism of the agriculturalist, Hsü Hsing.[37] Hsü Hsing believed a sovereign should till the soil alongside his subjects and prepare his own meals each day, in addition to carrying out his governmental duties. Mencius responded to this position with an argument for the division of labor. But he did not support his argument solely on the greater *utility* afforded by the division of labor; he argued Hsü Hsing's Way violated the *natural diversity of abilities* among people. It is in the nature of people that they differ in ability, and those who "work with their *hsin* (heart/minds)" realize this.

> Some labor with their hearts/minds and some labor with their strength. Those who labor with their hearts/minds govern, and those who labor with their strength are governed. Those who are governed provide for those that govern them. Those who govern are provided for by those they govern. This is a principle that operates throughout the world.[38]

The structure of Confucian society is not arbitrary or based on some externally derived principle, like utility. It is based on universal principles that are manifestations of our very nature. It is true that a division of labor is more efficient, but this is a *result* of its being right—not a justification of it. It is right by being the Way, and it is the Way by being the refined expression of what we, by nature, truly are.

When Ch'en Hsiang, a follower of Hsü Hsing's doctrine, argues for the uniform pricing of goods, Mencius responds with a similar argument:

> It is the very nature of things to be of unequal value.[39] Some things are twice, five, ten, one hundred, one thousand or ten thousand times as valuable as others. If you make them all of equal value, you will bring chaos to the world. If large shoes cost the same as small ones, who would make them? To follow the Way of Master Hsü is to lead people to act falsely to one another. How could his Way serve to govern a state?[40]

Again—as in every case—Mencius argues that the Confucian Way is the right way because it is the refined expression of what we, by nature, truly are. Just as goods, by nature, have different values, people, by nature, have different functions—in the family and in society at large. The Confucian Way provides the structure within which one can find one's destined role and the means by which one can cultivate himself to fulfill that role. This Way is decreed by Heaven; it is our destiny to realize it. It is the sole source of morality and is revealed by developing the innate moral sense we have within us.

It may appear that Mencius' view of morality amounted to a strict and inviolable traditionalism: a way of life that could not accommodate exception or change. But Mencius saw himself as one who fought this kind of thinking. His scheme located morality within the human agent: it was not a slave to some external standard. It alone allowed for exceptional circumstances to influence moral judgments. It was not strictly a rule-following morality; it was a morality of refined moral intuition.

One of Mencius' specific objections to those who based morality on some external standard was that such systems cannot account for the exceptional circumstances that make moral judgments so difficult. One example is Mencius' criticism of a philosopher named Tzu-mo. We do not know much about Tzu-mo's thought except that he advocated a position "midway between that of Yang Chu and Mo Tzu." [41] But from Mencius' criticism of him we can see that he—like Yang and Mo—held invariably to his standard. And holding invariably to any external standard will lead one astray. As Mencius said, "The reason I hate holding invariably to a single standard is that it *tse tao* (steals from the Way): it holds up one point and abandons a hundred others." This is the fate of anyone who seeks to embody morality in a doctrine; anyone who neglects the internal standard of the *hsin* (heart/mind).

Mencius uses similar language in his assault on a type of person he calls the *hsiang yüan* (the paragon of the village).[42] From his description, we see he is attacking those people who are ever-seeking to maintain their reputation as *proper people*. People who measure every word and action to be sure that it is in complete agreement with what is accepted as "proper," and that it will cause no offense. He calls such individuals the *te chih tse* (thieves of virtue), and he does so for the same reason he gave in his criticism of Tzu-mo. Such people *steal from the Way* by taking a part of it—a specific practice or notion—and following that part to the exclusion of everything else. Their fundamental error is looking for a practice to call the Way and ignoring the true source of the Way—one's innate moral sense. They fail to nourish the moral capacity they have within them and instead follow part of its manifestation. As a result, they fail. They become—like the others Mencius criticized—bound by rules; they never become true moral agents in Mencius' eyes.[43]

For Mencius, morality was grounded in human nature. The moral life is the life lived nurturing the moral sprouts that are the most important aspect of our nature: the part of us that makes us unique among creatures. As I shall explain in the chapters ahead, these sprouts are nascent dispositions, not latent capacities. They are available and active aspects of every human being by nature. However, they are weak, undeveloped and can be damaged. Without our constant attention, our moral sprouts may wither and fade. And when they are in such a diminished state, we can lose sight of them completely, in the rush of worldly events.

But if we constantly nurture our moral sprouts, they will mature into strong and lively moral dispositions. We will become consummate moral agents. Guided by a heart/mind that is the mature expression of our nature, we will spontaneously seek out, recognize and follow the moral path.

In grounding Confucius' vision in human nature and focusing attention on the central role of the *hsin* (heart/mind), Mencius not only responded effectively to the challenges of his day, he planted seeds that would later blossom into what we now call Neo-Confucianism. But in defending Confucianism, Mencius changed it. Mencius' claim that, by nature, each person had within himself a potentially perfect moral guide, must have breathed new life into the traditionalism Confucius had advocated. It added a new and vital personal autonomy to the Confucian notion of morality. Mencius' morality was psychologically based; it raised the heart/mind to a pre-eminent position. The heart/mind's reactions, to a large extent, came to replace the *li* (rites) as the guide for moral conduct.

This brought the promise—and the threat—of change. It surely must have breathed fear into the hearts of many rulers when Mencius claimed it was the responsibility of a ruler's relatives to dethrone him if he proves to be a bad king[44] and permissible, in extreme cases, for a minister to put his lord to death.[45] The burden for judging when such extreme measures were warranted now rested—as it must—on individual shoulders.

This was surely a new and revolutionary addition to Confucianism. We can see it as a direct result of the shift from Confucius' notion of morality, a morality based on a Heavenly-ordained social structure, to Mencius' notion of morality, a morality grounded in human nature.

This shift extended the range as well as the form of moral obligations. For example, Confucius never talked about our moral concerns extending beyond the human realm. In fact, he appears to have displayed a certain disregard for the lives of our fellow creatures.[46] Confucius might have admitted we all have *some* feelings for animals, but to him these feelings were not morally significant. Animals were significant only when they fulfilled a ritual need: as sacrifices, for food or as draft animals.

Since Mencius grounded his moral theory on the reactions of our heart/minds, he saw new dimensions to morality. Our feelings of distress for the suffering of animals, was, for Mencius, evidence for the existence of an innate moral sense. Such feelings took on new significance; they could serve as the beginning of the moral life.[47] Mencius describes precisely how our feelings for other creatures fit into a hierarchy of compassion.

> The superior man feels concern for creatures, but he is not benevolent to them. He is benevolent to the people but he does not love them. He loves his parents, is benevolent to the people and feels concern for creatures.[48]

This hierarchy does not violate Confucius' original vision, but Mencius has transformed and extended the vision. It is not wholly different, but it is no longer what it once was. This type of transformation continued throughout the tradition—as it does in every living tradition. We see an example of a more dramatic transformation—but a transformation that still preserves the vision—when we compare Mencius' notion of morality with Wang Yang-ming's.

The Nature of Morality:
Wang Yang-ming

Wang Yang-ming remained true to many aspects of the early Confucian notion of morality. He shared the utopian vision of a benevolent, hierarchical society in which all members worked together for the common good and found fulfillment in their individual contributions. But Wang's ideal society was quite different from Mencius' notion of society as a *great family*. Wang occasionally invoked the image of the family to describe the harmony of his ideal society, but this was not his central image.[49] Wang wanted more than a great family: he wanted to embrace the entire universe in his utopia: to *form one body with Heaven, Earth and all things*.[50]

For Wang, this was not just an ideal we might reach. The universe was actually united in this way. The nourishment we receive from plants and animals and the curative power of certain herbs and minerals was, for Wang, *evidence* of this underlying unity.[51] The universe was united in a fundamental and important way, and realizing this unity was the only way to bring peace and prosperity to the world; it was the basis of Wang's notion of morality.

Wang's utopian society is Confucian in its general structure, but it is predicated on metaphysical notions that were not part of Mencius' world. Wang's ideal society rests upon a different foundation, and this changed the traditional Confucian social model in important respects. It also altered the shape of traditional moral notions. In order to understand Wang's views concerning the nature of morality, we must examine carefully his utopian social model and the metaphysical foundation upon which it stood.

The early Confucian moral order, a society which modeled itself on the family, had been preserved by Mencius. He grounded the system in human nature by arguing that the structure of the family and of society were the developed manifestations of what we as human beings truly are. Though Mencius believed human nature was ordained by Heaven, his was very much a human-centered morality.[52]

Wang left much of this behind. He followed a way of thinking whose beginnings can be traced at least as far back as the Sung dynasty: to thinkers such as Shao Yung (1011-77),[53] Chou Tun-i (1017-73), Chang Tsai (1020-77), Ch'eng Hao (1032-85) and Ch'eng Yi (1033-1107). Wang inherited, from these thinkers and from the great Chu Hsi (1130-1200), a different view of the morally-ordered universe.[54] He saw the universe as a vast, integrated system ordered by *li* (principles). These principles gave shape—both physical and moral shape—to the universe; they found expression in every aspect of existence.

Confucius had appealed to tradition as support for his utopian vision, and Mencius grounded this tradition in human nature. But Wang, like other Neo-Confucians, offered a morality based upon a comprehensive metaphysical theory. Neo-Confucians had sought to defend their tradition in the language of their time, and under Buddhist influence, metaphysics had become the language of their time. Neo-Confucians not only developed an interest in metaphysics, they embraced the metaphysically-oriented methodology of Buddhism. They argued that an understanding of *reality* would lead to the confirmation of Confucian *values*, that their values were true because they represented the way the world truly is.

Wang's notion of principle was totally unknown to Confucius and Mencius.[55] For Wang, as for other Neo-Confucians, the concept was of paramount importance.[56] Principle was the universal organizer. But the shape it gave to the universe was not achieved through law; principle did not stand apart from the universe and decree its structure.[57] Principle played a role in the structure of the cosmos not unlike the role of DNA in biology. But there is one critical difference: the shape principle gave had moral as well as physical dimensions.

There was a happy compromise between freedom and necessity in following principle: one could transgress principle in a way one cannot transgress natural law. But going against principle placed the cosmos in tension, and in time its many aspects will conspire to undo the transgressor.[58]

The concept of principle comprehended many notions characteristic of early Confucian moral thinking. *Yi* (righteousness), *li* (rites), *hsiao* (filial piety) and *jen* (benevolence) all came to be viewed as specific expressions of principle. But principle accounted for more than the social realm—it explained both human form and human function, how long we lived as well as how we lived. It comprehended the animal, vegetable and mineral realms as well, ordered these realms and united them. It brought together the silkworm, the scholar and the stars, assigned them their respective functions and showed how they should work together to maintain a harmonious cosmos.

Wang no longer saw society as the family writ large. He no longer needed the structure of family relationships and the natural feelings of love between family members as an ultimate basis for his utopian vision or his moral notions. These were subsumed under the more comprehensive notion of *li*. Wang saw the universe unified, at every level, by principles, and he constructed his utopian society and his moral system upon this vision of unity.[59]

Wang saw the universe in terms of this new category, and this altered his perception of the old Confucian world. He no longer sought merely to mold the people of the world into a great family; he wanted to bring the entire universe together as a single body. Wang, of course, would insist that I say something like "realize that the universe *is united in this fashion*." For to him, this was the true state of affairs, and I only fail *to see* that this is so.[60]

The clearest and most complete statement of Wang's utopian vision can be found in his essay *Pulling Up the Root and Stopping Up the Source.*[61] There he describes how we are *to form one body with Heaven, Earth and all things* and how this is not just an ideal we should strive for; it is the true state of the universe. Wang retained a belief in the prior existence of a utopian society, and in this essay he describes life during the mythological golden age: when sages ruled the world and his utopian vision had been a reality. By looking carefully at certain aspects of his description, we can see how his utopian society differed from early Confucian visions.

Wang did not describe the people of his ideal society as individual members of a great family. In his vision, they became the parts of a single body: without independent existence, *being* only in relation to the other parts.[62] He retained the hierarchy of the early Confucian *great family*, but he expressed it in terms of the relative importance of different parts of a single body. There was still a Confucian hierarchy within this *great body*, and the arrangement of its elements followed the pattern established by principle.

> I asked, "The great man is one (lit. *forms one body*) with all things. Why then does the *Great Learning* say that there is a *relative importance* among things?"
>
> The teacher said, "Because of principle, there is naturally a *relative importance*. Take for example the body, which is one. We use the hands and the feet to protect the head and eyes, but does that mean we are prejudiced and treat the hands and feet as less important? We do this because it accords with principle."[63]

Wang believed principle extended throughout the universe and that it gives the universe both its physical and moral shape. *Hsin chih pen t'i* (The mind in itself)[64] is identical with *t'ien li* (Heavenly principle), and in its conscious aspect it is *liang chih* (pure knowing). Principle is the universal organizer and orderer. It extends throughout the universe, gives the universe its shape and texture, orders its tempo and in its conscious aspect—pure knowing—is aware of its work.

The mind in itself is not something which stands apart from the universe and observes it impassively. It "has no substance of its own,"[65] and yet it is an integral aspect of all existence. It is the clear, conscious aspect of the universe. It is clear, in the sense that it is without "obscuration"—it contains no trace of "selfish thoughts." And, as pure knowing, it is the conscious aspect of Heavenly principle: it is aware of *how things should be.*[66] Like a mirror, none of its images are its own.[67] When it is functioning freely, it accurately "reflects" every situation it encounters. The mirror metaphor may mislead us in one important respect: unlike a mirror, the mind in itself is not a passive receiver of images. Its "reflections" entail responding to each situation in the appropriate manner. But in an important way the mirror metaphor succeeds. The mind in itself *is passive* in the sense that none of its responses are its own. When it responds to a situation, it does so in accordance with Heavenly principle—not according to *its own* decisions.[68]

Wang was an idealist and a monist but both in his own unique fashion. He supported the Berkeleian notion that our knowledge of things is restricted to our perception of them, but his idealism was not a reduction of reality to mental events. Wang saw a single, unified source for the physical and moral structure of the universe—Heavenly principle—but he did not reduce the universe to this sole constituent. Wang's metaphysics closely resembles the general metaphysical system seen among Mahāyāna Buddhists.[69] They saw consciousness as the ordering principle of the world-as-perceived, but they did not deny the independent existence of the elements that composed this world.

Wang's metaphysics differed from the Buddhists in significant respects. Most importantly, for Wang, Heavenly principle described the physical and moral structure of a reality that was Confucian in nature. Pure knowing was an awareness of the truth of Confucian values: a truth all human beings inherently understand.

> The *relative importance* spoken of in the *Great Learning* is the natural order of *liang chih* (pure knowing). Not transgressing this order is called *yi* (righteousness). Following this order is called *li* (rites). Knowing this order is called *chih* (wisdom). Affirming this order, from beginning to end, is called *hsin* (faithfulness).[70]

Without principle, the universe would have no shape at all,[71] and without the conscious aspect of this principle, our pure knowing, its shape would not be known.[72] Without Heavenly-principle the universe would have neither form nor meaning.

The mind-in-itself is the conscious aspect of the physical and moral structure of the cosmos. It extends throughout the universe. It is not only transpersonal; it unites everything in the universe.[73] Because the mind extends throughout the universe, human beings are able to understand everything within it—at least *how everything should be*. Individual minds are instances of this universal mind, and in becoming aware of this they come to know their true form.[74] Here we see the intimate relationship between Wang's metaphysics and his ethics. We also see how his metaphysical views led him to describe the task of self-cultivation as a process of *discovery* rather than one of *development*.[75]

Wang's discussion of the alternation of day and night—how we understand it and why we follow this alternation with our states of sleeping and waking—is a wonderful example of how Wang weaves together empirical observations about the world and uses these to support his moral assertions.[76]

A student asserts—as an objection to Wang's claim that pure knowing is always aware of principle—that when we sleep, pure knowing is *unconscious*. But Wang shows that in "gathering itself together in a period of inactivity" during the night, pure knowing is not unconscious; it is, on the contrary, following Heavenly principle.

Wang argues that the alternation of light and dark, heat and coolness, describes periods of activity and inactivity; this is Heavenly principle. It is manifested in the alternation of the day and night, the yin and yang forces, the waxing and waning of the moon and the cycle of the seasons. The fact that it manifests itself throughout the universe "proves" that *Heaven, Earth and all things form one body*. The mind understands these different manifestations and the principle that unites them, and it naturally follows this alternating pattern of activity and inactivity. The properly cultivated mind accurately "reflects" the situation and responds by sleeping and waking in accordance with the pattern manifested in the world. Following this pattern accords with Heavenly principle; this is the world *as it should be*.

Wang asserts that his account of the phenomenon of sleep shows how the mind naturally knows Heavenly principle. According to Wang, we are not only *capable* of arriving at an understanding of how the world should be, we *already know*. Complete and perfect knowledge is inherent in the human mind; we fail to know only in not being aware of what we know. He explains our failure to know by invoking the well-known distinction between the *tao hsin* (mind of the Way) and the *jen hsin* (human mind) described in *The Counsels of the Great Yü* chapter of the *Shu Ching*.[77] Wang distinguished between *hsin chih pen t' i* (the mind in itself)—the mind of complete and perfect moral knowledge—and *jen hsin* (the human mind)—the mind in itself "obscured" by selfish human desires. The human mind is the mind of the Way covered over with obscuring selfish desires. Once these are removed, the mind in itself naturally operates as an infallible moral guide.[78]

Wang's concept of the mind has important consequences for his understanding of traditional moral notions; it is the source of his belief in the underlying unity of the universe. This belief, in turn, is the basis for his utopian vision and the foundation of his conception of the nature of morality. The morally cultivated person *forms one body with Heaven, Earth and all things*— he feels their pain as his pain—and this is only because they are all aspects of the universal mind.

Ch'eng Hao first developed the notion that the morally cultivated individual feels the suffering of the world as pain in his own body; he *regards all things in the universe as one body*. He presents this idea as part of his explanation of a passage in the *Analects*.[79] It was undoubtedly a great influence on Wang and is worth reproducing here:

> In medical books, a paralyzed arm or leg is said to be unfeeling (not *jen*).
> This expression is perfect for describing the situation. The benevolent
> person—(one who is *jen*)—regards all things in the universe as one
> body—there is nothing which is not (a part of) him. If he regards all things
> as (parts of) himself, where will (his feelings) not extend? But if he does
> not see them as (parts of) himself, why would he feel any concern for
> them? It is like the case of a paralyzed arm or leg: the life-force (*ch'i*)
> does not circulate through them and so they are not regarded as part of
> one's self. Therefore, *widely conferring benefits and helping the masses
> is the task of the sage.*[80] Benevolence is extremely difficult to describe,
> so Confucius said only that "one desires to be established and so
> establishes others; one wishes to advance and so advances others. To be
> able to draw the analogy from oneself can be called the art of
> benevolence."[81] Confucius wanted to lead us to see benevolence in this
> manner, in order for us to be able to attain benevolence itself.[82]

This view of benevolence is the logical extension of Wang's metaphysical
scheme. The feeling of benevolence extends to all creation *because* the mind
extends throughout the universe. To form one body with Heaven, Earth and
all things is to realize *the way things really are*. Those who don't feel this
unbounded connection, who feel no compassion for a world in pain, are like
a person with paralyzed limbs who cannot feel an injury inflicted upon his
hands or feet. He *is in pain*, but he simply *is not aware* of his true condition.[83]

Wang believed that human beings can become insensitive to the underlying
bonds that unite all creation, but they can never become completely numb.
They will always feel a tinge of shame for conduct that does not accord with
Heavenly principle. If you call a thief "a thief" to his face, he will blush—or
so Wang believed.[84]

In the previous chapter, we saw how Mencius extended the range of morality
when he shifted from Confucius' tradition-based morality to a morality based upon
the spontaneous reactions of the *hsin* (heart/mind). We see Wang took this process
several steps further, when we examine the scope of his notion of morality. Wang
argued that our feeling of concern extended down to plants, tiles and stones, that
benevolence extended to every corner of the cosmos.[85] This is consistent with his
argument for the basis of our benevolent feelings: that they reflect the universe's
underlying unity. But such a notion is completely alien to Mencius.[86]

Wang based his morality on the underlying unity of the universe. For him,
any injustice committed is a wrong against him, any disorder a disease he
suffers and any injury a pain in his own body.[87] This unites the tasks of personal
and worldly salvation in a fascinating way. It clearly is derived from Mahāyāna
Buddhist notions about the role of the Bodhisattva, an influence that was felt
throughout Neo-Confucianism.[88] We see this influence in early Neo-Confucian thinkers. For example, the Bodhisattva-like concern expressed by Fan

Chung-yen's description of the morally cultivated individual as one who, "worries before the whole world has worried and takes pleasure only after the whole world has taken pleasure" or the all-embracing utopian vision Chang Tsai expressed in his famous *Western Inscription*.[89] It also, to some degree, incorporates the Heavenly perspective of Taoism—a perspective that saw *all things as equal*.[90] This new metaphysical perspective added new dimensions to traditional Confucian morality.

Because Wang sought to form one body with Heaven, Earth and all things, his notion of morality became all-inclusive. The morally cultivated person felt distressed to see flowers trampled under foot or bricks and tiles wantonly destroyed.[91] It is not that he feels hurt to see them damaged—we might imagine Mencius agreeing to that—he feels the hurt as a personal injury: an attack on his own body.[92]

For Wang, moral perfection involved a loss of self—the loss of oneself as a person apart from other people and a loss of oneself as a being distinct from things. With Wang, the moral life became the realization of one's identity with all existence: one's sense of self expanded to embrace all reality. He defined the task of moral self-cultivation as the elimination of obstacles preventing this identification. Wang turned to the notion of selfishness—thoughts that drew a "false" distinction between oneself and others—as the object for attack. He argued that, by eliminating selfish thoughts, one preserves the Heavenly principle that is the mind in itself, and one realizes the goal of *forming one body with Heaven, Earth and all things*.[93]

Wang thought he was following Mencius. He argued that his attack on selfish thought continued the work Mencius had begun.[94] There is an apparent resemblance between Wang's assault on selfishness and Mencius' attack on profit. But I will show that this similarity has no solid basis, and that Wang failed to understand the motivation for Mencius' attack on the notion of profit.

As we saw in the previous chapter, Mencius attacked the notion of profit because it was *an external standard for morality*. It was the standard advocated by some of his most formidable opponents: the followers of Yang Chu and Mo Tzu. Of these two schools, the Mohists presented the greater threat. They were a highly organized and carefully articulated movement. And they offered a social order that purported to be *more benevolent* than the one offered by Confucians.

Mo Tzu argued that one should follow that course of action which results in the greatest material good for all with preference for none; he called this the practice of *chien ai* (impartial love). Mo Tzu argued that this was true benevolence and that the Confucian notion of benevolence, which was based upon a special regard for the members of one's own family, was divisive and misguided.[95]

Mo Tzu's doctrine of *impartial love* fascinated and confused Neo-Confucian thinkers. They failed to understand Mencius' refutation of the Mohist position because they had lost sight of Mencius' notions of morality and self-cultivation. They had shifted from Mencius' psychologically-based morality, which was grounded in a view of human nature, to a metaphysically-based morality, which was grounded in a belief in universal unity. This made Neo-Confucian descriptions of their ideal society difficult to distinguish from Mo Tzu's vision of the ideal state. According to Neo-Confucians, individuals were related to each other, and to everything in the universe, in an intimate and fundamental way. The elimination of selfishness, the force separating individuals from joining with the universe, became the task of moral self-cultivation.

The universal concern characteristic of Neo-Confucian thought made a rejection of Mo Tzu's notion of *impartial love* increasingly difficult. Criticism of Mo Tzu began to break down, and as prominent a Confucian as Han Yü (768-824) maintained that there was no essential difference between Mo Tzu and Confucius. Han Yü said:

> Confucians deride Mo Tzu for *identifying with one's superiors, loving impartially, honoring the worthy and explaining ghosts*.[96] But Confucius (taught) *to stand in awe of great men*,[97] and *when residing in a state one should not contradict its high ministers*.[98] The *Ch'un-ch'iu* casts blame upon tyrannical ministers[99]—Is this not *identifying with one's superiors*? Confucius (taught) overflowing with kindness (to all) and loving the benevolent.[100] He believed *extensively conferring benefits and helping the masses constitutes sagehood*[101]—Is this not *loving impartially*? Confucius *honored the worthy*.[102] He taught four courses of study to promote and reward his disciples,[103] and he taught them that they should be *anxious about dying and not having their names passed on*[104]—Is this not *honoring the worthy*?
>
> Confucius *sacrificed as if the spirits were present* and derided those who *sacrificed without participating in the sacrifice*.[105] He said, "I sacrifice and receive blessing."[106]—Is this not *explaining ghosts*?
>
> Both Confucians and Mohists affirmed Yao and Shun and condemned Chieh and Chou. They both cultivated the self and rectified the mind in order to bring order to the nations of the world. Why is this not a cause for mutual celebration? I believe that the dispute began in the later stages of these two schools. The ways of these two teachers were not originally (at odds) like this. Confucius must have made use of Mo Tzu's (teachings) and Mo Tzu must have made use of Confucius' (teachings). Had they not mutually used each other's (teachings), they would not have been Confucius and Mo Tzu.[107]

When Neo-Confucianism blossomed, during the Sung dynasty, Han Yü's statement came under criticism. But it was extremely mild criticism given the fact that these thinkers all took Mencius as their guiding light. When asked to comment on Han Yü's essay, Ch'eng Yi said:

> The intent of this essay is extremely good. But (Han Yü) was not sufficiently rigorous in what he said, and as a result, there are some errors.

> Moreover, Mencius said that Mo Tzu loved his elder brother's child no more than he loved his neighbor's child. But where in the text does Mo Tzu ever say anything like this?[108] Mencius was "pulling up the root and stopping up the source"[109] knowing that in the end it (Mo Tzu's teachings) would come to this. Any scholar, in his study of the way, can make a minute mistake that leads to a monumental error. Yang Chu originally studied *yi* (righteousness), and Mo Tzu originally studied *jen* (benevolence). But because what they studied was slightly prejudiced; they ended up *without a father and without a lord.*[110] Mencius wanted to rectify their basic principles; he knew they would end up like this.

> Han Yü like to select the best in people; we can say he was *chung* (loyal) and *shu* (altruistic). But in his support of teachings, he did not know how to be rigorous and so he erred to the point of saying things like "Confucious taught *identifying with one's superior* and *impartial love* just the same as Mo Tzu." This is truly inadmissible.

> Later-day students are not even equal to Yang and Mo. Yang and Mo originally studied *jen* (benevolence) and *yi* (righteousness). Later-day students do not (even) study these. But the faults of Yang and Mo were pointed out by Mencius. Later-day people have no one to point out (their errors), and so they do not see their own faults.[111]

Even with the most tortured interpretive contortions, Neo-Confucians could not ignore Mencius' utter rejection of Mo Tzu's position. But because their own positions were so close to Mo Tzu's notion of *impartial love*, they could not attack him too harshly without implicating themselves. In their writings, we see a domestication of Mencius' criticism of Mo Tzu. They don't deny that Mo Tzu was wrong, but they say his thought did little damage to the Way, especially in comparison to the damage done by the Buddhists. Ch'eng Yi had the following to say:

> The damage done by Yang Chu and Mo Tzu has already disappeared, while the damage done by Taoism is in the final analysis slight. Today, there is only Buddhism. It is discussed by everyone and is spreading every where. The harm it does is without end.[112]

> ...as things are today, even if there were several men each as great as Mencius, they would still be helpless. If we look at Mencius' time,

we see the damage done by Yang Chu and Mo Tzu was not great.
Compared with the situation today it was insignificant...[113]

In one of his most important works—his *Cheng-meng* (Correcting Youthful
Ignorance)—Chang Tsai went so far as to use Mo Tzu's term: *chien ai*
(impartial love),[114] and his *Western Inscription* —one of the most important
works of Neo-Confucianism—resembles Mo Tzu's thought in its advocacy of
a universal concern for all creation. Neo-Confucians came to regard Mo Tzu
as a thinker whose heart was in the right place; he simply "went too far". His
system wasn't bad *per se*: it just wouldn't work. Ch'eng Hao said:

> The good and evil in the world are all according to Heavenly principle.
> What is called evil is not fundamentally evil. Evil comes about only
> by going too far or failing to go far enough, as is the case with Yang
> and Mo.[115]

Neo-Confucians failed to understand both the gravity and the nature of
Mencius' criticism of Mo Tzu. For Mencius, Mo Tzu's thought failed utterly; it
was not *moral philosophy* at all.[116] Mo Tzu's theory defined morality on the
external standard of utility. It was not based upon human nature, and for this reason
Mencius felt it was something reprehensible.

Wang too failed to see this aspect of Mencius' criticism because he did not
understand Mencius' critique of morality. Wang did not see that Mencius
rejected every moral theory which sought to base morality on any standard
other than human nature. Wang condemned externally-grounded morality, but
he did not see the implications of Mencius' criticism—especially for his own
view on the nature of morality.[117]

Wang begins his discussion of Mo Tzu[118] by asserting that benevolence is "the
principle of unceasing production and reproduction," and "there is no place it does
not exist." It is woven into the very fabric of the universe; we have only lost sight
of its pattern. Benevolence grows naturally as the yang force begins to grow in the
dead of winter and as trees sprout and grow to maturity. Wang argues, because Mo
Tzu did not ground morality on the natural feelings of affection human beings
have for their parents, his notion of benevolence has not "root" or "starting point."
It will fail to develop and achieve the end Mo Tzu desired.[119] But it is interesting
to note the similarity between Wang's position and the revised Mohism that I-chih
presented as his counter-argument to Mencius.[120] I-chih accepted Mencius' point
concerning the natural feelings one has for parents and agrees that these are the
starting point of benevolence. But he argued one must build out from these natural
feelings. One must employ the Mohist doctrine of *chien ai* (impartial love) and
transform these feelings into a universal concern.

Wang's position appears to be quite similar to I-chih's, though his motivation for holding it was admittedly quite different. Wang grounded morality on
a metaphysical theory concerning the underlying unity of the universe. He

made Mencius-like appeals to our natural feelings—appeals I-chih accepted to a certain extent—but for Wang these were *evidence* for his metaphysical theory. It seems as if Wang too sought to ground morality in "two roots" (our innate moral feelings and a metaphysical theory). But Wang avoided this problem and in an interesting way. Wang's metaphysical theory not only yielded a Mencius-like view of human nature, it supported this view with a comprehensive argument linking human nature to the nature of the universe. For Wang, the mind was coextensive with the universe; there was nothing "outside" the mind. He offered not two roots, but a new and deeper root for Confucian morality.

The Nature of Morality:
Conclusion

Mencius retained much of Confucius' original vision of the moral life. For him, the moral society was still the family writ large; the family was the center and source of one's moral life. But Mencius offered new justification for Confucius' traditional vision. He grounded Confucius' system of *li* (ritual) in human nature itself: morality was the development of nascent *sprouts* that were part of our very nature. This new rationale for Confucian morality added new dimensions to the earlier vision, but the vision was intact and essentially unchanged.

Mencius vigorously attacked all attempts to ground morality in an external standard. No *yen* (doctrine) could ever replace the properly cultivated *hsin* (heart/mind) as one's guide to moral action. Especially pernicious were those doctrines which purported to determine what was right by measuring what was most *li* (profitable). And this criticism applied equally to the most altruistic (Mo Tzu and his followers) as well as to unabashedly selfish (Yang Chu and his followers) thinkers.

Wang had a very different notion of the nature of morality. He saw a universe united by *li* (principle), and principle gave the world both its form and its meaning. Wang believed the human mind itself was principle, and the mind's *liang chih* (pure knowing) was principle in its active, knowing aspect. The universe was defined by principle and the human mind was endowed with an innate ability to know exactly how the various parts of the universe should fit together; it was the sole source of moral knowledge.

Wang's new vision extended both the range and the quality of Mencius' notion of the nature of morality. The concern of Wang's new Confucian sage extended beyond anything Mencius had ever conceived. Wang's moral paragon was to see the entire universe as his body or, more precisely, see himself as part of the universal body. His great challenge was to eliminate the selfish thoughts that separated him from this universal embrace. And this embrace not only reached out to every human being; every animal, plant, tile and stone within his view became suitable objects of concern.

Wang attacked any philosophy which challenged his belief in an innate, perfect and fully-formed moral mind. He believed any philosophy which failed to embrace this view led to one of two errors. The first, characteristic of Buddhists and Taoists, was to search for the moral mind apart from the ordinary world. Because the mind itself was principle, it could never be found apart from the things in the world. Such a view turned one away from the world. It led to a forced and unnatural effort to still the mind and ended in the morally inert contemplation of emptiness. The second error, characteristic of Kao Tzu and the Ch'eng-Chu school, was to search for principles outside the mind. But because the mind was principle, such a search was futile. It only led one farther and farther away from what one needed most: the moral mind.

In the following chapters, I discuss some of the ways in which Mencius' moral vision was transformed by Wang. Mencius' view of our moral nature— as fragile sprouts that needed care and nourishment—became the view that people possess a fully developed moral sense. Evil came to be seen as a defilement of our naturally pure and perfect nature, rather than a failure to cultivate our nascent moral tendencies. Mencius' dislike of profit—a disdain for a false moral standard—was transformed into an obsession to eliminate all selfish thoughts. And the process of self-cultivation was changed from one of nurture and development to one of discovery and enlightenment.

The forces that shaped this transformation were many and diverse. But the differences in the view of Mencius and Wang concerning the nature of morality—the movement from a morality grounded in human nature to a morality grounded in metaphysics—was the theoretical change that most affected these other aspects of their moral philosophy.

Chapter 2

Human Nature:
Mencius

Mencius is renowned for advocating the theory that human nature is good. But exactly what his theory describes is a matter less well-known; arguably it is something widely appreciated but rarely understood.

Contrary to popular opinion, a belief in the goodness of human nature historically has not been characteristic of Chinese thought. From the time of Mencius until the resurrection of his theory by Ch'eng Yi in the eleventh century, almost no thinker in China advocated any version of the theory that human nature is good.[1] And there is little reason to believe such a theory was proposed prior to Mencius' statement of it.

As A. C. Graham has shown, Mencius formulated his theory of the goodness of human nature in response to a variety of contending theories, and these competitors deeply influenced Mencius' thinking.[2] In what follows, I focus my efforts on describing the important features of Mencius' theory—especially those features that distinguish it from Wang Yang-ming's later interpretation of Mencius. I explain Mencius' theory of human nature by describing three critical claims the theory entails: claims regarding human nature's *content, structure* and *proper course of development.*

An accurate picture of human nature must be comprehensive; it must account for every aspect of human behavior—the weak and subtle as well as the strong and manifest. It must especially be able to explain what might be described as "primitive behavior"—behavior that is basic to human beings and which cannot be explained in terms of other aspects of our nature. Such behavior is a most important clue to human nature. Our most obvious and dramatic appetites and instincts—such as hunger, a desire for sex and a sense of self-preservation—are examples of such behavior. But there are also subtle and less evident examples which reveal other aspects of human nature—such as a child's love for its parents or the feeling of alarm and concern one would experience if one were suddenly to see a child in imminent danger.[3] These characteristics have equal claim as parts of human nature and perhaps are of greater significance in the quest for human self-understanding. Mencius argued it is only these subtle and less obvious aspects of our nature that distinguish us from other animals; they reveal moral tendencies which are part of our constitution. Mencius supported this position by seeking for examples of these aspects of human nature in the inclinations of childhood and in certain spontaneous actions of adults.

29

According to Mencius, human beings begin life endowed with nascent moral "sprouts." These innate moral tendencies are active aspects of our nature, yet they do not exhaustively describe the moral nature of human beings. These "sprouts" are the beginning of morality; like all "sprouts," they require a period of growth in order to reach maturity. Mencius identifies four moral sprouts as essential parts of human nature:

> ...From this we see that the heart/mind of commiseration, the heart/mind of shame, the heart/mind of complaisance the heart/mind of judging right and wrong are essential to man.
>
> The heart/mind of commiseration is the sprout of benevolence, the heart/mind of shame is the sprout of righteousness, the heart/mind of complaisance is the sprout of propriety, and the heart/mind of judging right and wrong is the sprout of knowledge.
>
> Human beings have these four sprouts just as they have four limbs....[4]

In addition to using the metaphor of "sprouts," Mencius refers to these nascent moral tendencies in human nature as our *liang hsin* (innate heart/mind) or our *pen hsin* (fundamental heart/mind).[5] He also refers to them as our *ch'ih tzu chih hsin* (child's heart/mind).[6] These alternative names for the moral sense imply that it is part of our nature and yet an undeveloped part—something that is just a beginning.

The metaphor of the *child's heart/mind* must not be interpreted as a call to act childishly. It is possible to misconstrue Mencius' *child's heart/mind* as a call to revert to childhood—a position characteristic of works such as the *Tao-te ching*.[7] Mencius' metaphor describes something quite different. He points to childhood as an ideal state in which to observe the "sprouts" of human nature—not as the paradigm of human nature in its developed form. Mencius' point is that, in the pristine state of childhood, we can see clearly the early stages of our development—some of what we are meant to be.

In terms of a metaphor Mencius might have accepted, we can know something about human nature by observing it in its nascent stages of development just as we can know something about a seed planted in a garden by observing the sprouts as they first break through the soil. In neither case are we observing the adult form. We cannot see certain aspects of the mature person in the child any more than we can see every aspect of the mature plant in its sprout. The sprouts are evidence that morality is part of human nature and an indication of how we should develop.

Throughout our life, our moral "sprouts" are constantly springing up—even if we fail to cultivate them.[8] In certain contexts, in unguarded moments, they break through our accumulated bad habits and manifest themselves in spontaneous moral actions. Such actions escape the attention of most of us, because we have not learned to analyze these actions correctly. But they are "giveaways;" they reveal deeper aspects of our nature. And if a morally cultivated individual points them out to us and guides our understanding of them, we are able to recognize the innate, spontaneous moral inclinations that motivate such actions.[9]

Mencius also employs a kind of "testimonial argument" for the existence of a moral sense. He himself bears witness to his preference for righteousness over life itself. And he goes on to say such a preference is not his alone—others *have* chosen to die rather than violate righteousness. The existence of cases of supererogation are evidence of an innate moral sense, evidence that this moral sense—*shih hsin* (this mind)—is part of human nature.[10]

Mencius also supports his claim about innate moral tendencies by proposing hypothetical scenarios which illustrate the universal presence of moral feelings in human beings. His description of someone suddenly seeing a child about to fall into a well[11] is the best known example of this type of hypothetical scenario. Such "thought experiments"[12] lead one to affirm that benevolent feelings are a part of every person's nature. Contemplating such scenarios leads one to feel one's cohumanity with others and, like all of Mencius' cases, they elicit moral feelings in the person entertaining them.

Mencius uses these four types of evidence—the "inclinations of childhood," the spontaneous "give-away" actions of adults, the "testimonials" of those who choose the moral life and the results of his "thought experiments" to argue that human nature includes a specific set of moral "sprouts." Human nature has a specific *content*; it includes fundamental moral tendencies. Mencius grants that these moral "sprouts" are weak and fragile, that they are often overwhelmed by stronger appetites, instincts and passions. This, however, does not argue against the need to include them as part of human nature.

Had Mencius restricted his position to arguing for the *inclusion* of the moral sprouts as part of human nature, he would have established the possibility of moral action but not the stronger claim concerning the goodness of human nature. And there would have been another, more fundamental, criticism of the Mencian position, if it did nothing more than argue for the inclusion of moral capacities. For an adequate picture of human nature must do more than provide an inventory of its constituents. Such an inventory would simply be inadequate—just as it would simply be inadequate to describe the frescoes of the Sistine Chapel as "plaster, oils and pigments" or to describe an automobile by providing an inventory of its parts. Human nature is more than a collection of parts—its parts are arranged in a precise manner and there are important relationships among these parts. The arrangement of its constituent elements and the relationships that are defined by this arrangement define what it is as much as its discrete elements.

Mencius realized that the relationship among the parts was as important as the parts themselves, and he argued for more than the inclusion of the moral tendencies. He claimed that *human nature has a specific structure*, and that this structure affords a preeminent position to the heart/mind.

Mencius begins by arguing that there is a natural hierarchy within human beings. The various parts of human beings have relative values:

> Mencius said, "A man cares for every part of himself equally. Since he cares for every part equally, he nourishes every part equally. There is not an inch of skin he does not care for and so there is not an inch of skin he does not nourish. In determining whether a thing be good or bad, can there be any other way? A man must simply reflect upon himself.

> Some parts of a person are precious and others are base, some parts are great and others small. Do not injure the great for the sake of the small or the precious for the sake of the base. Those who nourish the small become small themselves; those who nourish the base become base.

> Now an orchard-keeper who neglects his valuable trees and nourishes the trees of lesser value is a poor orchard-keeper. One who nourishes a finger at the expense of his shoulder and back and does not realize what he is doing is like a crazed animal.

> A person motivated by hunger and thirst alone is regarded as base because he nourishes the small at the expense of the great. If a person motivated by hunger and thirst alone could avoid losing (what is great) then how could his mouth and belly be of no more value than an inch of skin?"[13]

Mencius assumes, and it seems quite reasonable to grant, that there is a natural hierarchy of importance among the various parts of the body.[14] He also seems to say that only one who is unaware of the relative values of these parts—one who fails to understand his own nature—could possibly act in such a way as to sacrifice something of greater value for something of lesser value. Even animals follow a natural hierarchy in the choices they make. Only when "crazed" are they driven to act in a manner contrary to this natural hierarchy.

In the passage that immediately follows the passage quoted above, Mencius argues that each of our parts has a natural function and this function determines its place within the natural hierarchy. Moreover, he maintains it is the function of the heart/mind to reflect on and determine the relative value of different actions.

> Kung-tu Tzu asked, "All are equally human. Why is it that some become great and others small?"

> Mencius replied, "Those who follow what is great within them become great; those who follow what is small become small."

Kung-tu Tzu then said, "All are equally human. Why is it that some
follow what is great and others follow what is small?"

Mencius replied, "The ear and the eye cannot think and become
obsessed by things. When one thing comes in contact with another, it
leads it away. The office of the mind is to think. When it thinks, it gets
things right; if it does not think, it cannot get things right. These are
what Heaven has given us. If one takes his stand in the great that is
within him, the small cannot take it away from him. This is what
makes one great."[15]

Mencius saw that the natural function of the heart/mind is to think. It alone
can entertain options, weigh their relative merits and choose among alternatives. He believed this was a uniquely human ability, a distinctive feature of
human nature. In order to be true to our nature, we must exercise each of our
various parts according to its natural, its Heavenly endowed, function. And
since the mind's function is to think and choose, we must exercise it in this
manner and follow the guidance it provides.

According to Mencius, the heart/mind is naturally the governing organ; it
organizes and gives direction to the rest of the self. Though our appetites and
instincts are powerful parts of human nature, it is not their natural function to
govern the self; they are, by nature, subordinate to the heart/mind.[16] This hierarchy
is part of human nature; it is the decree of Heaven. It is also the principle which
governs human organization writ large. Human society, properly organized,
repeats this hierarchy on a grander scale: thinking men govern society just as the
organ of thought governs the self.

Some labor with their hearts/minds and some with their strength.
Those who labor with their hearts/minds govern, and those who labor
with their strength are governed. Those who are governed provide for
those that govern them. Those who govern are provided for by those
they govern. This is a principle that operates throughout the world.[17]

If the heart/mind thinks it will "get things right"—it will choose the right
course of action.[18] But the choices the heart/mind makes are not free in an
important sense. Morality is not "existential;" it is not established by the
choices we make. Nor is it the result of reason alone. For Mencius, morality
is the manifestation of human nature. The moral-religious life is the life lived
following the natural course of human development, guided by the Heavenly-
endowed heart/mind.

Fully realizing one's heart/mind is the way to know one's nature. Fully
knowing one's nature is the way to know Heaven. To preserve one's
heart/mind and develop one's nature is the way to serve Heaven.
When dying young or living long do not cause one to be double

minded, cultivating oneself and awaiting whatever is to come—this
is the way to establish one's destiny.[19]

Though there is only one moral Way and we are endowed with the
beginnings of morality, we do not come into the world as full moral agents.
We grow into morality as we mature. As our nature develops, if it follows the
proper course of development, we realize our destiny as moral creatures. For
Mencius, this *proper course of development* defines human nature.[20]

Mencius used a variety of agricultural metaphors to describe the proper
course of human development.[21] These metaphors present a picture of human
nature that is distinctively Mencian, and we will see in the following sections,
The Origin of Evil and *Self-Cultivation*, that seeing this picture in all its details
is essential to understanding his moral philosophy.

Mencius believed that if human beings developed "normally," if they
followed the course Mencius saw as defining their nature, they became morally
good. This process of development embraced both the physical body and the
heart/mind. Mencius drew no hard line between these two; to do so would have
been anathema to his claim that moral goodness is the natural outgrowth of
human nature.

We are not born good; we are born for goodness. Our moral sprouts must
ripen, as grain must ripen, before our mature nature is revealed.[22] Mencius'
explanation of his claim that human nature is good clearly reveals he meant
the *proper course of human development* leads to goodness.

> Mencius said, "Now as for his *ch'ing* (true essence), a man may
> become good—this is what I mean when I say (man's nature) is good.
> His becoming bad is not the fault of his endowment."[23]

In the case of plants, we know how they should grow because we have seen
the adult form of healthy specimens of the same plant. By analogy, Mencius
pointed to the sages of classical times as the "healthy specimens" of what
human beings should be. But one might ask how the sages knew how they
should be? Though never asked the question, Mencius had an answer. He
argued the sages were moral connoisseurs, but he insisted their intuitions on
moral taste were available to us all. Through reflection, we could discern which
actions were right and wrong, and if any person were to so reflect he would
arrive at the same judgments as the sages. He would know what is right by the
instinctive joy that accompanies the contemplation of morally good action.

> ...All palates agree in savoring the same flavors, all ears agree in
> appreciating the same sounds, and all eyes agree in enjoying the same
> beauties. Is it only in the case of our hearts/minds that there is nothing
> shared in common? What is it about which our hearts/minds agree? I
> say it is concerning what is right and proper. The sages were the first

to grasp what my heart/mind shares in common with other human beings. That is why what is right and proper pleases my mind just as grain and grass fed meat pleases my palate.[24]

As I pointed out in the first chapter, the pleasure of moral action is not what makes it right. The sense of pleasure that accompanies moral action marks the moral life as the "natural" course of human development.[25] It eliminates the need for coercian and shows that the development of morality is natural to human beings. The moral life is an active process of growth encouraged by an attendant feeling of joy; it has behind it the force of nature.

The lesser sensory pleasures we enjoy are enhanced when they are experienced in the course of morally correct behavior.[26] Mencius even insists they can only be *truly* enjoyed when experienced in the course of morally correct behavior. He insists the joy that accompanies the moral life is "the greatest joy of all."[27] It marks the natural course of human development; it is also the force that draws people irresistibly to the side of the virtuous leader.[28]

Mencius believed the proper course of human development embraces both physical and moral aspects; allowing the moral aspects of human nature to grow is as much a part of normal human development as is physical growth. There is no way to separate the various strands of human nature. The moral nature reveals itself in the physical body: in the "clear and bright pupils" of the moral individual,[29] in his face and in his figure.

> The superior person takes benevolence, righteousness, ritual and wisdom as his nature. These are rooted in his heart. They manifest themselves in the gentle harmony of his face and the fullness of his back. They spread throughout his four limbs, and without speaking, these express his meaning.[30]

Mencius summed up this symbiosis between the moral and physical development in a short but important passage:

> Our physical shape and faculties are given by Heaven. But only the sage brings himself to completion.[31]

Our physical power and abilities naturally increase in the course of normal development. For example, in the course of normal human growth, we crawl, toddle and then walk. Mencius argued there is a similar course of proper moral development that parallels this physical growth. The affection an infant displays to its parents naturally develops into filial piety, and as the child grows, it naturally develops respect for its elder brother. If this process continues along its proper course, the child develops an awareness of his obligations to other members of society as well. He matures and enters into new relationships—he becomes a sibling, a friend, a spouse, a parent and a member of society. As this process unfolds, his moral behavior naturally

extends beyond love for his parents and out to society at large. He becomes a
loving brother, a faithful friend, an attentive husband, and affectionate parent
and a loyal subject. One can know the correct course of human development
by observing the "best specimens" of the past: the sages. But one cannot attain
the ideal they represent merely by copying their actions. One must look within
and find the nascent moral sensibility inside oneself. One must exercise and
nurture one's moral capacity; developing these moral sprouts leads one along
the Way.[32]

Mencius' view of human nature is one of the guiding principles of his
thought; understanding it is the key to understanding his moral philosophy.
Most importantly, for the purpose of the present study, his notion of human
nature, and the ways this notion gets played out in other aspects of his thought,
is arguably the most significant difference between Mencius and Wang Yang-
ming.

Human Nature:
Wang Yang-ming

To be a follower of Mencius, one must, among other things, hold some version of the claim that human nature is good. And in this regard, Wang Yang-ming remained true to the Mencian tradition. But Wang had a very different view of human nature and a very different understanding of what it meant to describe human nature as good. These differences are best understood in terms of Wang's metaphysical orientation—an orientation deeply influenced by Buddhist thought.[33] In order to understand Wang's view of human nature, we must see it in relation to his metaphysics. Specifically, we must understand it in terms of his notion of *li* (principle).

Li (principle) gives the world both its physical and moral shape; it is manifested everywhere and can be viewed from an infinite variety of perspectives. These different views of *li* are commonly referred to as if they were separate and distinct phenomena. For example, the *hsin* (heart/mind), its *i* (thoughts) and *wu* (things)—the objects of these thoughts—appear to be separate and distinct. But Wang claimed these are all just different aspects of *li* (principle). He also believed human nature itself is simply one more manifestation of *li*.

> ...*Li* (principle) is one; that is all. If one speaks of *li* coming together (to form a person), one calls it *hsing* (nature). If one speaks of the master of this accumulation, one calls it *hsin* (heart/mind). If one speaks of the operation of this master, one calls it *i* (thought). If one speaks of the consciousness of this operation, one calls it *chih* (knowing). If one speaks of the stimulation and response of this consciousness, one calls it *wu* (things).[34]

Just as human nature is but one manifestation of *li* (principle), the form, features and character of human beings are but manifestations of human nature.

> ...*Hsing* (nature) is one; that is all. As (man's) bodily form one calls it *t'ien* (the Heavenly/Natural). As master (of the body), one calls it *ti* (lord). As actions, one calls it *ming* (destiny). As man's endowment, one calls it *hsing* (nature). As master of the body, one calls it *hsin* (heart/mind). As the mind's operation—encountering the father, one calls it *hsiao* (filial piety) and encountering the ruler, one calls it *chung* (loyalty). Proceeding in this way, its descriptions extend on indefinitely. But the nature is one; that is all.

> Similarly, a man is one; that is all. In relation to his father, he is a son; in relation to his son, he is a father. Proceeding in this way, his descriptions extend on indefinitely. But a man is one; that is all. All

one need do is direct effort toward (understanding) one's nature. If one can understand *hsing* (nature), the myriad principles will be clear and distinct.[35]

It might seem that Wang has preserved Mencius' model of human nature; that Wang's *li* describe for human nature a similar *content, structure* and *proper course of development*. But this is not so.

Wang's view of the original *content* of human nature was quite different from Mencius'. Wang believed the moral heart/mind was an innate, perfect and fully-formed endowment. This heart/mind is received at birth and remains constant throughout one's life. One become moral by becoming aware of this endowment, and one becomes aware by eliminating the obscuration of selfish desires.

Mencius believed we are born with sprouts of moral virtue; Wang believed these virtues are fully-formed. For Mencius, these sprouts develop or fail to develop as a function of their environment and the effort applied to cultivating them. For Wang the virtues are present whether we develop them or not. As we will see below, Wang did not believe there was a *proper course of development* for the moral nature, and this belief is reflected in his view of human nature's content.

Wang did share with Mencius a similar view of the *structure* of human nature. He believed the heart/mind commanded the preeminent position and governed the lower aspects of human nature. But Wang afforded the heart/mind this status because of its position within his metaphysical scheme. The heart/mind was principle—in its conscious aspect. It was the heart/mind of the universe, not just of human beings. It was not merely the key to knowledge—the means which can lead one to understand—it was that knowledge itself.

The difference between Wang's view of human nature and Mencius' is most clearly seen in terms of the third feature: *the proper course of development*. Wang's view of human nature did not fully incorporate Mencius' notion of a *proper course of development*. The notion was preserved in one respect: Wang would have described the normal physical growth of human beings as a process governed by *li*. But in the critical aspect of *moral growth* the notion of a *proper course of development* is nowhere to be found. For Wang, the moral aspects of human nature were fully formed at birth; they were an endowment of mature moral dispositions. We can see how Wang subtlety changed Mencius' notion of human nature even as he paraphrased his mentor:

> ...*Chih* (knowing) is the conscious aspect of *li* (principle). If one speaks of it as master (of the body), one calls it *hsin* (heart/mind). If one speaks of it as (man's) endowment, one calls it *hsing* (nature). *Young infants all know to love their parents and respect their elder brothers.*[36] If only one can keep this consciousness free from the

obscuration of selfish desire and *extend* it fully, it will be the mind in itself. It will then join with Heaven and Earth...[37]

Comparing this passage with *Mencius* 7A15, we see Wang has left out an important feature of Mencius' original thought.

Mencius said, "Those things which men do not study yet are able to do, are *liang neng* (innate abilities). Those things which they do not ponder yet know, are *liang chih* (innate knowledge). Young infants all know to love their parents. *When they are older*, they all know to respect their elder brothers. Loving one's parents is benevolence. Respecting one's elder brother is righteousness. All that remains is to extend (these feelings) to everyone in the world.[38]

Wang eliminated the all-important *interval of growth* explicit in this passage from Mencius, and this omission is symptomatic of Wang's different view of human nature. Wang did not believe the moral aspects of human nature needed development. He interpreted the terms *liang neng* (pure ability) and *liang chih* (pure knowing), seen in the passage above, as designating *fully-formed*, innate aspects of human nature.

Wang also gave new meaning to another important notion in Mencius' thought: the notion *k'uo erh ch'ung* (to enlarge and fill-out).[39] For Mencius, this meant to *develop* the four moral sprouts to their mature and proper state. Wang did not believe any development was necessary or even possible. For him, *k'uo ch'ung* meant to extend *liang chih*: to apply the pure knowing one already possessed to the situation at hand.

As for the principles of all events and every thing; they are not outside my mind. To insist (one must) *investigate all the principles in the world*,[40] is to risk giving the impression that the pure knowing of my mind is insufficient, and that I must seek throughout the wide world in order to supplement and augment it. This seems to separate the mind and principle and to regard them as two things. As for the tasks of study and inquiry, reflection and discrimination, and earnest action—it may be that one must exert one hundred times the effort of another.[41] But when *k'uo ch'ung chih chi* (fully extended) to the point where one has *exhausted one's nature and knows Heaven*,[42] it never goes beyond the *chih* (extension) of my mind's pure knowing. How could an iota be added to my pure knowing![43]

Wang's understanding of *k'uo ch'ung* goes over without remainder into his interpretation of the *Great Learning's* doctrine of *chih chih* (the extension of knowledge). In firm opposition to Chu Hsi, who believed one must seek for principles in things and events, Wang believed one must simply extend one's pure knowing.

Chih (to extend) is *chih'* (to reach the ultimate limit).[44] It is like saying: "Mourning is *chih* (extended) to *chih* (reach the ultimate limit) of grief;" and the line in the *I Ching*: "(He) knows *chih'* (the ultimate) and *chih'* (reaches to the ultimate).[45] "Knowing the ultimate" is *knowledge*, and "reaching to the ultimate" is *extension*. The *extension of knowledge* is not—as later scholars say it is—*ch'ung kuang* (filling-out and broadening) one's knowledge. It is simply to extend the pure knowing of my own mind. Pure knowing is what Mencius spoke of when he said, "The heart/mind of right and wrong is something all men possess."[46] The heart/mind of right and wrong does not need to think in order to know and does not need to study before it can perform. This is why it is called pure knowing![47]

Wang's notion of *liang chih* was central to his view of human nature. He understood *liang chih* as an endowment—a perfect and fully-formed moral disposition innate to human beings. It was akin to vision—a faculty one possessed and that naturally operated flawlessly. The goal of self-cultivation was to restore this faculty to its original state by eliminating the interference of "selfish thoughts."

> The mind in itself is nature; nature is principle. To completely realize the principle of benevolence, one must extend one's benevolence to the ultimate of benevolence. To completely realize the principle of righteousness, one must extend one's righteousness to the ultimate of righteousness. Benevolence and righteousness are nothing other than my nature. Therefore to completely realize principle is to completely realize my nature.[48]

> *Chih shan* (the highest good) is the nature. The nature, in its original state, is without the slightest trace of evil. Therefore we call it *chih shan* (the highest good). To abide in it (the highest good) is to return to its (the nature's) original state.[49]

Wang's view of the moral aspects of human nature is revealed clearly in the metaphors he uses for *liang chih*. His central metaphors—the moral mind as the sun (which is obscured by "clouds" of selfish desires)[50] and as pure gold (which is tainted by the base impurities of selfish desires)[51]—are both taken from Buddhism.[52] Both metaphors show Wang believed the moral nature was a fully-formed and perfect *lost endowment*.[53]

The *sun obscured by clouds* is by far Wang's most common metaphor for the moral mind (obscured by selfish desires).[54]

> The master also said. "Pure knowing is within human beings. No matter what you do, you cannot deceive or destroy it. Even a thief knows he should not be a thief. If you call him a thief, he still will blush."[55]

Yü-chung said, "(He steals) only because (his pure knowing) is covered over and obscured by material desires. But pure knowing is within him; it can never be lost. It is like when clouds obscure the sun—how could the sun ever be lost!"

The Master said, "How brilliant is Yü-chung! Others do not see it as clearly as he does."[56]

Wang viewed the moral nature as every person's innate endowment, but an endowment most people lose sight of.[57] All people have within them this innate moral "self," and this inner self—their true self—is wholly good. This is Wang's very different understanding of the innate goodness of human nature, described by Mencius.

Though everyone is endowed with an innate, perfect and fully-formed moral nature, everyone is not equally endowed. *Qualitatively* human nature is common to all human beings, but individual endowments of nature differ *quantitatively*.

A sage is a sage because his mind has been purified; (it is pure) Heavenly principle and is without the slightest trace of selfish human desires. It is like what makes pure gold pure; it has been completely purified and is without the slightest trace of copper or lead. When a man has purified his (mind's) Heavenly principle, he is a sage. When gold is purified it is pure (gold).

However, sages differ in ability and strength just as different amounts of gold differ in weight. Yao and Shun were like ten thousand pounds (of gold). King Wen and Confucius were nine thousand pounds. Kings Yü, T'ang and Wu were seven or eight thousand pounds. Po-i and I-yin were like four or five thousand pounds. Though they differed in ability and strength, the Heavenly principle of (their minds) was equally pure. All of them can be called sages. It is like (different) amounts of (gold) being different (in weight) but equal in purity. (The different amounts) are all pure gold. If five thousand pounds of (pure) gold is mixed with ten thousand pounds (of pure gold), the purity would be the same. If Po-i and I-yin were to mingle with Yao and Confucius, the purity of each one's Heavenly principle would be the same. For the purity of pure gold depends on its purity and not its quantity. Being a sage depends on the purity of one's Heavenly principle and not on one's ability and strength.

Therefore, anyone willing to study and purify his mind's Heavenly principle can also become a sage. It is like comparing a tael of gold to ten thousand pounds (of gold). Though there is an immense difference in terms of quantity, in terms of purity there is nothing wanting. Thus it is said, *Anyone can become a Yao or Shun.*[58]

As I pointed out in the previous section, Mencius too believed human beings share a common nature, but that there is a natural diversity of abilities among human beings. Mencius believed some people were better endowed to be the moral elite of their age. This belief in a natural hierarchy might lead one to ask for an explanation—why were some born with superior abilities? But such a question is compelling only to those who believe in the complete natural equality of all human beings. To Mencius, and to Confucian thinkers in general, a natural diversity was self-evident, everywhere in nature. To them it was obvious that, among human beings, there was a natural diversity of abilities: physical, mental, artistic and most importantly, moral.[59]

Wang understood this natural diversity in terms of a difference in endowment, and he used this analysis to explain differences in moral performance while retaining a belief in an innate, fully-formed and wholly-good nature common to all human beings. Wang believed there were two ways in which one's endowment could be better or worse. There can be a *quantitative* difference in one's endowment of moral nature: this was expressed in the above passage with the metaphor of varying amounts of "gold." Later in the same passage, and in other places throughout his recorded sayings, Wang refers to a second factor. There can be—it is natural that there is—a difference in the purity of one's physical nature.

Wang relies upon the distinction between *hsing chih pen t'i* (the nature itself) and *ch'i chih chih hsing* (the physical nature) in order to explain this second factor. Wang, and Neo-Confucians in general, seem to have borrowed this particular form of the distinction between a pure, original nature and an impure physical nature from Buddhism, specifically from Buddhist *tathāgatagarba* literature.

The notion of the *tathāgatagarba* was introduced into China as early as the third century, when the *Tathāgatagarbha Sūtra* was first translated into Chinese.[60] The notion was further developed in texts such as *The Lion's Roar of Queen Srīmālā*[61], and it is a central notion in such texts as the *Laṅkāvatāra Sūtra*[62] and *The Awakening of Faith.*[63] Wang was well-versed in the Buddhist literature of his time as were the Neo-Confucian thinkers who preceded him.[64] This view of human nature—the opposition of a pure, original nature and an impure, physical nature— was established long before Wang's time.

The version of this distinction which became characteristic of Neo-Confucianism was first proposed by Ch'eng Yi, and it became the dominant view under the influence of Chu Hsi.[65] Ch'eng Yi claimed the nature itself (the original nature) cannot be known apart from its manifestation in living human beings (the physical nature), and that this manifestation is necessarily a diminished form of the nature. However, he insisted that any discussion of human nature must embrace both these aspects.

To discuss *hsing* (the nature) without discussing *ch'i* (the physical) is incomplete. To discuss *ch'i* (the physical) without discussing *hsing* (the nature) is unenlightened.[66]

Wang embraced this aspect of Ch'eng Yi's teaching: any discussion of human nature must employ this "balanced" approach.

Your letter says, "Someone quoted Ch'eng Hao's remark: 'Men are tranquil at birth. The state preceding this is beyond description. As soon as one talks about *hsing*[67] (the nature) it is not *hsing* (the nature).' Why is it (the nature) 'beyond description' and why is it 'not the nature?' Chu Hsi responded (to Ch'eng Hao's remark) by saying the nature is 'beyond description' because there is not yet anything of which one can speak. And it is 'not the nature' because (if we can talk about it) it must already be mixed with *ch'i*.[68] I do not understand the remarks of either of these gentlemen. Whenever I come across this point in my readings, I become confused. Please explain this to me."

"Inborn" is what is called "nature."[69] The word "inborn" is the same as (the word) "physical." (Kao Tzu's remark) is like saying the "physical" is the "nature." If (one says) the "physical" is the "nature," then the state before *man is tranquil at birth*[70] is beyond description. As soon as one says that the *physical* is the *nature*, one has fallen to holding a one-sided view. It is not the nature's original state.

When Mencius claimed human nature is good, he was discussing it from the perspective of the nature's original state. Nevertheless, the signs of human nature's goodness can only be seen in *ch'i* (the physical). If there were no *ch'i*, they could not be seen. The feelings of commiseration, shame, complaisance, and right and wrong are all *ch'i*. Ch'eng Yi said, "To discuss *hsing* (the nature) without discussing *ch'i* (the physical) is incomplete. To discuss *ch'i* (the physical) without discussing *hsing* (the nature) is unenlightened." He said this because students only recognize one side. When one understands one's own nature, "*Ch'i* is *hsing* and *hsing* is *ch'i*."[71] Fundamentally, these two cannot be separated.[72]

In many respects, Wang's view of human nature is remarkably close to Ch'eng Yi's. Even Wang's controversial notion that *hsing chih pen t'i* (the nature in itself) is without good or evil[73] finds precedent in Ch'eng Yi's thought. The following quote from Ch'eng reveals how closely Wang followed Ch'eng Yi's precise wording, when discussing the relationship between nature and *ch'i*.

"Inborn" is what is meant by "nature." *Hsing* (the nature) is *ch'i* (the physical) and *ch'i* (the physical) is *hsing* (the nature). Inborn refers to man's endowment at birth. According to principle, this contains both good and evil. Thus it is not that men are born with these two in mutual opposition originally within the nature.[74]

The moral nature in itself is the mind in itself, and though Wang characterizes this as *chih shan* (the highest good), he denies one can ascribe goodness to it.[75] All descriptions of human nature which ascribe features or qualities to the nature must be understood as referring to *ch'i chih chih hsing* (the physical nature): the original nature as manifested in human form.

The distinction between the original nature and physical nature was central to Wang's thought.[76] He relied upon it to explain both Confucius' and Mencius' statements concerning human nature. He understood Confucius' statement, "By nature human beings are close; through practice they grow far apart,"[77] as referring to these two states of nature. We are "close" from the point of view of original nature, and "far apart" from the point of view of the physical nature. And Wang understood Mencius' claim that human nature is good as a description from the point of view of the original nature.

> Confucius' saying "by nature men are close" is the same as Mencius' saying "the nature is good". One cannot understand (these remarks) exclusively from the perspective of the physical (nature). If we try to explain them in terms of the physical nature, in which there is the mutual opposition between *firm* and *weak*,[78] how can (men) "be close (by nature)?" Only in terms of their (originally) good nature are men alike. When first born the goodness of human beings is originally the same. By firmly practicing goodness, one becomes firmly good. And by firmly practicing evil one becomes firmly evil. If one weakly practices the good, one becomes weakly good. And by (weakly) practicing evil, one becomes weakly evil. Thus day by day, men grow "far apart."[79]

Wang also used this distinction to explain the difference between Mencius and Hsün Tzu. According to Wang, they did not disagree about the essence of human nature; they merely viewed it from different perspectives.[80]

> (Wang said), "Mencius discussed human nature directly from the perspective of its original source and said, broadly speaking, people are like this (good by nature). Hsün Tzu's doctrine that human nature is evil was arrived at from the perspective of its errors. One cannot say he was entirely wrong, only that his understanding was not refined. Most people have lost the mind in itself."

> (I) asked, "In discussing human nature from the perspective of its original source, Mencius wanted people to apply their efforts toward achieving a complete understanding of its source. In discussing human nature from the perspective of its errors, Hsün Tzu defined the

task (of moral self cultivation) solely in terms of correcting the errors one had already made. This requires too much effort."

The Master said, "That is correct."[81]

Wang embraced Ch'eng Yi's explanation of the difference between the original nature and the physical nature. As we have seen above, Ch'eng Yi appealed to Kao Tzu's position, as found in the *Mencius*, in order to establish the physical nature side of this dichotomy. He understood Kao Tzu's statement—that *sheng chih wei hsing* (inborn is what is called the nature)—as a description of the physical nature. According to Ch'eng Yi, the disagreement between Mencius and Kao Tzu turned on their different perspectives on human nature: Mencius spoke of human nature in its original state; Kao Tzu spoke only of the physical nature. Wang accepted this explanation, making sure to point out that Mencius did not neglect to mention the physical nature as well.

> I asked, "In saying, 'Inborn is what is meant by nature,' Kao Tzu was, after all, correct. Why did Mencius criticize him?"

> The Master said, "What is inborn is of course nature. But Kao Tzu recognized only one side (of the nature) and failed to recognize its original state. If he had understood its original state, what he said would have been fine. Mencius also said, 'Our form and complexion are Heavenly nature.'[82] His (understanding) included the physical nature."[83]

Wang criticized both Hsün Tzu and Kao Tzu for failing to realize human nature included an innate, perfect and fully-formed moral sense. They mistakenly believed the physical nature was all there was to know. This led Hsün Tzu to describe human nature as evil[84] and Kao Tzu to claim righteousness is external.[85] Their views of human nature were "one-sided," and this led them into error.

Here again, we see the domestication, by Wang and earlier Neo-Confucians, of Mencius' harshest enemies and critics. This was only possible because of the radical changes that had occurred in Confucian thought. The shift to metaphysically based moralities distorted the Neo-Confucian interpretation of Mencius. He was no longer fundamentally opposed to thinkers like Kao Tzu and Hsün Tzu. On their interpretation, Kao Tzu and Hsün Tzu were half-right. Mencius was superior only because he had seen the whole truth.

Wang criticized Chu Hsi for making the same kind of mistake. Wang objected to Chu Hsi's insistence on the need to investigate things in order to understand principles. Wang believed the original nature was complete and perfect, that all principles were already present. The mind in itself was principle; there was no need to augment one's *understanding* of principle by searching outside one's own mind.[86]

Searching for principles outside the mind implied the mind and the nature were deficient in some respect. And Wang argued this was precisely the error Kao Tzu had committed when he claimed righteousness was external.

> Exclusively to seek the mind in itself and thereby abandon the principles of things is to lose the mind in itself. The principles of things are not outside my mind. If one looks outside the mind and seeks for the principles of things, one will find no principles. (On the other hand) to abandon the principles of things and seek for my mind—what would I find?

> The mind in itself is nature. Nature is principle. The mind of filial-piety to one's parents is the principle of filial-piety. Without the mind of filial-piety to one's parents, there is no principle of filial-piety. The mind of loyalty to one's sovereign is the principle of loyalty. Without the mind of loyalty to one's sovereign, there is no principle of loyalty. How could principle be outside my mind?

> Chu Hsi said, "One studies the mind and principles; that is all. Though the mind is lord of (only) a single body, it governs the world's principles. Though principles are scattered throughout the myriad phenomena, they are not outside a person's mind." This describes well the aspects of universal dispersion and unity (of principle), but it does not avoid the error of leading students to regard the mind and principles as separate. This is why later generations have the misfortune of exclusively seeking for the mind in itself and abandoning the principles of things. It is precisely because they don't understand *mind is principle*. As for looking outside the mind and seeking for the principles of things, this is to believe there are things (the mind) cannot understand. This is Kao Tzu's theory that righteousness is external. This is why Mencius said he never understood righteousness.[87]

Wang believed human beings were endowed with a perfect and complete moral nature at birth. This moral nature was identical with principle. One became aware of principle through its conscious aspect: *liang chih* (pure knowing) which is the mind in itself in its active, knowing aspect. Seeking this inner moral light and letting it shine was the task of moral self-cultivation. Any practice that led one away from *liang chih* was incorrect and revealed a fundamental misunderstanding of human nature.

Human Nature:
Conclusion

According to Mencius, human nature has a specific *content*: human beings are born with a well-defined set of physical, mental and emotional capacities. These different parts are arranged in a very special *structure* and the shape of this structure emerges as an individual matures. Human nature has a *proper course of development*; it grows to maturity slowly and only if raised in an appropriate environment and given proper care. This is why Mencius used so many agricultural metaphors in his discussions of human nature.

If human nature develops as it should, the mind will take its rightful place as governor of the self. It will function in its natural capacity and guide one through a life of moral self cultivation. Only in this way can human nature achieve its full form.

In Wang Yang-ming's time, the Buddhist notion of an original, pure and fully formed inner nature—an inner nature which was obscured by an outer, defiled physical nature—had become the dominant view among Confucian thinkers. Wang accepted this view of human nature. For him, the original, pure and fully formed nature was Heavenly principle, and this principle defined the Confucian Way.

Principle described human nature in a way remarkably close to Mencius' view. If we compare their accounts of morally *perfected* individuals, it becomes extremely difficult to describe the differences between Mencius' fully-developed sage and Wang's fully-discovered sage.[88] But this should not obscure the profound differences which distinguish their separate views of human nature. In Wang's account of human nature, there was no *proper course of development*. No development was necessary or even possible, for the moral nature was a complete and perfect endowment. The *content* of one's moral nature remained unchanged throughout one's life and regardless of the level of cultivation one achieved. Moral principles may be brought to the surface, refined and polished, but they remained fundamentally unchanged throughout one's life.

Wang's belief in an original, pure and fully-formed inner nature, hidden beneath an impure physical nature, is totally alien to Mencius' thought. His interpretation of human nature dramatically changed fundamental features of Mencius' view, and these changes had profound consequences for other aspects of Wang's thought. I will examine some of the most important consequences in the following two chapters: the *Origin of Evil* and *Self Cultivation*.

Chapter 3

The Origin of Evil: Mencius

Religious traditions, such as Christianity, which claim the world was created and is sustained by an omniscient, omnipotent and compassionate God have found the existence of manifold evil in the world especially bothersome. The existence of evil in the world seems to indicate the creator God must not know of it, cannot eliminate it or chooses not to eliminate it. Each of these explanations appears to undermine some aspect of their beliefs concerning the nature of God and His relationship to the world.

Mencius had a remarkably different picture of the world. His world was not the creation of an omniscient, omnipotent and compassionate God. And because of this, he was not compelled to explain certain types of evil, types that many in the West have found particularly disturbing and difficult to explain. On the other hand, his doctrine of the innate goodness of human nature presented him with his own version of this problem. For in Mencius' time, no less than in our own, examples of human ruthlessness and cruelty were far too abundant. Mencius could not—and he did not—simply ignore the gulf between his theory about human nature and the actual behavior of human beings. Reconciling these two required a convincing account of the *Origin of Evil*: how evil was possible and why it was so widespread.

Mencius did not postulate the existence of radical evil in the world. He never offered an explanation for the existence of what we might describe as fundamentally evil things or events. He did not see such creatures as mosquitoes and poisonous snakes as inherently evil. And he did not, like the Buddha, regard the existence of sickness, old age and death as signs that life is somehow fundamentally flawed.

What may seem even more remarkable, Mencius did not regard as problematic the possibility that a morally good person could, for no apparent reason, be bitten by a mosquito or poisonous snake, or suffer death from some horrible disease. He had no eschatology to balance a misfortune suffered in this world, and he did not deny that such misfortunes are sometimes the plight of even the best of human beings.[1]

A morally excellent person could die an early and horrible death. Mencius did not see such events as inherently evil, unjust or as indications Heaven was displeased and against the morally good person. Mencius' explanation of situations in which very bad things happen to very good people—an explanation he inherited from Confucius—is simply that these actions are decreed by

49

Heaven. Such events are beyond human control. They are misfortunes, but they are not evil.

The good fortune one enjoys or the misfortune one must endure was a separate issue entirely for Mencius. Good and evil were measured exclusively in reference to the Way, and as I discussed in chapter one, the Way had no direct connection with one's material well-being. There was no calculus insuring that the good were also fortunate, and being well-off was no sign that one was being rewarded for good behavior or chosen by Heaven.

Evil *per se* was not part of the fabric of Mencius' world. Evil was defined exclusively in terms of the failure, on the part of human beings, to accord with the Way. And for Mencius, the necessary and sufficient condition for according with the Way was realizing the full potential of one's innate nature. How well one followed the proper course of human development determined if one was good or evil—if one's actions were to be applauded or condemned. Nothing else entered the moral equation.

> Fully realizing one's heart/mind is the way to know one's nature. One who knows one's nature knows Heaven. To preserve one's heart/mind and develop one's nature is the way to serve Heaven. When dying young or living long do not cause one to be double minded, cultivating oneself and awaiting whatever is to come—this is the way to establish one's destiny.[2]

The morally cultivated individual recognizes that Heaven is the source of every event in the world not initiated by a human being.[3] He recognizes that the ultimate course of events in the world are beyond his control, but he chooses to participate only in those events which accord with the Way. The morally correct person is neither resigned nor reckless. He doesn't accept things as fate, unless they accord with the Way. He doesn't throw his life away, but he will sacrifice his life for the Way.

> There is nothing that is not decreed. One should accept anything, as long as it is proper. Therefore, one who understands the decree does not stand beneath a wall which is about to collapse. To die following the Way is a proper destiny. To die in fetters and handcuffs is not a proper destiny.[4]

Mencius accepted the possibility of unjustifiable suffering, but he denied that this in any way should affect the actions of the morally upright individual.

Such suffering is not without a discernible purpose. Moral heroes, like all heroes, are revealed by their deeds. It is their courage and fortitude under adversity that throws them into bold contrast with most of their fellow men. It is also arguably true that adversity helps to forge such individuals: like great artists, moral heroes need to suffer in order to understand.

Those who understand virtue and the conduct of affairs often have suffered adversity. The estranged minister or the son of a lowly concubine, because he is constantly attentive to dangers and deeply ponders the difficulties, he succeeds where others fail.[5]

Mencius seemed to say even more than this. For him, adversity not only strengthened one's moral qualities; it served as a sign that Heaven had chosen the suffering individual as its champion.

Shun rose from his fields; Fu Yüeh was raised-up from his frames and scaffolds; Chiao Ko from his fish and salt; Kuan I-wu from the hands of his jailer; Sun Shu-ao from the shores of the sea and Po-li Hsi from the market-place. From these examples, we know that when Heaven is about to entrust a man with a great mission, it first exercises his mind with suffering and his muscles with toil; it forces him to suffer starvation and hardship. It confounds his undertakings so as to unsettle his mind, toughen his nature and improve his deficiencies....[6]

Heaven challenges the righteous; it tests them and tempers them for the difficulties which lie ahead. Here Mencius offers an explanation for a certain type of undeserved pain and suffering. Suffering is a means through which one can improve his practice of the Way. This explanation does not account for cases in which the good die young, without having the opportunity to exercise their well-tempered moral courage. But if such a case is offered as an objection to Mencius, it is an objection which goes beyond a bound he himself recognized.

Mencius restricted evaluations of good and evil exclusively to the realm of human action. Unjustified pain and suffering exist; things occur which are beyond human control. But such events, by definition, were not candidates for praise or blame. These were things "outside" of human beings, and the origin of both good and evil was "within" us.

Seek and you will get it; let go and you will lose it. In this case, seeking helps you get it, and what you seek is within yourself. There is a proper way to seek it, but whether you get it or not is a matter of destiny. In this case, the seeking does not help you get it, and what you seek is outside of yourself.[7]

Mencius restricted questions of moral value to the realm of human actions. He believed those actions which promote the proper development of human nature result in good and those which inhibit or distort this growth result in evil. But even if we grant this understanding of morality there are still questions to be answered. To begin with, how could the innate good nature of human beings ever fail to develop? There was abundant evidence, in Mencius' time, that human beings were in fact much less than he claimed they were *by nature*.

Since most people seemed not to follow the development Mencius claimed as natural—in what sense was it human nature? Mencius needed to explain the gap between his theory and the reality around him. He needed to present an account of the *origin of evil*, and he did so by way of the familiar plant metaphors he had used to explain human nature.

In one of his most powerful images, Mencius draws an analogy between the moral barrenness of society and the barrenness of Ox Mountain—a deforested hillside on the outskirts of a large city.[8]

> The trees of Ox Mountain once were beautiful. But because it is located on the outskirts of a large city, it was attacked with axes and bills—could it retain its beauty? With the periods of rest it was granted each day and with the moisture provided by rain and dew, it was not without growing sprouts and buds. But then cattle and sheep came to graze upon these; this is why it now appears so barren. People see its barrenness and think it never had any trees upon it. But is this the *hsing* (nature) of a mountain?
>
> So too (is this the case with) what is within human beings—can human beings be without the heart/mind of benevolence and righteousness? The way one loses one's *liang hsin* (innate heart/mind) is like the way the trees (were attacked with) axes and bills. Day by day one's heart/mind is attacked—can it retain its beauty? With the periods of rest it is granted each day and with the salubrious effect of the early morning *ch'i* (psycho-physical energy),[9] a person's heart/mind comes close to having those likes and dislikes which all men share in common. But these feelings are arrested and destroyed by his activities during the day. When (their growth) is arrested repeatedly then the evening's *ch'i* cannot preserve them. And when the evening's *ch'i* cannot preserve them, then he becomes not much different from an animal. People see him behaving like an animal and think he never had (any other) capacity. But is this the *ch'ing* (true essence) of a human being
>
> Truly, if it receives its proper care there is nothing that will not grow, and if it loses its proper care there is nothing that will not perish. Confucius said, "Hold it fast and it will be preserved, let it go and it will be destroyed. Its coming and going has no specific time and no one knows its place."[10] Was he not speaking of the heart/mind?[11]

In the *Ox Mountain* parable, Mencius argues that though the mountain appears to be without trees, such is not its true nature. Originally, it was covered with a lush forest, and only through years of abuse—the uncontrolled deforestation by humans and relentless grazing of livestock—has it been reduced to its present state.

Ox Mountain was stripped of its trees by axes and bills. The trees continually tried to reemerge, sending forth new sprouts, but these were quickly gnawed
away by grazing animals. Only through this prolonged process of systematic
abuse was the true nature of the mountain ground away. But, Mencius argues,
viewing the mountain in its present, denuded condition gives no clue as to its
true nature.

Similarly, Mencius goes on to argue, pointing to the lack of morality, which
appears to be the norm among people, gives no clue as to their true nature. Due
to the prolonged and systematic abuse they have suffered, living in a society
hostile to moral development, their true nature, their moral nature, has been
ground away. To the untrained eye, people appear to be callous and cold, by
nature.

The *Ox Mountain* parable illustrates that the absence of moral qualities in
mature adults is not necessarily an indication of the character of human
nature.[12] It also shows the nature's tenacious and continuing effort to reassert
itself, even in the harshest conditions. It warns us of the frailty of human nature
and urges us to preserve and nourish our innate moral sense.[13]

Mencius argued that the moral sprouts need a proper environment in order
to grow, and he likened this need to the need plants have for their growth:
proper soil, temperature and timely rain.

> Do not be puzzled by the King's lack of wisdom. Even the most easily
> grown thing in the world will not grow if it is given one day of warmth
> and ten days of cold. I seldom have an audience with the King, and
> when I leave, those who expose him to the cold approach. Though I
> bring forth a few moral shoots, what good does it do?[14]

But the moral sprouts need something more—they need the right kind of
human attention. If we examine the *Ox Mountain* parable carefully, we see it
is one of only a few cases in which Mencius describes human nature with a
vegetative metaphor that does not assume human attention. As we look at his
other vegetative metaphors we will see that they are taken from *agriculture*
not *Nature*; cultivation is an integral part of the imagery.[15] The trees of Ox
Mountain grow wildly and without a pattern, and Mencius sees human
development much differently.

Mencius argued evil was the result of the failure of human nature to develop
along its proper course. This failure occurred because certain essential conditions had not been met: certain ingredients were absent, certain steps were not
followed or were performed out of sequence, or some harmful action—an
unnatural action which interfered with the process of growth—had been
performed.

Mencius placed great emphasis on the need for a proper, nurturing, environment. If human nature is to develop properly, the society in which one grows

up must be conducive to moral growth. In the following passage, he makes it clear that only those who are already firmly established in the Way can withstand an environment hostile to the growth of human nature.

> Only a superior individual can have a constant heart while lacking a constant means of support. Most people will not be able to maintain a constant heart if they lack a constant means of support. Without a constant heart, they will be led astray and fall into excesses—stopping at nothing. To punish them after they fall afoul of the law is to entrap them. How can a benevolent ruler allow himself to entrap his people?[16]

Providing the essentials of life is the beginning—not the end—of the ruler's responsibilities. Careful attention to the task of moral cultivation is part of a nurturing environment; a ruler must provide his subjects with a proper education.

> The minister of agriculture taught the people to sow and reap, cultivating the five kinds of grain. When the five kinds of grain were brought to maturity, the people all obtained a subsistence. But men possess a moral nature; if they are well fed, warmly clad, and comfortably lodged, without being taught at the same time, they become almost like beasts. This was a subject of anxious solicitude to the sage Shun, and he appointed Hsieh to be the Minister of Instruction, to teach the relations of humanity: how, between father and son, there should be affection; between sovereign and minister, righteousness; between husband and wife, attention to their separate functions; between old and young, a proper order; and between friends, fidelity. The highly meritorious sovereign said to him, "Encourage them; lead them on; rectify them; straighten them; help them; give them wings. Bring them to understand this for themselves. Then follow this up by stimulating them, and conferring benefits on them."[17]

From these passages, we see Mencius believed most people were incapable of overcoming a hostile social environment. A minimal level of worldly comfort is a prerequisite for moral cultivation. Providing the necessities of life, prevents the desperation of struggling for survival from interfering with moral growth. In addition, education must be provided as part of a *nurturing environment*. Most people's moral sprouts are simply not strong enough to grow on their own: they require care and nourishment.

Mencius argued that the rulers of his day failed to provide these minimal requirements for moral growth, and the result was a widespread lack of morality. In an environment hostile to moral growth, a lack of morality becomes the rule. Society becomes morally barren—barren as Ox Mountain.

We can understand why Mencius and Confucians in general have tended to be "social philosophers," philosophers who aim at *social change from the top down*. As Mencius explained in the passage above, it is rulers who provide

the environment for their subjects. Someone with Mencius' view of morality—
the blossoming of the unequally distributed but universally present moral
tendencies of human nature—is forced to conclude that the best strategy for
inculcating morality in society is to win over a ruler who will provide the
environment necessary for moral growth. The Confucian view of morality had
a strong affinity for this type of strategy. Though one of its primary goals was
to provide for the masses, it did not appeal to them directly—it was not a
populalist movement.[18] On the other hand, it did not patronize the common
man. It sought to provide him an opportunity for personal development, not
just food, clothing and shelter.

But not all people require a benign environment in order to develop into
moral agents; as I mentioned earlier, overcoming difficulties is characteristic
of the morally exceptional person. Mencius believed some people are just born
with more moral courage and a greater ability to withstand adversity than most
other people. Such a difference in ability does not contradict his "holistic"
understanding of human nature. Human nature is defined by a specific content
arranged in a precise structure and following a proper course of development,
but this does not preclude some having greater capacities in a given aspect of
human life.

When we consider passages in which Mencius compares the sages to great
musicians and chefs, it is clear that he thought of them as *moral connoisseurs*.
The sages were people with an enhanced sensibility, people who possessed a
gift which we all can recognize, participate in and appreciate as fellow human
beings, but one to which we cannot lay equal claim.[19]

If this were not how Mencius thought of things, it would be difficult for
him to provide a satisfactory explanation of how the sages first managed to
grow into moral heroes. If they were no different from other people—if they
were not morally stronger than most of us—then the only explanation for their
exceptional achievement would seem to be, they were fortunate enough to
grow up in a *fortuitously* nurturing environment. Such an explanation would
render human destiny precarious at best. And it simply does not reflect
Mencius' view of history, particularly his description of the sages.

For Mencius, the sages were divinely endowed men of heroic stature. They
worked relentlessly to drain away and control the raging waters of pre-civilized
China. They drove off the primitive beasts which threatened mankind, and they
invented the rudiments of civilization. The sages molded civilization out of
primordial chaos.[20]

The sages overcame incredible obstacles in their struggle to bring order and
peace to the world. Their virtue thrived in the most hostile of environments.
Shun, the epitome of filial-piety, purportedly earned his living as a farmer, a
potter and a fisherman—hardly regal professions.[21] He was hated by his
parents and elder brother, who conspired and attempted to murder him on at

least two occasions.[22] And yet Shun was the model of the filial son and affectionate younger brother. He overcame astounding obstacles and became a moral paragon. This was characteristic of the sages; Mencius consistently depicts them as men who overcame the harshest of circumstances.

Mencius thought that every human being would respond to morality in a similar fashion, and that all were capable of attaining moral perfection. But he also believed that some were better able to lead the way to morality:

> Heaven, produced mankind in such a way that those who first under-
> stand, awaken those who are slow to understand; and those who first
> awaken, awaken those who are slow to awaken.[23]

Mencius' view, that there is a difference in capability, in no way undermines his claim that the sage and I are the same *in kind*.[24] The sage is not different in kind; he is more of what, by nature, human beings are. He is the moral equivalent of a gifted composer or artist, an insightful mathematician or physicist, a creative chef or an athletic champion. The sage is a more concentrated and refined expression of what is most distinctively human. As expressed by one of his disciples:

> ... The unicorn is the same in kind as other four-footed animals, the
> phoenix is the same in kind as other birds of flight; Mount T'ai is the
> same in kind as small mounds of earth and ant-hills; the Yellow River
> and the Sea are the same in kind as puddles of rain. The sage, too, is
> the same in kind as other men. But he stands out among them; he is
> above the crowd. Ever since man first came into the world, there has
> never been one greater than Confucius.[25]

Mencius believed the evil which dominated his world was largely, if not completely, the result of a loss of moral leadership. People were not good because of a decline in the social environment which resulted from a lack of good rulers. The early sages had succeeded in molding a society which provided everyone the opportunity to nurture their moral sprouts and realize their nature, and the result was a happy and prosperous society. Mencius offered this golden age as a paradigm for his own disordered time to emulate.

Here, much of Mencius' argument turns on the credibility of his historical vision. If there never were sage kings in antiquity and a golden age in the past, he has only proposed a world that might be—not described the way the world was and how human beings really are. Even if we grant his vision of the past, there is still one critical issue that requires our attention.

Mencius needed to explain how it was possible for society to decline morally. If there were good leaders in the past, leaders who led their society to moral excellence, how did things go so wrong?[26] Mencius explained one form of the problem of the *origin of evil*: the ill effects of a hostile environment explained the existence of human beings who were good by nature but bad in fact. But given his view of history the problem of the *origin of evil* is not so much *why aren't people good* but rather *how could they possibly have become bad?*

Mencius did not believe civilization was in an uninterrupted downward spiral. Between his age and the sage-emperors Yao and Shun, there had been alternating periods of order and disorder.

> ... After the death of Yao and Shun, the Way of the sages declined. Tyrants arose one after another. They pulled down houses in order to make (pleasure) ponds and lakes, and the people were without a place to rest. They abandoned the fields, turned them into parks and gardens, and the people were unable to secure food and clothing. Heresies and violence arose again. With so many parks, ponds, and lakes, birds and beasts flourished. By the time of (the tyrant) Chou, the world was again in great disorder. The Duke of Chou assisted King Wu in punishing Chou. He attacked (the state of) Yen and within three years put its ruler to death. He drove Fei Lien to the edge of the sea and executed him. He destroyed fifty states, drove tigers, leopards, rhinoceroses and elephants to the distant wilds, and the world rejoiced...
>
> (Again) the world declined and the Way faded into obscurity. Heresies and violence arose once again. There were ministers who murdered their kings and sons who murdered their fathers. Confucius grew apprehensive and composed the *Ch'un-ch'iu*...
>
> No sage-king has yet appeared. The feudal lords do whatever they please, itinerant scholars indulge in senseless debate, and the words of Yang Chu and Mo Ti fill the world...[27]

Exactly how the "way of the sages declined" is left unexplained. But Mencius did say more about the alternating periods of moral order and decay.

> ...Every five hundred years a true King should arise, and in the interval there should be those who are famous in their time. From the Chou dynasty to the present, over seven hundred years have passed. The five hundred year period has been exceeded; the time is ripe. Heaven must not as yet wish to pacify the world. If it did, who is there in the present age other than myself?...[28]

Mencius believed in a recurring pattern of alternating order and disorder, a pattern begun by the world-ordering sages of antiquity. Beginning with these sages, the moral order of the world has waxed and waned. Every five hundred years, a sage emerges to rectify the world, only to be followed by a period of decay and an age of disorder.

This belief in a golden age followed by a fixed period of gradual decline is a very old idea in Chinese thought. It is easy to see how the early Chinese, with their agriculturally inspired world-view and their firm belief in the correspondence of the celestial and terrestrial realms, might seek to find a recurring pattern in history—a pattern that recurred with the regularity of celestial phenomena. Though the precise origins of this belief may never be known, it is supported by another very old idea—the notion of *te* (virtue).[29]

In its earliest stages, *te* was conceived of as a psychic power: a power which a ruler received from Heaven and which allowed him to attract and command others. This power was granted by ancestral spirits and was associated with the ruler's line as well as the ruler himself. But Heaven granted a fixed allotment of *te*, and as the rulers of a given line succeeded one another, they "spent" this allotment. As it diminished so too did their power to rule. The power of the ruling family gradually declined until they could no longer sustain their rule.

As the ruling house declined in power, there was a concomitant decline in society. The peace and order which the founding figure had established began to unravel, until violence and disorder again dominated the world. At this point, Heaven would raise up a new ruler—a ruler whose *te* was strong. This new ruler would receive Heaven's *ming* (mandate), found a new ruling line and begin the cycle again.

In the earliest examples, it seems a ruler could not augment his allocation of *te*. But he could preserve it by strictly observing proper ritual form—most importantly the ritual obligations to his ancestors. With Confucius, this notion underwent radical change. Confucius identified *ritual behavior* with *morally good behavior*, extending the range of ritual across every aspect of social life and down to every member of society.[30] By being morally good an individual not only preserved his *te*, he augmented it.[31] One's ability to rule thus became a function of one's moral development.

This notion of *te*—the moral power which enables a ruler to attract and retain the support of his subjects—may have been the inspiration for Mencius' cyclical view of history. The founding figures of the golden reigns of antiquity were men whose *te* was great—they were the moral heroes of their time. It was their *te*, a kind of *moral charisma*, that propelled them to positions of authority and sustained their rule. This moral charisma gave them a power over others and this power continued, after their deaths, to sustain those who followed them. Mencius seems to have believed that the influence of both good and evil individuals extends beyond their time and fades gradually.

> The influence of a gentleman extends for five generations and then ceases. The influence of a petty person (also) extends for five generations and then ceases. I was never a disciple under Confucius; I have learned of him from others.[32]

Gradually, even the influence of a sage-king diminishes, his power fades and the world begins to slide into disorder. Evil appears and culminates in the rule of a despicable tyrant. Heaven then selects a new champion who overthrows the tyrant, punishes him in the name of Heaven, and restores the moral order.

When we examine Mencius' thought carefully, we see that it is a mixture of new and old. Mencius was seeking to defend Confucianism. In fashioning his defense, he retained much that was old, but he also introduced several monumental innovations. Perhaps his greatest innovation was the development of a rich and persuasive argument grounding the Confucian vision in human nature itself.

But this innovation required additional explanations. How could human beings, who are good by nature, develop into bad people? How could some individuals (the sages) overcome an originally hostile environment and realize their innately good nature? And how could the moral society they fashioned ever go awry? Mencius answered the first question with his explanation of the ill effects a hostile environment could have on the proper growth of human nature, an explanation he advanced with his agricultural metaphors. He explained the sage's original conquest over chaos by granting them exceptional moral strength, and this he could do within the structure of his view of human nature. But to explain how human beings could become bad once society had been made good, Mencius reached back for a very old belief, a belief in cyclical periods of social order and chaos.

This belief seems to be related to the ancient concept of *te*, which since the time of Confucius had come to be thought of as a kind of *moral charisma*: a power which enabled a ruler to reign by moral force. This power was at its peak with the founding figure. But after his reign it began to fade, and as it diminished, the light with which he had illuminated the Way grew dim and eventually went out. Evil emerged and increased: gradually becoming dominant in the world. Heaven then raised up a new champion and the cycle began anew.

Mencius seems to have believed this process was somehow built into the very structure of the cosmos. The moral society had a natural life-span of five hundred years. It was like a plant, which is born, matures, grows old and dies. And, like a plant, in its death it carried the seeds of its regeneration. Like the procession of the four seasons or the waxing and waning of the moon, the cycle ended only to begin again.

But this leaves Mencius with a strange picture. If the five hundred year cycle is part of Heaven's plan, then Heaven seems to be responsible for evil as well as for good. Heaven encourages human beings to be good, it provides them with a good nature, but it also imposes a cycle of moral light and darkness upon the world. The five hundred year cycle seems to grant those who catch the cycle on the moral "up swing" a tremendous advantage and seems to doom those who are drawn under on the "down swing" to a horrible disadvantage. If this too is a matter of *ming* (fate), then fate can indeed be cruel. This picture seems fatalistic in a way not usually associated with Mencius.[33]

The Origin of Evil:
Wang Yang-ming

W ang did not share Mencius' agricultural model of moral self-cultivation. He did not believe evil arose in the world because a poor environment or lack of the right kind of care stunted or warped the proper course of human nature's development. Wang believed all people possess a perfect and fully-formed moral nature: a moral endowment which he called the *mind in itself*. He believed evil came into being when people failed to heed the guidance of this innate moral mind, and that such failure occurred when their *liang chih* (pure knowing) became obscured by selfish desires. When people lose sight of their moral minds, they lose their innate moral guide. They lose their way on the path of morality and turn to evil.

> Someone said, "All people have *shih hsin* (this mind). Since the mind is principle, why is it some people become good and others become evil?"
>
> The Master said, "The mind of the evil person has lost its original state."[34]

Explaining how this is possible—how selfish desires arise and how we lose sight of the guidance of *liang chih* is Wang's particular form of the problem of the *origin of evil*.

Wang, like Mencius, did not believe in radical evil. The world was not a battleground upon which two mutually opposed forces fought for the hearts and minds of human beings. Evil was not a separate principle fundamentally opposed to the innate moral mind. Evil was a consequence of a dysfunctional mind; it arose when the mind became imbalanced.

A person's mind becomes imbalanced when he becomes attached; when he performs an action for himself, rather than because it should be done. The action itself may be morally impeccable, but if it is motivated by personal desire, it becomes a source of evil. Acting out of personal desire, defiles the innate purity of the mind. It obscures pure knowing by "adding something to the mind in itself." And according to Wang, nothing may be added to the mind in itself without inducing an imbalance.

> The Master once said to his disciples, "No thought should stick to the mind in itself, just as not the least bit of dirt should stick to the eye. It requires very little dirt to cover the eye and blot out Heaven and earth."
>
> He also said, "The thought need not be a selfish thought. Even good thoughts should not become stuck in any way. It is like putting gold or jade dust in the eye, just the same it cannot open."[35]

The perfectly cultivated moral individual acts only in accordance with principle, motivated only by the mind's pure knowing. In an important sense, his actions are not his own. The more advanced his spiritual development, the weaker his sense of acting for himself. It becomes increasingly difficult for him even to describe his actions, because they become less and less *his actions*.

> The Master said, "As one's *kung fu* (practice) becomes refined, it becomes more difficult to capture in words and harder to explain. Attaching any thought to what is refined and subtle, undermines the entire *kung fu*.[36]

If we examine cases of undeserved suffering described in Wang's writings, we see he shared, with Mencius, certain beliefs concerning the moral character of such events and the role of suffering in the world. We also begin to see his explanation of how the mind first loses its innate balance and allows evil to arise.

The first case involves his disciple, Lu Ch'eng, whose son had become critically ill.

> I was living temporarily at the bureau of state ceremonials, when, unexpectedly, I received a letter from home saying my son was critically ill. I was extremely saddened and unbearably depressed. The master said, "This is precisely the time you should exert effort. If you let this opportunity slip away, what use is all your learning? People must train and polish themselves at just such times as this..."[37]

The second case is the illness of the disciple Ch'en Chiu-ch'uan.

> I was bedridden in Ch'ien-chou. The master said, "Sickness is something difficult to rectify. How do you feel?"

> I replied *kung fu* (practice) is extremely difficult."

> He said, "Remain cheerful. That is (your) practice now."[38]

In neither case does Wang offer any justification for the occurrence of these illnesses. He remains true to the tradition, begun by Confucius, of not regarding such events as candidates for moral praise or blame.[39] The only moral dimension to such events rests in how the individual reacts to the situation into which he is thrust. Wang urges Lu and Ch'en to use their calamities as *opportunities to practice*. He shared Mencius' belief that adversity is an opportunity to temper one's character.

We see this belief again in Wang's description of how the sage Shun reacted to his brother's attempts to kill him.[40]

> Initially, Shun contributed to Hsiang's desire to kill him; he was too anxious for Hsiang to become good. In this, Shun was mistaken. After

gaining experience, he realized *kung fu* (practice) was simply to rectify himself—not to admonish others. This was the way to achieve harmony. This was where Shun could *stimulate his mind, harden his nature and improve his deficiencies.*[41] The words of the ancients all concern their personal experiences. That is why we feel them so deeply.[42]

Wang did not explicitly advocate Mencius' belief that Heaven purposely burdens those destined for greatness, but he did believe adversity was central to the task of moral self-cultivation.[43] For Wang, difficulties were not punishment from Heaven or a sign that Heaven was displeased. They were opportunities to temper one's character, chances to *stimulate the mind and harden the nature*. Wang used this expression, from the *Mencius*, to describe his own most difficult period: his banishment in Kuei-chou.

Later, I was transferred to Lung-ch'ang. I lived among barbarian people and faced great difficulties. After *stimulating my mind and hardening my nature* it seemed I had become enlightened...[44]

It was only when Wang was stripped of every comfort and advantage—when he was armed only with his *liang chih* that he found the truth. The passage continues.

I searched for personal realization for yet another year and looked for confirmation in the Five Classics and the Four Books.[45] It was like a raging river bursting its banks and rushing to the sea. I realized—to my joy—that the Way of the sage is level, like a broad highway. But contemporary Confucians have recklessly forged narrow pathways. They tread on thorns and brambles and fall into pits and trenches. In the final analysis, their teachings are inferior even to Buddhism and Taoism. No wonder the best scholars reject Confucianism and hasten to these teachings. Is this the fault of Buddhism and Taoism?

Wang admired aspects of Taoist and Buddhist practice; the followers of these schools had managed to attain certain limited goals—such as lessening selfish desires and maintaining a sense of concentration and inner peace. But their achievement was not without cost. They attained these goals by following a forced and unnatural path which was fundamentally flawed. Wang argued Buddhists were motivated by a selfish desire: a desire to escape from *samsara* and Taoists sought to attain the selfish goal of personal immortality. They both sought *personal salvation*, and this was anathema to the goal of non-attachment to which they, as well as Wang, aspired.[46]

Taoists discuss vacuity motivated by a desire to *yang sheng* (nourish life). Buddhists discuss emptiness motivated by a desire to escape the sorrowful sea of life and death. Both add selfish thoughts to (the mind) in itself. (The mind) thereby loses its original vacuous and empty nature and is obstructed. The sage simply returns to the original state of pure knowing and does not add any selfish thoughts.[47]

This was not the only error the Buddhists had made. They were attached to the idea of purity itself. Wang argued they sought to maintain purity instead of realizing they were innately pure. Their effort itself was an impurity and interfered with the operation of *liang chih*—it was like jade or gold dust in the eye.

...Buddhists differ from us; their minds are motivated by selfishness. Now to desire to think of neither good nor evil and thereby keep the mind's pure knowing clear, tranquil, and at ease is to have a mind of selfishness and greed, to be arbitrary and dogmatic...[48]

Wang seems to have adopted this criticism, almost without modification, from the *Platform Sūtra*, a text he had read and at times quoted.

Suppose someone holds the doctrine of clinging to purity. But the nature of man is fundamentally pure. It is only because of deluded thoughts that the *tathatā* is covered over and obscured. Apart from deluded thoughts, the fundamental nature is perfectly pure. If you make an effort to cling to purity this will only give rise to the delusion of purity... Those who advocate this view obstruct their original nature and end up being bound by purity.[49]

Buddhists and Taoists had upset the original balance of the mind by adding selfish thoughts of personal salvation and false notions of purity to the mind in itself. They became attached to these notions, and they thereby obscured their pure knowing.

But to Wang, the Buddhists and Taoists were not the source of the world's problems. They were symptoms of a disordered world but not the causes of that disorder.[50] The Buddhists and Taoists were ineffective; they could not govern the world and their methods would not lead one to the truth, but they would not lead one to extreme evil. The real culprits, the source of the world's evil were degenerate Confucians. Their perverse practices failed to enlighten; they had allowed Buddhism and Taoism to flourish and caused positive harm in the world. This idea is expressed clearly by one of Wang's students.

Wang Chia-hsiu asked, "Buddhists entice people to enter their way with the prospect of leaving the cycle of life and death. Taoists entice people to enter their way with the prospect of achieving immortality. (But) in their hearts, they do not wish people to do evil....

... Confucians of later generations have only gotten hold of the lower parts of the sage's doctrine, and it is fragmented and mutilated. They have lost the truth and drifted into the four schools of memorization and recitation, composition, success and profit, and textual criticism. In the final analysis, these cannot but be regarded as heterodox schools... When compared to the followers of Buddhism and Taoism—whose minds are pure, desires few and who have transcended worldly concerns—surprisingly (these later Confucians) seem inferior in certain respects...[51]

The "four schools" described in the passage above are the root cause of the evil Wang saw in the world. These four fundamental errors are all cases of seeking form over content, mistaking attendant features of the moral life as goals in themselves.[52]

Of these four, (pursuing) *success and profit* is the only one for which precedents can be found in Confucius or Mencius.[53] And if we examine this notion carefully, it becomes clear that *success and profit* is simply an alternative expression for Wang's old enemy: "selfish desire." The other three errors clearly are not separate types; they are the handmaidens of this central error of selfishness. They aid and abet the practice of selfishness by legitimizing it and by distracting attention from the business of moral self-cultivation. They replace *real learning* with purely *academic learning*, and this, according to Wang, is the root cause of evil.

Wang displayed a certain anti-intellectual persuasion.[54] He believed society exclusively and wrongly emphasized knowledge, in the sense of information, at the expense of wisdom (moral knowledge) and style, in composition and presentation, over moral content. True learning was moral learning. It produced a belief in the truths of Confucianism and not simply knowledge of those truths and an ability to describe them.

Wang distinguished between true knowledge, the moral knowledge innate to human beings, and acquired knowledge: knowledge of the world, including knowledge of moral standards. True moral knowledge is the beginning of proper action; knowledge and action, in their original state, cannot be separated. Knowledge separated from action is simply not true knowledge; a separation of the two is symptomatic of obscuration by selfish desires. One of Wang's students, Hsü Ai, once asked:

"Now there are people who, despite knowing they should be filial to their parents and respectful to their elder brother, cannot be filial or respectful. From this it is clear that knowledge and action are two separate things."

The master said: "They have already been separated by selfish desires; this is not the original state of knowledge and action. There have never been people who know but do not act. Those who know but do not act, simply do not yet know. Sages and worthies taught people about knowledge and action, so people would return to the original state of knowledge and action and not just do what they could and quit. Thus the *Great Learning* gives us examples of *chen chih hsing* (true knowledge and action) saying, it is 'like loving a beautiful color or hating a bad odor.'[55]

The person who "knows" parents should be served with filial piety but doesn't proceed to serve them in this manner simply does not possess *chen chih* (true knowledge). Wang discusses *true knowledge* in several passages,[56] and from these discussions it is clear he means by *true knowledge* an understanding that embraces, in addition to a cognitive awareness of a situation, a corresponding and appropriate emotional response.

Selfish desires subvert the unity of knowledge and action by interfering with the mind's innate ability to know. Like foreign matter in the eye or congestion in the nose, selfish desires disrupt the normal operation of a natural human faculty: the mind's *liang chih* (pure knowing). From his theoretical claim about the nature of knowledge and action, Wang moves to the practical conclusion that one cannot possess *true knowledge* unless one has *already* acted.

> It is like a person with a stuffed up nose. Even if he sees a malodorous object before him, he does not smell it, and so he does not hate it. This is simply not to know the odor. This is just like the case of saying someone knows filial piety or brotherly respect. That person must have already acted with filial piety or brotherly respect before he can be said to know them. One cannot say he knows filial piety or brotherly respect, simply because he knows how to say something filial or brotherly.[57]

The notion that true moral knowledge embraces both cognitive and emotional components and the specialized use of the term *chen chih* (true knowledge) to refer to this type of knowledge did not originate with Wang. Ch'eng Yi used it in one of his most memorable passages:

> *True knowledge* is different from ordinary knowledge. I once met a farmer who had been mauled by a tiger. Someone said that a tiger was mauling people in the area, and everyone was alarmed. But this one farmer had on his face an expression that differed from the rest. Everyone, even a child, knows a tiger mauls people, but they do not possess *true knowledge*. It is only true *true knowledge* if it is like that of the farmer. When men continue to do what they know they should not do, this is because they do not truly know it is wrong. If they truly knew, they would not do it.[58]

Wang believed Confucianism had degenerated because it had come to regard moral learning as something one obtains from academic study—that it is acquired knowledge, something added to one's nature. Learning had become the pursuit of information, the ability to catalogue and compare passages from the classics and the ability to compose clever compositions, loaded with literary allusions. It was no longer the quest for *true knowledge*. *True knowledge* included an appropriate emotional response and the motivation needed to act; it was the beginning of the appropriate action. But knowledge and action had become separated. People had become infatuated with the intellect and lost sight of the moral guidance provided by the heart/mind.

But how did people, who are endowed with a pure and perfect innate nature, ever go astray? How did their pure knowing ever become beclouded? What caused them to turn from true learning and pursue false doctrines?

A good place to start, in approaching this problem, is Wang's *Four Sentence Teaching*.

> The mind in itself is without good or evil,
> Good and evil are thoughts in motion,
> Knowing good and evil is pure knowing,
> Doing good and getting rid of evil is *ko wu*.[59]

The mind in itself is beyond description; it can only be known as it is manifested in actual human beings. But when the mind is manifested in human form, it loses its original perfection. It is no longer *tao hsin* (the mind of the Way); it is *jen hsin* (the human mind). These are not two different minds; they are the mind in two different states.

> The mind is one. Before it is mixed into human beings, it is called *tao hsin* (the mind of the Way); after it is mixed with human falsehood, it is called *jen hsin* (the human mind). When the human mind attains what is proper, it is the mind of the Way; when the mind of the Way forsakes what is proper, it is the human mind. From the start, there are not two minds. Ch'eng Tzu said, "The human mind is human desire. The mind of the Way is Heavenly Principle."[60] His wording appears to divide them (into two minds), but his idea is correct.[61]

The movements of the human mind naturally produce both good and evil thoughts. But *liang chih* is also an aspect of every movement of the mind. It is aware of the goodness or evil of each and every thought. If unobstructed, pure knowing will rectify each thought as it arises, and one will then act only in appropriate ways.

> Whenever we become attached to any of the seven emotions, this is a (selfish) desire. Yet the instant there is any kind of attachment, *liang chih* is naturally aware of it. When *liang chih* is aware of it, the impediment is removed and *liang chih* resumes its original state.[62]

Evil actions can only arise if *liang chih* somehow becomes obstructed. If we examine further Wang's understanding of the two states of the mind we see how pure knowing becomes obstructed.

Wang explained the two states of the mind by adopting Ch'eng Yi's scheme, which described a pure and perfect innate nature defiled—as it comes into being—by *ch'i* (psycho-physical stuff). This *ch'i* is not evil per se; but it does obscure the clear perception of our perfectly pure nature. Because of the interference of *ch'i*, we fail to see our fundamental unity with and our true place in the universal order. We begin to generate selfish thoughts and desires, and these further obscure the perception of our innate nature. Moreover, *ch'i* naturally occurs in varying degrees of "coarseness," and the coarseness of one's *ch'i* determines how clearly principle is perceived.[63] All people face the difficult task of refining their endowment of *ch'i*, and most have an endowment that requires concerted effort to refine. But even a person with exceedingly refined *ch'i* is subject to the pull of physical desires. It is part of the human condition to continually confront the danger of losing sight of the mind in itself.

> There is nothing evil in the nature. Therefore there is no knowledge that is not pure. *Liang chih* is the equilibrium before the feelings are aroused. It is broad and impartial, the original state of stillness and inactivity. It is possessed by all men. However, it cannot but be darkened and obscured by physical desires. Therefore, one must study, in order to eliminate the darkness and obscuration.[64]

For Wang there were two factors which contributed to the emergence of evil. First, there was the interference of *ch'i*. *Ch'i* necessarily "darkens and obscures" one's pure knowing. And since *ch'i* occurs in various degrees of "coarseness," it seems different people are "obstructed" to varying degrees as a matter of principle. Second, there were the different endowments of abilities each person received.[65]

As I noted earlier, this second factor presents problems for Wang's claim that everyone can become Yao or Shun and raises serious questions about how much of the task of moral self-cultivation is truly within an individual's power to control.[66] It also seems to leave Wang saying that evil, as well as good, exists as a matter of principle. But there is another problem with Wang's explanation that becomes apparent when we examine his notion of history and compare it to Mencius'.

Wang shared Mencius' belief in an historical golden age, but unlike Mencius, he did not believe in a five hundred year cycle describing the growth and decay of the moral society. For Wang there was no cycle. The Way had been in force in highest antiquity—during the golden age of Yao and Shun and during the following period of the Three Dynasties. Since that time, society had been in a constant downward spiral.[67]

...With the decline of the Three Dynasties, the kingly way expired and the art of hegemony flourished. Since the passing of Confucius and Mencius, the learning of the sage has been covered in darkness and depraved teachings have spread across the land.[68]

As Wang traces the path of this decay, he reaches a time when the three academic "errors" arose.

...The learning of the sage was long past and the art of hegemony became well established and deeply ingrained. Even the worthy and wise could not avoid being tainted by it. Their attempts to clarify, repair, and embellish (the Way) in order to restore its joyous light to the world, only strengthened the hegemon's defenses.[69] No one could even glimpse the gate or wall of the sagely Way. Thereupon, those who practiced the learning of textual criticism came to be regarded with renown. Those who advocated the learning of memorization and recitation came to be regarded as learned. And those who indulged in writing compositions came to be regarded as refined. Thus with great bluster and noise the members of this herd began to compete with one another, each trying to establish himself in the world. No one knows how many schools there were. There were ten thousand paths and a thousand trails, but no one knew which one to take...[70]

This was the final blow to the Confucian way; it marked the beginning of the triumph of selfishness and profiteering.

It has been several thousand years now since the poison of success and profit has soaked into the very marrow of man's heart and through practice become part of his nature. People boast to each other of their knowledge, crush each other with power, wrangle through every means and struggle for fame and glory...[71]

Wang's account offers no explanation for society's decline. Why did those who were once so vigilant become so lax? How did the people of the golden age manage to unlearn the Way. In the first half of this chapter, I showed how Mencius' explanation of the existence of a five hundred year cycle carried with it the difficulty of fatalism, but at least Mencius attempted an explanation. Wang seems to be without any explanation for his view of history.

If Wang believed the people of later ages had been overwhelmed by the drag of physical desire, then he needed to explain how the ancient sages ever managed to overcome it and create the golden age in the first place. The only possibility would seem to be that somehow either the "quality" of people's *ch'i*, the "quantity" of their endowed abilities or both varies over time and had been in steady decline. But if this is true then it seems the moral decay which Wang so roundly condemned was according to principle. Wang left no clue as to his position on this issue. He seems to be unable to account for either the rise or fall of his golden age.

Wang simply asserted that over time the Way had decayed and at a point in this downward spiral the "four schools" of false learning had emerged. But he gives no explanation of why they came into being. Like many Buddhists of his time, Wang believed he lived in a degenerate age. His Way had fallen from the golden heights of high antiquity to the nadir of contemporary existence.[72] He also shared with them a similar form of the problem of the origin of evil. Like them, he believed the source of the evil which had gradually taken over the world was a kind of self-deception. Human beings had somehow managed to lose sight of something they had once seen clearly. They had unlearned what they once knew so well—something they still knew in the depths of their heart/minds. Evil was the result of a self-imposed ignorance. But what was the cause of this ignorance? In the final analysis, Wang did not have an explanation; he could not explain how things originally went awry. He shared this burden with the Buddhists. And he also shared with them a conviction that answering such questions was not conducive to alleviating the problem. Like them, his concern was *therapeutic* and not *theoretical*;[73] he sought a cure for the evil he perceived but he had no explanation of its origin.[74]

The Origin of Evil:
Conclusion

Mencius viewed human nature as a course of development which if allowed to reach its natural conclusion would result in fully moral human beings. He saw as evil, any disruption of or deviation from this natural course of development. This could occur in a variety of different ways. Denying individuals the necessities of life and an environment conducive to moral growth caused most to abandon the true course and fall into evil ways. A failure to devote enough of the right kind of attention to moral self-cultivation, a failure to afford the heart/mind its proper place as guide and governor of the self, also led to evil. One became seduced by lesser pleasures or false doctrines, and one's moral sprouts withered and died from neglect. And finally, the wrong kind of effort, artificially helping the moral sprouts to grow, not only does not contribute to moral development, it does positive harm.

Mencius believed some individuals were morally gifted, they had a greater natural ability to withstand the hardships of an environment hostile to moral growth. They were able to develop despite the hardships they faced. And they led others to the moral life by creating a society conducive to moral growth, a society in which each individual found the material necessities and moral guidance required for their development. Such a society had existed in high antiquity, during the reigns of Yao and Shun, and again during the early years of the Chou dynasty.

But why did society decay? How could the ideal society created by the early sages ever go awry? If human beings naturally grew into moral agents, the society which provided an ideal environment for their moral growth should have continued to produce greater and greater numbers of morally cultivated individuals. Mencius taught that the morally perfected societies of antiquity had decayed, and he needed to explain how this was possible.

Mencius believed there was a natural cycle of five hundred years describing the rise and fall of the moral society. The moral society had a finite life. It flourished, and after a period of decay and collapse it rose again. This belief is easily seen as yet another manifestation of Mencius' tendency to see things in terms of agricultural metaphors. And it may also be related to much older notions in Chinese thought.

But this view leaves Mencius in an awkward position. It leaves him attributing to Heaven the boon of human nature's goodness and the bane of an unavoidable, moral dark age. His explanation carries with it the difficulty of fatalism.

Wang had a very different notion of human nature. He did not believe in Mencius' natural course of moral growth. He believed the innate moral nature was a perfect, fully formed endowment. But this endowment was lodged in *ch'i* (psycho-physical stuff). When combined with *ch'i*, the *tao hsin* (mind of the Way) becomes *jen hsin* (the human mind). And the movements of the human mind naturally give rise to both good and evil thoughts. Monitoring these thoughts is *liang chih* (pure knowing). This moral faculty immediately knows good or evil and when aware of evil immediately eliminates such thoughts from the mind. But *ch'i* interferes with the operation of this moral faculty. This allows selfish thoughts and desires to arise. These further interfere with the functioning of *liang chih* and allow evil to flourish.

The degree to which an individual's *liang chih* is so "obscured" depends upon two factors. the "quality" of his *ch'i* and the "quantity" of his innate abilities. But these are both part of an individual's endowment. It seems evil—as well as good—is a matter governed by principle.

There is another, more dramatic, problem with Wang's explanation of the origin of evil. It fails to account for his description of history. Like Mencius, Wang believed in a past golden age, the time of the sage kings Yao and Shun. But Wang could not explain how this golden age had declined, how the morally perfected individuals of the ideal past had unlearned the Way and allowed the golden age to fade away. Wang did not believe in Mencius' five hundred year cycle. He saw a steady, uninterrupted downward spiral, propelled by a deepening ignorance of the Confucian Way. In the course of this decline, the three "academic errors" arose and completely blocked the learning of the sage. By Wang's time, the pursuit of success and profit had won and completely dominated the world for more than fifteen hundred years.

But nowhere, in Wang's works, do we find an explanation of how this ignorance first arose, what series of events caused the glory of the golden age to sputter and eventually die out. In this respect, Wang's view seems very similar to certain aspects of Buddhist thought. They too lacked an adequate explanation of the origin of evil. Like Wang, they claimed their approach was *therapeutic* and not *theoretical*. And like the Buddhists, Wang believed he saw what was wrong with the world and knew how to "cure" its condition. In the following chapter, I examine the cure he prescribed, his method of self-cultivation.

Chapter 4

Self-Cultivation:
Mencius

Mencius and Wang Yang-ming were equally optimistic about the prospect of human perfectibility. Both believed human beings were uniquely equipped for the task of moral self-cultivation: human beings were moral creatures, *by nature*. But, as we have seen in the previous chapters, their view on the *nature of morality, human nature* and the *origin of evil* differed remarkably, in spite of Wang's self-avowed allegiance to Mencius. This difference is equally manifest in their respective views on *self-cultivation*.

We can distinguish, in their thought, two separate models of self-cultivation: Mencius' *development* model and Wang Yang-ming's *discovery* model.[1] Like their differing views on the *origin of evil*, these two models reflect distinctly different views on *human nature* and the *nature of morality*. A clear understanding of these models helps us to understand some of the significant similarities and important differences between Mencius and Wang.

Mencius taught that all human beings are born with nascent moral tendencies and that these fragile moral *tuan* (sprouts) are the only legitimate source of morality.[2] He pointed to a variety of paradigm cases as evidence for the existence of these innate moral tendencies, and he used these as starting points for the process of moral self-cultivation. These cases fall into several distinct types. There are: the *indications of childhood*, the *give-away actions* of adults, *testimonials* to the moral life and the results of his *thought experiments*.[3]

Mencius never claimed these spontaneous moral actions and feelings will, of themselves, result in complete moral cultivation. For Mencius, these were only the beginnings of virtue; examples of man's moral "sprouts." He insisted these "sprouts" need to be developed; not developing them results in moral failure.

> All men have these four sprouts in themselves. If a man develops them fully, they will be like a fire that has begun to burn or a spring that has begun to find vent. If they are developed fully, he can protect all within the four seas. If they are not developed, he will be unable even to serve his mother and father.[4]

For Mencius, the task of self-cultivation is the development and extension of the innate moral sense. His method for helping someone follow the path of moral self-cultivation begins by eliciting spontaneous moral feelings in the person. He does this by identifying the person's own *give-away* actions, as these present themselves, and by relying upon his repertoire of other types of paradigmatic cases. Mencius points to these examples as evidence that each person possesses the moral sprouts within himself. Mencius then leads people to focus attention on actual examples of proper moral action which they themselves have performed and to fully savor the good feelings that naturally accompany such actions. The contemplation of such examples, in awareness of their true motivation, elicits a feeling of joy, and Mencius believed this joy nurtures the innate moral sense. Such contemplation provides conclusive evidence of one's innate moral sense and the positive feedback which accompanies it reinforces one's moral tendencies. Mencius believed the moral sprouts grow when nurtured in this way.

As the moral sense develops, Mencius encourages the person to *extend* these moral feelings, by pointing out other situations worthy of a similar moral response; situations Mencius knows will elicit the same positive feedback. He urges the person to continue this process of nurturing and extending the innate moral sprouts. One must "accumulate righteousness"[5] by constantly attending to the task of moral self-cultivation. One is to *pi yu shih yen* (pay constant attention to the task).[6] If the innate moral sense is nurtured and extended to its full potential it will eventually inform all of one's actions. The result is a perfectly virtuous individual.[7]

> All men have some things which they cannot bear; extending that feeling to what they can bear results in benevolence. All men have some things which they will not do; extending that feeling to what they will do results in righteousness.[8]

Overcoming moral failure involves two basic steps: *recognizing* one should do some action and then finding the *motivation* to perform the action. The rational judgment that one should do a given action is often not motivation enough; one often needs to *grow into* the idea of acting morally. Mencius believed people are, by nature, disposed to *grow into* the idea of acting morally, but they need time, the proper environment and some effort in order to accomplish this.

The effort needed, in order to grow into the idea of acting morally, consists of focusing one's attention on the task of nurturing and extending one's moral feelings. If one can focus one's attention on this task, the moral sense will grow spontaneously and, with continued effort, will inform every aspect of one's life. Everyone possesses the ability to make this effort; becoming adept at extending one's moral feelings is what distinguishes morally superior individuals. As Mencius tells King Hsüan of Ch'i:

> Hence one who extends his compassion can take care of all the people within the Four Seas. One who does not cannot even care for his own family. There is just one thing in which the ancients greatly surpassed

others, and that was in being good at extending what they did. Why is it then that your compassion is sufficient to reach animals yet you do no good acts that reach the people?[9]

The task of focusing attention on the responses of one's innate moral sprouts and the effort of extending these feelings by discovering them in other appropriate situations is the "weeding and hoeing" of moral self-cultivation. One must exert oneself in this manner, even in the most benign social environments.

Mencius said, In years of plenty, many young people are reliable, but in years of want many cannot control themselves. It is not because of their Heavenly conferred endowments that such differences exist. It is because (some) have allowed their hearts to become mired.

Now take the case of barley. Sow it and cover it up. If the soil is the same, and the time of planting is also the same, it will sprout and grow. And when its proper time has come, it all will be ripe. Though there are differences (in the yield of barley), these are because the soil was rich or poor, there was unequal nourishment by rain and dew or unequal application of human effort.[10]

The growth of the moral sprouts is a natural process. It extends through time, has definite stages and follows a pattern of gradual *development*. The process, as Mencius describes it, is reminiscent of Confucius' account of his own spiritual development.

At fifteen, I *chih yü hsüeh* (set my heart on learning). At thirty, I stood firm. At forty, I had no more doubts. At fifty, I understood Heaven's decree. At sixty, I followed it obediently. At seventy, I could follow my heart and never stray beyond what was right.[11]

For Mencius, moral self-cultivation is a long and gradual process of growth. One ripens in the course of self-cultivation just as barley ripens as it matures. As one advances, more of what human beings are destined to be becomes manifest. Human nature is revealed, in this process, and if the process runs its full course, human nature blossoms into sagehood. A life of self-cultivation is the natural course of human development.

There is an order and sequence to this development. The process of learning the Way consists of a series of definite steps, none of which may be skipped over. Mencius illustrates this point with a metaphor of flowing water.

Hsü Tzu said, "Confucius often expressed his admiration for water, saying: 'Oh water! Oh water!' What did he see in water?"

Mencius replied, "Water from a spring gushes forth—never stopping day or night. It advances only after filling every indentation, flowing

> to the sea. Anything with a source is like this—and this is what he saw in it."[12]

> .... Flowing water is such that it does not advance until it has filled every indentation. A gentleman who has *chih yü tao* (set his heart on the Way) does not advance until he has perfected each lesson.[13]

One does not advance until one has fulfilled every requirement of each stage of the process, until one has "perfected each lesson." One cannot attain the ultimate goal of self-cultivation suddenly. Learning the Way is like cultivating a garden, it is a gradual process of growth. One cannot expect to attain full growth instantly. But, in the course of the process of growth, one gains greater and greater moral strength. Mencius borrowed a term from Chinese physiology to describe this moral strength; he called it *hao jan chih ch'i* (flood-like energy).[14]

> (Mencius said)... "I am good at nourishing my *hao jan chih ch'i* (flood-like energy)."

> Kung-sun Ch'ou asked), "I would like to know what you mean by *flood-like energy."*

> (Mencius replied), "It is difficult to put into words. It is the greatest and most unyielding of energies. If one nourishes it with integrity and does it no harm, it will fill up the space between Heaven and earth. This energy is the companion of righteousness and the Way. Without them, it will starve. It is nurtured by an accumulation of righteousness; it cannot be obtained through a quick display of righteousness. If one's actions do not rest well with one's heart, then (this energy) starves. That is why I say Kao Tzu never understood righteousness—he viewed it as something external...[15]

Mencius' *hao jan chih ch'i* is the moral courage which grows within a person who practices the Way. Mencius believed this moral courage grows naturally within anyone who freely acts in accordance with the Way. Such action nourishes the moral sprouts within us and helps them to grow. Righteousness nourishes the *flood-like energy*, just as rain, sunshine and fertile soil nourish the "energy" of a growing plant. As one's moral strength grows, one is able to perform more, and more difficult, moral actions. The effect builds and "flood-like" it overcomes all obstacles; it then "fills up the space between Heaven and earth."

But this moral energy will not grow if one forces oneself to comply with the Way. Following a prescribed course of action without having an accompanying emotional commitment to that action not only will fail to nourish the moral sprouts—it injures their growth. The passage, quoted above, continues by presenting the parable of the *Farmer of Sung*.

...Pay constant attention to the task. Do not neglect the mind; do not (make an artificial effort to) help it grow. Do not be like the man of Sung. There was a man of Sung who pulled at his shoots of grain, because he was anxious for them to grow. Having done this he went home, not realizing what he had done. He said to his family, "I am worn out today; I have been helping the grain to grow." His son rushed out of the house to look at their plants and found that they all had withered.

There are few in the world who can resist the urge to help their grain to grow. Some think there is nothing they can do to help. They leave their grain unattended, not even bothering to weed. Others try to help their grain to grow. They go out and pull at the shoots. Such actions not only fail to help the grain, they harm it.[16]

Mencius encourages us to "pay constant attention to the task." We must never neglect the task of moral self-cultivation. We must reflect, searching for our moral sprouts and experiencing the joy of moral thought and action. And we must look at the world around us to discover other suitable objects for the effort of extending our moral feelings.

But self-cultivation is a gradual process of development, and we must not skip any step in the process. We must not make an artificial effort to force the growth of the moral sprouts. Mencius' warning not to make an artificial effort, urges us to avoid attempting a morally correct action, if we are not emotionally ready to perform it. He would rather we start by performing those actions which we can do with a full-blooded commitment. He believed only such actions nourish the moral energy within us and helps our moral sprouts to grow. He held this belief, confident they would grow and propel us to ever greater moral achievement.

There is an obvious danger inherent in this approach. One could end up waiting forever to perform one's first moral action. One could always put off making the difficult choice to act morally and claim one is "just not ready" for such an action. This is a difficulty Mencius recognized and responded to but did not fully resolve. He insisted there were cases where one just had to "bootstrap" oneself into action. Moral self-cultivation cannot accommodate perpetual procrastination.

Tai Ying-chih said, "I am not able, at the present time, to implement a tax of (only) ten percent *and* abolish the customs and market duties. Could I just lighten these and wait until next year to abolish them completely?"

Mencius said, "Take the case of a man who each day steals one of his neighbor's chickens. Someone tells him, 'This is not the way a gentleman behaves.' And he replies, 'Could I just cut down on how

many I steal? I'll only take one each month and wait until next year
to stop completely.' If you know something is not right, stop it as soon
as you can—why wait until next year?"[17]

The *development* and *discovery* models are two ideal types of self-cultivation. But in practice, things are never quite so neatly divided. In one respect,
Mencius' developmental method of self-cultivation resembles the discovery
model: one must realize that *one has* the nascent moral sense. Without this
discovery, the task of moral self-cultivation cannot even begin. But in order
for the moral task to continue and succeed, one must not only *realize* one has
innate moral dispositions, one must also *believe* that these nascent moral
tendencies will grow, if only given the chance. This belief is what propels one
to *pi yu shih yen* (pay constant attention to the task). Without this belief, there
is no way to pursue Mencius' path of moral self-cultivation with the lively
interest necessary for its success.

The case of King Hsüan of Ch'i provides an excellent example of Mencius
at work and a clear illustration of his method of self-cultivation. When Mencius
explained to the king the hidden reason which had motivated the king's
exchanging a sheep for an ox—the king's spontaneous sprout of compassion—
he helped the king discover his "lost heart", his innate moral sprout.[18]

> The king was pleased, and said, 'It is said in the *Book of Poetry*, "The
> minds of others, I am able by reflection to measure;"—this describes
> you. I indeed did the thing, but when I turned my thoughts inward,
> and examined into it, I could not discover my own mind. When you
> spoke those words, they struck a chord in me.'[19]

One might question whether the king's sparing of the ox was indeed a *moral
action* after all, for he did so without being aware of his motivation. But for
Mencius, the king's action was moral, because it was motivated by the innate
moral sprout of compassion. Mencius' aim was to reveal to the king the
existence of his moral sprouts, even though—in this particular case—they
were not properly applied.[20]

Mencius succeeded in helping the king discover his sprout of compassion,
and he urged the king to extend this compassion to his subjects. Indeed it seems
the similarity between the ox's suffering the people's suffering was already
becoming apparent to the king, for the king himself likened the ox's frightened
appearance to, "an innocent *person* going to the place of death".[21] But here is
where the real difficulties began. The king found himself without the corresponding emotional reaction; he lacked the motivation necessary for action,
in the case of his people.[22]

The king goes on, in the latter half of Book I, to offer reasons why he can't
carry out a benevolent rule: he is fond of power, the pleasures of his park, valor,
wealth, women and song. Interestingly, Mencius does not counsel the king to

give up these desires but only to share them with his people, for this is the only way to *really* enjoy them.

Throughout their encounters, Mencius keeps pointing to the people—the oppressed, suffering people—confident that if the king would only focus his attention on *them* his moral sprouts would grow and motivate the king to proper action. Mencius was trying to get the king on the road to moral self-cultivation; he knew it was a long and difficult road, but he believed that if only the sprouts of morality were given an opportunity, they would grow into a strong and lively disposition.

King Hsüan discovered his moral sprouts, he could *see* that he had a moral sense, but he did not *believe* that these sprouts would grow and extend to every aspect of his life. As a consequence, he did not pursue Mencius' program of moral self-cultivation. Mencius was careful to distinguish these two distinct aspects of the task of moral self-cultivation—the *seeing* and the *believing*—and he had specific terms to describe failure in either case. The first he called *tzu pao* (doing violence to oneself); and the second *tzu ch'i* (throwing oneself away) or *tzu tsei* (robbing oneself).[23]

> With those who do violence to themselves, it is impossible to speak. With those who throw themselves away, it is impossible to do anything. To disown in his conversation propriety and righteousness, is what we mean by doing violence to one's self. (To say), "I am not able to dwell in benevolence or pursue the path of righteousness," is what we mean by throwing one's self away.[24]

Mencius was able to help the king avoid the first defect: the king discovered compassion in himself, but Mencius could not get the king to take the second step: to believe in Mencius' method of self-cultivation. Mencius must have believed that had the king given his program a fair chance, if the king had made a sincere effort, virtue would have come forth "like a fire which has begun to burn, or a spring which has begun to find vent."

Mencius believed one's moral sprouts will grow, one's flood-like energy will increase, if one practices the Way. Like an agricultural endeavor, moral self-cultivation requires hard work, constant attentiveness and patience. Again, like agriculture, it is a fragile task; it can be destroyed by a hostile environment, neglect or improper effort. Most importantly, it is a long and gradual process of *development*.

In the case of King Hsüan, there was no progress at all, and in the end Mencius was forced to leave the king behind. But he also left behind an example of moral teaching unique in character.

Self-Cultivation:
Wang Yang-ming

W ang Yang-ming's *discovery model* of self-cultivation differs in significant ways from Mencius' *development model*. For Wang, there is no need for development of the moral nature; such development is not even possible. All human beings are endowed with a perfect and fully formed moral nature: the mind in itself. In its active, knowing aspect, the mind is *liang chih*; it is fully cognizant of every moral principle. It can guide one to a perfect moral life and it will do so *spontaneously* once the interference of selfish desires has been eliminated. For Wang, human nature is a *lost endowment* and evil results from the *interference of selfish desires*—desires which obscure our innately good, fully formed nature.

As a consequence of these beliefs, Wang sees the task of self-cultivation as a paring away rather than a building up; a reduction of interference rather than a process of nurture and growth. For Wang, there is no need to cultivate the innate moral mind; it is perfect and complete in every respect. For him, the task of moral self-cultivation consists of eliminating the obscuration of selfish desires, allowing the mind to shine forth in all its glory.

Like Mencius, Wang believes we all perform spontaneous moral actions, and that these provide an important clue to our true nature. But, for Wang, these actions are not fragile moral sprouts that need to be nurtured and cultivated; they are the tips of a massive moral iceberg: the visible manifestations of a fully-formed moral disposition that lies hidden below a sea of selfishness. Mencius used his repertoire of examples of spontaneous moral feelings to argue the moral sense was a vital part of human nature. The moral sprouts were indications of what is to come, what human nature will be if it develops properly. But for Wang, such examples were clues of what already is, glimpses of something lying just below the surface of our normal activity.

Wang believes all human beings are endowed with a complete and perfect moral mind, but like some ancient lost city, overgrown and choked with weeds, the moral mind has become hidden beneath a mass of selfish desires. In most people, it is rarely and only partially visible. In order to see the moral disposition in its full glory, we must clear away the obstructions that cover it over by getting rid of selfish desires. For Wang, the task of moral self-cultivation is exclusively concerned with the elimination of these interfering desires.

Wang's overriding concern with the removal of selfish desires finds no precedent in Mencius. Aside from a single reference [25] to the benefit of having few desires, Mencius has nothing bad to say about desire, *per se*. The right kind of desires are the very basis of Mencius' moral philosophy; they guide us and encourage our progress along the moral path. The pleasure we experience by

heeding these desires marks morality as the natural course of human life and makes moral self-cultivation possible. These common desires bind us together with other human beings, and the shared enjoyment of them is the force which enables the moral ruler to reign.

For Mencius, the natural development of human nature—not the elimination of selfish desires—defines the task of moral self-cultivation. In his conversations with King Hsüan of Ch'i, Mencius invokes the fact that people all share common desires, desires for personal pleasures, as proof of their co-humanity and as a prod to get the king thinking about his responsibilities to his subjects. Nowhere in Mencius do we find Wang's call for the extinction of "selfish desires;" Wang's term *ssu yü* (selfish desire) never even appears in the *Mencius*.[26]

For Wang, the goal of moral practice is the preservation of the originally pure character of the mind in every aspect of one's behavior. In this state, the mind is like a mirror. It reflects each situation properly: it neither adds to nor diminishes the images which come before it. Its reflections include the proper response to each situation, but once the appropriate response has been made and the situation is resolved, no trace of it remains behind to impair the operation of the mind. In this state, the mind responds spontaneously, in every circumstance, with the morally correct action. Once all selfish desires have been eliminated, the innate mind, one's pure knowing, provides an infallible guide for the moral life.

Wang bases his method of moral self-cultivation on his interpretation of the term *ko wu* in the *Great Learning*. The process of moral self-cultivation, the elimination of selfish desires, is carried out through the process of *ko wu*.

The term *ko wu* has enjoyed a wide range of interpretations.[27] In Western sources, it is most widely known by Legge's translation: "the investigation of things."[28] Legge bases this translation mainly on Chu Hsi's commentary on the *Great Learning*:

> *Ko* is *chih* (to reach); *wu* (thing) is like *shih* (affair). *Ko wu* is to reach into the principles of things and affairs.[29]

It is probable that Chu Hsi was following Ch'eng Yi's interpretation. In one passage Ch'eng says:

> *Ko* is *chih* (to reach); and *wu* is *shih* (affair). Affairs all have their principles; to reach into their principles is *ko wu*.[30]

In another passage Ch'eng says:

> ...*Ko* is like *ch'iung* (to exhaust); *wu* is like *li* (principle). *Ko wu* is like saying, "to exhaust their principles."[31]

Wang gives a very different interpretation of the term *ko wu*. For him, *ko wu*, the process of moral self-cultivation, is the task of constant internal

scrutiny. Wang defines *wu* (a thing) as the locus of one's attention and understands the character *ko* as "to rectify." Wang's "things" are not the objects and events of the word, as they are for Chu Hsi, but rather one's thoughts, both in regard to the objects and events in the world and in the internal operation of imagination. *Li* (principles) are not to be found in the outside world; the mind itself is principle. For Wang, *ko wu* is not "the investigation of things"— but the "rectification of thoughts." It is the task of rectifying one's thoughts, both the mind's responses to the objects and events one encounters and its own internal musings, through the elimination of all selfish desires.

> (One) *ko* (rectifies) *wu* (things), as in Mencius' expression, "The great man *ko* (rectifies) the ruler's mind.[32] (One) eliminates whatever is incorrect in the mind and maintains the correctness of its original state. Wherever there is a thought, eliminate whatever is incorrect and maintain the correctness of the mind's original state. Then nowhere, at no time, will Heavenly principle not be preserved. This is to exhaust principle. Heavenly principle is bright virtue. And exhausting principle is shining with bright virtue.[33]

If one has a thought that is not in accord with principle, it must be "rectified:" it must be purged of the impurity of selfishness. Strictly speaking it would be inaccurate to describe any thought that is completely in accord with principle as "one's own." Such a thought is without the slightest trace of selfishness. It is pure knowing; it is Heavenly principle. Because it is Heavenly principle, like a mirror, it immediately and accurately reflects the situation at hand. Such a thought will, of itself, constitute the beginning of action, and the action it initiates will be the morally correct response to the situation at hand.

Wang does not think of moral action in terms of contemplating, willing and performing an action. For him, the necessary and sufficient condition for moral action is a *true perception* of a situation.[34] When we truly see, we not only believe—we act. For Wang, true perception involves the proper emotional response, and this emotional response entails the proper action. He does not distinguish between feeling the proper moral response and performing the proper action. This is the essence of his teaching of *chih hsing ho i* (the unity of knowledge and action). It is this view of moral action that leads him to describe *affections* such as "loving beautiful colors" and "hating bad odors" as *actions*.[35]

> Thus the *Great Learning* gives us examples of *chen chih hsing* (true knowledge and action) saying, it is 'like loving a beautiful color or hating a bad odor.' Seeing a beautiful color is a case of knowing, and loving a beautiful color is a case of acting. One need only see a beautiful color, and already he loves it. It is not that after seeing it he then makes up his mind to love it. Smelling a bad odor is a case of

knowing, and hating a bad odor is a case of acting. One need only smell a bad odor, and already he hates it. It is not that after smelling it he then separately makes up his mind to hate it.[36]

A true perception of one's selfish attachments has the power to relieve them instantly. There is no additional work to be done, no action to be taken, if one's *liang chih* is operating freely.

Whenever we become attached to any of the seven emotions, this is a (selfish) desire, and this acts as an impediment to *liang chih*. Yet the instant there is any kind of attachment, *liang chih* is naturally aware of it. When *liang chih* is aware of it, the impediment is removed and *liang chih* resumes its original state.[37]

Pure knowing never fails to know, but we do not always perceive this knowledge. And despite the interference of *ch'i*, we are always able to perceive it. We fail only because of a lack of attention; we either make no effort to see or we are distracted from seeing by making the wrong kind of effort. For Wang, the task of moral self-cultivation consisted of becoming attentive to the ever present and perfect moral guidance of *liang chih* as it operates in the actual affairs of one's own life. Wang believed the problem with the people of his time was they either failed to look for this guidance or they looked for it in the wrong places. In either case, he believed the remedy for their difficulty was Mencius' teaching of *pi yu shih yen*.[38]

For Mencius *pi yu shih yen* meant to "pay constant attention to the task." He wanted people to be attentive to moral self-cultivation, to seek every opportunity to practice morality and nurture the moral sense. But he also warned them of the danger of making an artificial effort to help the moral nature grow. Since Mencius believed in a natural course of development, he believed any effort to rush the growth of the moral sprouts was as harmful as neglecting to care for them. In terms of his agricultural model, he urged people to attentively and patiently tend their moral sprouts.

But Wang believed the innate moral nature was fully formed; there were no sprouts to grow. For him, *pi yu shih yen* meant "always *have* a task." One must be constantly attentive to the operation of pure knowing *in the actual events of one's own life*. Pure knowing offers us guidance in every action we take. So, on the one hand, we must strive to be attentive to it, we must "not neglect" its guidance. On the other hand, we must seek the guidance of *liang chih* only in the events of our own lives. *My* pure knowing operates to guide *me* in *my* particular situations in life. If I abandon this guidance and seek for moral knowledge somewhere else, it will not only fail to help me, it will lead me farther astray. This happens when I over-intellectualize the task of moral self-cultivation, when I try to "help it grow." Wang believed one must avoid

practicing self-cultivation in the abstract and concentrate on the actual events in one's own life. These contained the true lessons one needed to learn.[39]

> ... *Kung fu* (practice) lies completely in "always having a task." "Not to neglect" and "not to help" are only additional warnings. If there is never any interruption of *kung fu*, there is no need to speak of "not neglecting." And if there is never any desire to see quick results, there is no need to speak of "not helping." How clear and simple is *kung fu*! How free and natural!

> If one does not exert effort to "always have a task" and instead, while suspended in a vacuum, one sticks solely to "not neglecting" or "not helping," it is just like *cooking rice by heating a pot*. If one does not put in water and rice, and only concentrates on adding fuel and starting the fire, I don't know what kind of thing he will cook up. I am afraid the pot will crack before the fire can be properly adjusted.

> Nowadays, those who concentrate their efforts solely on "not neglecting" or "not helping" have precisely this kind of problem. All day long, suspended in a vacuum, they practice "not neglecting" or "not helping." They chase about, all over the place, but they have nothing real to work on. In the end, their effort leads to submerging into emptiness and preserving quietude or learning to become silly, stupid fellows. When they finally confront some actual affair, they hunker down in confusion, unable to manage or control it. These are all ambitious scholars, but throughout their lives they must toil bitterly, wrapped and bound, forever waiting to act. This is all because their method of study has ruined them. What a great pity![40]

Wang believed people had been led astray by over-intellectualizing the process of self-cultivation. They failed to practice morality in the concrete situations of daily life and instead sought the contemplation of morality in the abstract. This led to the morally inert practice of quietude, characteristic of Buddhists and Taoists, and the more pernicious, merely academic study of morality, characteristic of degenerate Confucians.

In this re-interpretation of Mencius' teaching of *pi yu shih yen*, we again see clear indications of Buddhism's influence on Wang. The need for concrete practice and the criticism of over-intellectualizing one's spiritual development and pursuing it "in a vacuum" are central themes in the *Platform Sūtra*, a text Wang knew well.

> A deluded person recites; a wise man puts his mind to practice. There are also deluded individuals who empty their minds, sit in tranquility and think of nothing. They call themselves "great." Because of their deviant views, one cannot even talk with this kind of person.[41]

Wang did not believe in the natural growth of the moral sprouts. He wanted something quite different from Mencius' attentive and patient gardener. Wang wanted complete concentration on the task of moral self-cultivation, and this meant absolute and uninterrupted attention to the guidance of *liang chih* in the affairs of one's own life.

> This effort must be carried out continuously. Like eradicating robbers and thieves, one must resolve to wipe them out completely. In idle moments, one must search out and discover each and every selfish thought for sex, wealth, fame and the rest. One must resolve to pluck out and cast away the root of the sickness, so that it can never arise again. Only then may one begin to feel at ease. One must, at all times, be like a cat catching mice—with eyes intently watching and ears intently listening. As soon as a single (selfish) thought begins to stir, one must conquer it and cast it out. Act as if you were cutting a nail in two or slicing through iron. Do not indulge or accommodate it in any way. Do not harbor it, and do not allow it to escape...[42]

Mencius understood moral failure as a disruption of the natural development of human nature and sought to overcome moral failure by nurturing the innate moral sprouts. Wang used the distinction between ordinary knowledge and true knowledge to provide an explanation for moral failure. His method of self-cultivation consisted of eliminating the obscuring selfish desires which interfered with the operation of *liang chih*. To illustrate the difference between Mencius' and Wang's explanations of moral failure, let us imagine how Wang might have responded to the case of King Hsüan of Ch'i.

For Mencius, the king failed because his moral sprouts never had the chance to grow into the full-fledged moral dispositions that are the culmination of their natural development. They were, like the trees on Ox Mountain, hewn down and gnawed away by hostile forces. Mencius sought to protect and nurture the king's moral sprouts, confident they would grow and lead him to the moral life. But Wang would say the king did not possess *true knowledge* of the moral obligations incumbent upon him as ruler, because he was blinded by his selfish desires; his pure knowing was obscured by his own selfish thoughts.

Had Wang faced King Hsüan, he would have sought to eliminate the selfish desires obscuring the king's innate moral sense, this is Wang's refrain, again and again, to his students. This is his only response; he did not believe in the *growth* of the moral sense, and so he could not hope for progress from any other quarter. Mencius gave no such counsel to the king. He encouraged the king to enjoy his many pleasures and did not see these necessarily as impediments to moral progress. Quite the contrary, Mencius felt that such pleasures were a way to focus the king's attention on the moral task. Mencius believed that if he could lead the king to think of his people being without these pleasures, the king's moral sprouts would break through and develop into a full-fledged, functioning moral disposition. Mencius could follow this course because he believed in the natural growth and development of the moral sense.

Mencius believes we all have nascent moral sprouts, Wang that all human beings possess a fully formed moral mind. Mencius says that we can all *become* a Yao or a Shun—that we are all *potential* sages.[43] Wang believes that all people *are* sages; they are endowed with a complete and perfect moral mind.[44] His words must not be glossed as merely a more enthusiastic statement of Mencius' position; they reveal a fundamental difference between these two thinkers.

Wang's method of self-cultivation consisted exclusively of the elimination of selfish desires. He trained each student to seek out and recognize the operation of *liang chih* in that student's life. The deluded student needed a teacher; a teacher who could distinguish between good and evil, lead the student to recognize the response of pure knowing and identify when the student is being misled by selfish desires. In this capacity the teacher is like a coach, helping the student utilize the gifts he has in order to realize a goal he desires. Wang was in fact most like a guru, a spiritual guide who adjusts his pedagogic tactics to the needs of individual students and who relies on his personal charisma to inspire faith in his methods.

It is here, in teaching others his method of moral self-cultivation, that Wang borrows from the *development* model. He believed that for those who had lost sight of pure knowing through the accumulation of selfish desires, a gradual method of self-cultivation is necessary. For such individuals, the task of moral self-cultivation, the extension of pure knowing, is a gradual process, and he invokes the plant metaphors so familiar in Mencius.[45]

> Establishing a commitment and applying effort are *ju chung shu jan* (like planting a tree). When the root first sprouts there is still no trunk. Then there is a trunk, but there are still no branches. After there are branches, then there are leaves. And after there are leaves, then there are flowers and fruit. When one first plants the root, one should only be concerned about nourishing and caring for it. Do not think about the branches. Do not think about the leaves. Do not think about the flowers. And do not think about the fruit. How does dreaming about these things help in any way? Do "not neglect" the work of nourishing and caring, fearing there will be no branches, leaves, flowers, or fruit.[46]

Though the similarity with Mencius is clear, the difference must not be obscured. For Mencius, the moral sense grows and matures: extending out to cover all our actions. For Wang, the growth of plants is a *metaphor for progress* in moral self-cultivation; concentrating on the task of moral self-cultivation is *ju chung shu jan* (*like* planting a tree). For Wang, the extension of pure knowing is the application of knowledge one already possesses. One gains nothing in the process, one simply loses one's delusions. For Mencius, our innate moral tendencies aren't *like sprouts*—they *are sprouts*.

Wang didn't believe the moral tendencies were sprouts. He never used Mencius' term *tuan* with its special sense of "sprout." The only passage in the *Ch'uan-hsi lu* in which Wang comes close to Mencius' special use of this term reveals clearly the difference between these two thinkers.

> ...Mencius' claim that human nature is good refers to the nature in its original state. But the *tuan* (clues) of human nature's goodness can only be seen as manifested in *ch'i*. If there were no *ch'i*, these could not be seen...[47]

Wang understood Mencius' "four sprouts" of virtue as "four clues" to the underlying character of human nature. This was the common interpretation among Neo-Confucian thinkers. Chu Hsi understood the term *tuan* in precisely this way. His comment on the *locus classicus* of the term, *Mencius* 2A6, says:

> Commiseration, shame, complaisance and (judgments) of right and wrong are emotions. Benevolence, righteousness, propriety and wisdom are human nature. The heart/mind is what unites the emotions and human nature. The *tuan* are *hsü* (the ends of threads, clues). One can see what is fundamental to the nature by observing its expression in the emotions. It is like when there is something within and one can see *hsü* (clues) of it on the outside.[48]

Mencius' method of self-cultivation sought to develop the moral sprouts, to help them grow to maturity. Wang's method sought to discover the moral nature and restore it to its original state.

> The "highest good" is the nature. In its original state, it is without the slightest trace of evil. That is why it is called the "highest good." To "rest" in it is to return to its original state.[49]

But here Wang's method becomes obscure. In order to "return" to the nature's original state, we must eliminate the "obstructions" which interfere with the natural functioning of pure knowing. This requires that we "establish a commitment." But how does one accomplish this? And how is "establishing a commitment" like planting a tree? Wang doesn't believe in the growth of the moral sprouts. From his descriptions, "establishing a commitment" seems to be like lighting a fuse or starting a fire.[50] Mencius has moments in which he insists we must simply make ourselves follow a certain course of action, but Wang's entire enterprise seems to consist of repeated acts of sheer will. He tells us, cryptically, that this will, this commitment, is the task of "creating something out of nothing."

One who plants a tree must nourish its roots. One who plants virtue must nourish his mind. One who wishes a tree to mature must, in the early stages of its growth, prune away the many branches. One who wishes virtue to flourish must, in the early stages of study, eliminate his love of external things. For example, if he loves poetry and literature, then his spirit, each day, will be drained away in these pursuits. Thus is it with the love of all external things.

This study that I speak of is the task of *wu chung sheng yu* (creating something out of nothing). You gentlemen must have faith. The task is simply to establish a commitment. As soon as a student is committed to the thought of doing good, it is *ju shu chih chung* (like the planting of a tree). As long as one neither makes an artificial effort to help it grow nor neglects it, as long as one cares for it and nourishes it, naturally it will grow both day and night. Its vital energy will be greater each day and its branches and leaves more luxuriant. In the early stages of growth, it will produce many branches, and these must be cut off. Only then can the roots and trunk grow large. In the early stages of study the same is true. Thus in establishing a commitment, singleness of purpose is to be valued.[51]

Mencius' underlying beliefs concerning human nature led him to describe a gradual method of self-cultivation. Moral self-cultivation was a process of growth and development. It must not be neglected, but it cannot be rushed.

Wang presented a very different picture. Human nature was a lost endowment. The process of self-cultivation was the recovery of this lost endowment by discovering the moral mind—paying attention to the operation of *liang chih*. One had to awaken to knowledge which one already had.

This awakening could be long in coming. If the accumulated obstructions were great, their removal would require time and great effort. In such cases, Wang relies on the agricultural metaphors characteristic of Mencius to describe the task of self-cultivation. But in individuals who are not deeply deluded, the awakening could be sudden and complete, as it was for Wang during his banishment in Kuei-chou. Such an enlightenment, in a flash of insight, removed all doubt. It empowered the individual as the absolute arbiter of right and wrong, and obviated the need for further self-cultivation. All that remained was to demonstrate one's moral perfection or, perhaps more accurately, to allow it to operate freely in the world. This aspect of Wang's thought gave his teachings an intense and dynamic quality: complete enlightenment could be in the next moment of thought. Perhaps more than any other aspect of his thought, this belief in the possibility of sudden moral enlightenment distinguishes Wang from Mencius.

Self-Cultivation:
Conclusion

Mencius' method of self-cultivation reflects his beliefs about human nature and the nature of morality. He believed in Confucius' vision of the moral life, and he saw it as the blossoming of human nature. But in addition to the proper kind of environment, human nature required continual care in order to mature properly and fully.

One needed to cultivate moral strength, one's *hao jan chih ch'i* (flood-like energy) by "accumulating righteousness." The more moral actions one performed, the greater one's moral strength became. But in order to perform moral actions, one needed to nurture one's moral sprouts, these provided the motivation for moral action. The moral sprouts grow naturally, if one affords them the proper amount of attention. If one seeks out the nascent moral tendencies in one's own heart/mind and feels the joy of acting in accordance with these moral feelings, the moral sprouts will be nourished and will grow.

Mencius attempted to lead people to pursue a life of moral self-cultivation with his array of different paradigm cases of moral feelings: the *indications of childhood, give-away actions* of adults, *testimonials* and his *thought experiments*. Once he was able to lead a person to recognize and enjoy the innate moral sense, Mencius encouraged him to nurture and extend these feelings. Mencius believed if he could keep a person engaged in this task, the moral sprouts would be nourished and would grow, until they extended to and informed every action.

Self-cultivation was a long and difficult process of *development*. It must not be neglected, and it could not be hurried along. We must *pi yu shih yen* (pay constant attention to the task). Mencius urged us to adopt the attitude of an attentive and patient gardener, confident our moral sprouts would grow and yield a fully developed moral disposition.

Wang Yang-ming's method of self-cultivation was also based upon his beliefs about human nature and the nature of morality. He believed in the Confucian vision, but he saw it as the manifestation of our innate, fully formed and perfect nature. There were no "sprouts" to nurture, the moral disposition was ready and available, one just had to find it.

Wang understood Mencius' paradigmatic cases of moral feelings as clues in the search for the innate moral mind. The moral mind is lost, hidden beneath a mass of selfish desires. Moral self-cultivation is the task of removing these obstructions and *discovering* the innate moral mind. But selfish desires are removed when one recognized them for what they are. They are burned away when exposed to the cleansing light of *liang chih* (pure knowing)—the "sun behind the clouds." The task of self-cultivation is to pay constant attention to the operation of pure knowing in the events of one's own life. One may "not neglect" its guidance—even for a moment—and one must "not (make an artificial effort to) help" it grow, by over intellectualizing the task. Wang understood Mencius' teaching of *pi yu shih yen* as "always *have* a task." One must not seek for moral guidance outside of one's own actual experiences. Pure knowing teaches the lessons one needs to learn, each and every moment of one's life.

Wang did not want an attentive and patient gardener. He wanted us to awaken suddenly to the moral guide within and to follow it wherever it led. We were to seek this guide in the activities of our daily lives—we were not to "cook rice by heating a pot." We were to pay constant attention to this guide and remain ever vigilant—"like a cat catching mice"—on guard for the appearance of selfish desires.

Chapter 5

Sagehood:
Mencius

In the preceding chapters, I have traced a number of key differences between the moral philosophies of Mencius and Wang Yang-ming, and tried to show how their different views fit together as systems of thought. But despite their differences, Mencius and Wang shared many beliefs and goals in common. Most importantly, for both thinkers, an individual's ultimate goal in life was to attain complete moral perfection, the state of *sagehood*.[1]

For Mencius, this goal was attained by the *development* of an innate capacity, brought to fruition through a long process of nurture and growth. For Wang, the goal of sagehood was the *discovery* of a lost endowment, a sudden awakening to the moral guidance of one's *liang chih*. It is difficult, but not impossible, to distinguish Mencius' fully *developed* sage from Wang's fully *discovered* sage. In this chapter, I will separate these two views of sagehood by describing them in terms of the notions of *power* and *doubt*. By *power*, I mean both the accessibility of sagehood and the range of prerogatives a sage enjoys. And by *doubt*, I mean a sage's confidence in his own sagehood: how much authority for the determination of sagehood rests within the autonomous judgment of the individual.

Mencius changed Confucius' notion of sagehood. It is not at all clear Confucius would have agreed with Mencius' claim that "anyone can become Yao or Shun."[2] For Confucius, the sages were the semi-divine architects of the golden age. They discovered the *li* (rites), the terrestrial constellations describing human life, and they provided them for all human beings to follow. Mencius brought Confucius' sage down to earth. He believed sagehood was accessible to everyone; it was grounded in human nature itself.

Mencius granted every person the possibility of sagehood, people had within them the *power* to become morally perfect. With the passing of the classical sages, the ideal of sagehood had changed. Sages were no longer semi-divine creators of the ideal society. Their work had changed from creation to restoration. To become a sage meant to resurrect the ideal society which once had been, to repeat a pattern that had already been discovered and practiced. This change had begun with Confucius himself, who believed that the key to restoring the Way of the former sages was the study of their documents. Their Way was embodied in their writings, and the preservation and study of these writings was a critical part of the greater goal of restoring the Way. To Mencius, the work of preservation and study became at least as

91

important as the task of restoring the Way. He believed Confucius was the greatest sage of all.

> ...Mencius said, "Tsai Wo, Tzu Kung, and Yu Jo[3] were wise enough to recognize a sage, and they would never stoop to praising a person just because they liked him. (Yet) Tsai Wo said, 'In my opinion, my master is vastly superior to Yao and Shun.' Tzu Kung said, 'By viewing their rites, he knew their government. By hearing their music, he knew their virtue. Looking back over a hundred generations of kings, he could rank each one, and no one could show him to be wrong.[4] Since the birth of man, there has never been one like my master.' Yu Jo said, 'The unicorn is the same in kind as other four-footed animals, the phoenix is the same in kind as other birds of flight; Mount T'ai is the same in kind as small mounds of earth and ant-hills; the Yellow River and the Sea are the same in kind as puddles of rain. The sage, too, is the same in kind as other men. But he stands out among them; he is above the crowd. Ever since man first came into the world, there has never been one greater than Confucius.'..."[5]

Confucius did not create or modify the original pattern; he preserved the records of the ideal society that once existed. He was a traditionalist; his Way was learned by *study*—not by *thought*. One was to learn the *li* (rites) of the ancients and repeat their ideal pattern.

> I once spent an entire day without eating and an entire night without sleeping—engaged in *ssu* (thinking). It was of no help. It is better to study.[6]

Mencius introduced a novel idea by grounding the Confucian vision in human nature itself. He shifted the authority for moral decisions from the *li* (rites) to the *hsin* (heart/mind). He believed the pattern described by the rites was encoded in the heart/mind of each and every person. If one cultivated one's moral sprouts, one could find the Way within. And the key to nurturing one's moral sprouts was to exercise the heart/mind in its proper role: to think.

> ...The office of the heart/mind is *ssu* (to think). When it thinks it gets things right; if it does not think, it cannot get things right...[7]

Thinking became the key to both the method for attaining sagehood and the practice of the developed sage. But Mencius was certain such thought would lead to only one conclusion: the Way Confucius had described. He did not abandon the tradition or ignore its precedents. However, his view did diminish the stature of both the sages and the rites. If everyone is capable of deciphering the eternal patterns, it is easy to see how one might begin to question the importance of the sages and the rites to one's quest for sagehood. And such questioning could pose a serious threat to the tradition itself.

One of Mencius' fiercest critics, Hsün Tzu (fl. 298-238), used this very point to argue against Mencius' view of human nature.[8] He argued that if human nature is indeed "good," there would be no need for the sages and the rites. Human beings would guide themselves along the Way.

> Mencius says human nature is good, but I say this is not so. In every age and throughout the world "good" has meant that which is correct, peaceful and orderly and "evil" has meant that which is prejudiced, unruly and chaotic. This is the distinction between good and evil. Now if human nature were truly correct, peaceful and orderly, then what would be the use of sage kings and what would be the use of rites and righteousness? What would these add to (man's) correctness, peacefulness and orderliness?...
>
> ... if human nature is good, we could do away with sage kings and eliminate rites and righteousness. If human nature is evil, we must honor sage kings and cherish rites and righteousness...[9]

But Hsün Tzu misunderstood—or misrepresented—Mencius' position on human nature. He refused to allow Mencius to use the term *hsing* (human nature) to describe a *process of growth*. For Hsün Tzu the term could only be used for "that which is given by Heaven; you cannot learn it; you cannot acquire it by effort."[10] Mencius did not believe human nature was complete at birth. He believed the moral sprouts required nourishment and cultivation in order to reach their destined state. In the past, a few uniquely endowed individuals were born whose moral sprouts were exceptionally strong. Their moral sprouts were able to mature, and this enabled them to create the ideal society. These sages provide the perfect model for human self-cultivation, and the rites and practices of the societies they created provide the perfect plan for society.

But most people's moral sprouts are weak and easily damaged, they need help in the work of moral self-cultivation. Because people require an extensive period of nourishment and cultivation in order to realize their true nature, because throughout this period they are vulnerable to a variety of hostile forces, most everyone needs help. And help comes in the form of guidance from the sages and from the rites.

This is where Mencius stayed close to Confucius' early vision. His view did not pose the threat Hsün Tzu claimed it did. For Mencius, the early sages retained their prestige; they were the paragons of human development. And the rites retained their lustre; they provided the guidelines for human conduct and social organization. Most people need the support these offer, at least in the initial stages of self-cultivation. The sages and the rites are like braces, carefully placed to support a young, weak plant. They facilitate the growth of the moral sprouts by giving the mind proper objects of contemplation: nourishing food for thought. They guide and support their development until the sprouts are able to stand on their own. But these supports do not alter or inhibit natural growth. A healthy, vital specimen which grows undamaged, will follow the course and assume the shape described by these supports.

Mencius extended the accessibility of sagehood to every person. Everyone had the *power* to become a sage. But being a sage was to be the guardian of a tradition; someone who preserved the classical patterns of culture. Mencius' sage developed an innate capacity which became the judge in moral decisions, but the mature expression of this capacity fulfilled a well articulated, traditional ideal. One didn't devise some novel way of being; one *grew into* an existing ideal. There was a balance, in Mencius' thought, between the *power* of the individual and the *pressure* of tradition. Tradition could only be violated in certain extraordinary cases.

> Shun-yü K'un said, "A man and a woman should not touch each other's hands when giving or receiving[11]— this is the proper rite, is it not?"

> "Yes, this is the proper rite," said Mencius.

> (Shun-yü K'un) said, "If my sister-in-law is drowning, should I rescue her with my hand?"

> Mencius said, "Not to rescue her would be to act like a wild animal. That a man and woman should not touch each other's hands when giving or receiving is the proper rite, but rescuing a drowning sister-in-law with one's hand is *ch'üan* (weighing the circumstances)."[12]

In this case, exceptional circumstances compel an individual to suspend the standing taboo prohibiting contact between a man and a woman. The taboo itself is not modified or challenged, it is judged inappropriate in a new and unusual set of circumstances. The taboo remains, but its application is *fine tuned* to adjust for a novel situation.[13]

Mencius sought to preserve the classical patterns. His faith in the tradition motivated him to seek an understanding that both preserved the ancient *li* (rites) and satisfied his moral intuition.[14] He sought to balance these two forces in his understanding of the Confucian tradition. The ways Mencius responds to the tension, between individual moral intuition and traditional pressure, is revealed in his interpretation of ancient texts. In some cases the moral intuition prevails over a text.

> Mencius said, "It would be better to be without the *Book of History* than to completely trust in it. In the chapter *The Completion of War*, I would take only one or two passages. A benevolent man has no enemy anywhere in the world. When the most benevolent fought the least benevolent how could it be that 'the blood flowed until it floated the pestles in their mortars'?"[15]

Mencius felt enough confidence in his developed moral sense to dismiss a great deal of well established history from a highly regarded text: the *Book of History*. And yet it is absolutely essential to realize that this is the only case in which Mencius completely rejects a classical source. It is also important to note that Mencius did not believe there was any direct connection between Confucius and the *Book of History*. It lacked the authority Mencius accorded to certain other classical texts.

Mencius did think highly of parts of the *Book of History*.[16] On two occasions, he quotes from the *Book of Poetry* and the *Book of History* in quick succession, in order to support an argument he was advancing.[17] But he did not accord the *Book of History* the high regard he reserved for the *Book of Poetry* and the *Spring and Autumn Annals*. Mencius believed Confucius had composed the *Spring and Autumn Annals*[18] and he regarded the *Book of Poetry* as Confucius' fundamental text of instruction. Mencius' regard for the *Spring and Autumn Annals* was something new, but his distinction between the *Book of History* and the *Book of Poetry* can be found in the sayings of Confucius himself. If we examine the evidence in the *Analects*, we see a clear difference between Confucius' use of the *Book of History* and his esteem for and use of the *Book of Poetry*.[19]

Confucius once quoted the *Book of History* and once answered a question about it.[20] And the beginning of chapter twenty in the *Analects* is assembled mostly from passages taken from the *Book of History*.[21] The only other possible reference to the *Book of History* shows Confucius did accord it respect; he always used *ya yen* (the proper pronunciation) when he quoted from it.[22] But this is rather sparse mention especially, as we shall see, when compared with Confucius' use of the *Book of Poetry*. And there is an important question to be asked regarding these passages in the *Analects*. Was Confucius referring to a text called the *Book of History* or was he, as Legge suggests,[23] referring to ancient records in general? Nowhere in the *Analects* does Confucius describe or praise a text called the *Book of History*. There is almost no evidence in the *Analects* to support the claim that he was referring to an established text. If he was, it was a text he respected but rarely quoted. At most we might suppose it was a text, *parts of which* he admired but much of which he held suspect. In an case, it was not a text central to his thought or teaching.

The *Book of Poetry* is a different story altogether. Throughout the *Analects*, Confucius and others quote from the text and paraphrase its verses.[24] Almost all of these references are found in the present version of the *Book of Poetry*. We also find several references to individual sections within the present version of the text.[25] Twice, Confucius tells us *the text* consists of three hundred verses.[26] He sings its praises again and again.[27] And most importantly, he describes it as a necessary part of a gentleman's learning, and urges his disciples to study it.

> The Master said, "My children, why do you not study the *Book of Poetry*? The odes serve to stimulate the mind. They may be used for the purpose of self-contemplation. They teach the art of sociability. They show how to regulate feelings of resentment. From them you learn the more immediate duty of serving one's father, and the remoter one of serving one's prince. From them we become largely acquainted with the names of birds, beasts and plants."[28]

Confucius told his eldest son that one who does not know the *Chou-nan* and *Shao-nan* (the titles of the first two books of the first part of the present version of the *Book of Poetry*) is "like one who stands with face against a wall."[29] And on another occasion, Confucius told him, "one who does not study the *Book of Poetry* is not fit for conversation."[30]

Most importantly, we see repeated cases of the *Book of Poetry* being used, in actual practice, as the text of study among Confucius' disciples. For example. Tzu-hsia asks for an explanation of some lines from the *Book of Poetry*. After Confucius answers him, Tzu-hsia inquires further concerning Confucius' explanation. The master is pleased and says:

> Shang (Tzu-hsia) is the one who stimulates me! With him, I can begin to discuss the odes![31]

Similarly, in a conversation with Tzu-kung,[32] Confucius is pleased that his disciple has been able to select from among the odes, one that illustrates the significance of Confucius' earlier remarks. Confucius can "begin to talk with him about the odes."

Confucius demanded more than just the memorization of the odes. A student had to be able to apply the lessons contained in the *Book of Poetry*.[33] We see Confucius admonishing another disciple, Tzu-lu, for his mindless repetition of some lines from the *Book of Poetry*.

> Neither dissatisfied nor covetous,
>
> How could he do wrong?
>
> Tzu-lu kept repeating (these lines). The master said, "How can *this* lead you to do right?"[34]

Learning the true import of the odes was an accomplishment of the highest order. A disciple could move the master deeply by displaying the right sensitivity to this text.

> Nan Jung repeated the lines about the white jade scepter three times. The master gave him his elder brother's daughter as a wife.[35]

The *Book of Poetry* was central to Confucius' teaching. It was the closest thing he had to "scripture." And this fact was not lost to Mencius. He accorded it the highest prestige, on par with Confucius' own "creation"—the *Spring and Autumn Annals*.

Mencius not only often quoted the *Book of Poetry* to illustrate his arguments,[36] he defended the odes from "clumsy" interpretations.

> Kung-sun Ch'ou asked, "Kao Tzu said, 'The Hsiao P'an is the ode of a little man.' *What do you think about this*?"
>
> Mencius said, "Why did he say that?"
>
> (Kung-sun Ch'ou) said, "Because of the murmuring it expresses."
>
> Mencius said, "How stupid was old Kao in regard to this ode!" .... The dissatisfaction expressed in the Hsiao P'an is the working of relative affection, and that affection shows benevolence. Stupid indeed was old Kao's criticism of the ode."[37]

Most important of all, Mencius twice quotes Confucius praising the author of an ode as one who "knows the Way."

> The *Book of Poetry* says: "Heaven created the teaming masses, And for each creature, there was a standard. The people's invariable principle, is to love this admirable virtue." Confucius said, "Did not the author of this ode, know the Way!"[38]

Mencius never rejected any part of either the *Spring and Autumn Annals* or the *Book of Poetry*. These texts were too closely linked to Confucius. They had attained the status of scripture and could not be rejected or modified. But they still were open to *interpretation*, and Mencius was the first to begin carefully arguing for the proper interpretation of classical texts.[39] He argued for his interpretations on several grounds. In some cases, he sought to "clarify" the meaning of terms.

> King Hsüan of Ch'i asked, "Is it true that T'ang banished Chieh and King Wu attacked Chou?"
>
> Mencius said, "So it is written."
>
> (King Hsüan) said, "Then may a minister kill his lord?"
>
> Mencius said, "A thief of benevolence is called a thief. A thief of virtue is called a bandit. A thief or a bandit is called an outcast. I have heard, in the case you cite, that an outcast was put to death. I have not heard of the killing of a lord."[40]

In other cases, Mencius sought to provide the proper historical context to recorded events, a context which supported his interpretation.

Wan Chang said, "When Confucius received his lord's order to appear at court, he went without waiting for his carriage.[41] Was Confucius then wrong?"

Mencius said, "At the time, Confucius was in office and had specific duties to perform. He was summoned on official business."[42]

Most importantly, Mencius relied on his intuition to determine the meaning of metaphors and to interpret the "essence" of a passage from the classics.

Hsien-ch'iu Mang said, 'I take your point on the issue of Shun's not treating Yao as a minister, *but* it is said in the *Book of Poetry*:

"Under the whole Heaven, Every spot is the sovereign's ground; To the borders of the land, Every individual is the sovereign's minister;"—and Shun had become sovereign. I venture to ask how it was that Ku-sau was not one of his ministers.'

Mencius answered, 'That ode is not to be understood in that way:—it speaks of being laboriously engaged in the sovereign's business, so as not to be able to nourish one's parents, *as if the author* said, "This is all the sovereign's business, and *how is it that* I alone am supposed to have ability, and am made to toil in it?" Therefore, those who explain the odes, may not insist on one term so as to do violence to a sentence, nor on a sentence so as to do violence to the general scope. They must try with their thoughts to meet that scope, and then we shall apprehend it. If we simply take single sentences, there is that in the ode called "The Milky Way,"—"Of the black-haired people of the remnant of Chou, There is not half a one left." If it had been really, as thus expressed, then not an individual of the people of Chou was left.' [43]

Mencius relied upon his developed moral intuition to interpret the classics, but he did this with a measure of *fear and trembling*. He was compelled, by an overriding faith in the tradition, to verify his intuitions with authentic classical precedents. His work of interpretation was a measure of his ability to understand the truth embodied in the classics, not a confirmation of their truth.[44] Mencius' moral intuition never replaced the writings of the *Spring and Autumn Annals* or *Book of Poetry* as the source of moral knowledge. Mencius harbored a healthy *doubt* about anyone's ability to question the authority of the tradition. It was not possible for him to imagine someday a sage would arise who would reject the teachings of former sages, regardless of the distance in place and time. Things just couldn't change *that much*.

Shun was born in Chu Feng, moved to Fu Hsia and passed away in Ming T'iao. He was an Eastern Barbarian. King Wen was born in Ch'i Chou and passed away in Pi Ying. He was a Western barbarian. The distance separating them was more than a thousand *li* and the time between them more than a thousand years. And yet the ways in which they ruled over China fit together like two halves of a seal. The former sage and the later sage had a single standard.[45]

We see this attitude manifested again in Mencius' faith in his own ability to see the Way. His mission against the teachings of Yang Chu and Mo Tzu had earned him the reputation of one who "likes to argue."[46] And in defending his actions, Mencius insisted future sages would see he was correct in the course he took.

> (I) defend the Way of the former sages and resist Yang and Mo. I banish licentious words and ensure depraved talk cannot arise. Such talk arises in men's minds and injures their affairs. It arises in their affairs and injures their government. If another sage should come forth, he would not alter what I have said.[47]

Mencius had great confidence in his ability to determine what was right and what was wrong. This confidence was based upon his belief in an innate capacity to know and on many years of study and reflection. But doubt outweighed conviction throughout the process of self-cultivation. Confidence grew only after a long and arduous apprenticeship with the sages as teachers and classics as lessons. And it could never move him to act contrary to this heritage. Unwavering fidelity to one's tradition and especially to one's master was central to Mencius' teaching. And instilling this fidelity in one's students was part of being a true master.

> P'eng Meng studied archery under Yi. When he had mastered every-thing Yi had to offer, he thought, "In all the world, only Yi is better than I." Thereupon, he killed Yi.
>
> Mencius said, "Yi shares the blame in this."
>
> Kung Ming-yi said, "It seems to me he was blameless."
>
> Mencius said, "You should simply have said, 'Was his blame not slight?' The men of Cheng sent Tzu-cho Ju-tzu to invade Wei, and Wei sent Yu-kung Chih-ssu to pursue him. Tzu-cho Ju-tzu said, "Today I am suffering from an old complaint and am unable to hold my bow. I shall surely die." He asked his driver, "Who is pursuing me?" The driver said, "It is Yu-kung Chih-ssu." Tzu-cho Ju-tzu said, "Then I shall live!" His driver said, "Yu-kung Chih-ssu is Wei's best archer. How can the master say, "I shall live?" Tzu-cho Ju-tzu said, "Yu-kung Chih-ssu studied under Yin-kung Chih-t'o and Yin-kung Chih-t'o studied under me. Now, Yin-kung Chih-t'o is an upright man; his friends too must be upright." Yu-kung Chih-ssu approached and said, "Master, why are you not holding your bow?" Tzu-cho Ju-tzu said, "Today I am suffering from an old complaint and am unable to

hold my bow." Yu-kung Chih-ssu said, "I studied archery under
Yin-kung Chih-t'o and Yin-kung Chih-t'o studied under you, master.
I cannot bear to take your Way, turn it against you and do you harm.
However, today, I am on my lord's business, and I dare not be remiss."
He then drew several arrows, knocked off their metal tips on the
carriage wheel, fired four and withdrew.[48]

We see Mencius' fidelity to Confucius displayed throughout the *Mencius*.
In one passage, Mencius rejects a story about Confucius which claims Confucius associated with some unsavory characters.

> Wan Chang asked, "Some say that when in Wei Confucius lodged
> with Yung Chu and when in Ch'i he lodged with the attendant Ch'i
> Huan— are these things true?"
>
> Mencius said, "No, it was not like that. These are the stories of gossip
> mongers. ... had Confucius lodged with Yung Chu or the attendant
> Ch'i Huan, it would have been in accordance neither with righteous-
> ness nor fate. ... If Confucius had lodged with Yung Chu or the
> attendant Ch'i Huan—how could he be Confucius!"[49]

In another conversation, Mencius rejects a passage purported to be the
words of Confucius.[50]

> Meng of Hsien-ch'iu asked Mencius if the following passage were an
> authentic conversation of Confucius'. "The knight replete with virtue
> is a loyal subject however much his prince may fail him, and a loyal
> son no matter what the father does! When Shun stood with his face
> to the south and Yao, at the head of the feudatory princes faced north
> and paid him homage, Ku-sou too faced north and paid (his son)
> homage. When Shun saw this his discomposure showed on his face.
> Confucius said, 'At that moment, the world was in grave peril, most
> grave.' Is this authentic?"
>
> Mencius said, "No it is not. The True Gentleman would not say such
> a thing. This passage emanates from some village pedant of eastern
> Ch'i. (What really happened was this).....[51]

In both these cases, Mencius defends Confucius against any hint of im-
propriety. Confucius could never be wrong, he was the perfect sage.[52] His
words could never be mistaken or contradicted.

Mencius was not an explorer or a pioneer; he was a guardian, a guide and
a witness. He sought to protect the Confucian Way, lead others along it and
personally manifest it. The Way he followed had been forged by the ancient
sages, and its lessons had been preserved by his master, Confucius. Confucius
had distilled and refined the Way of the ancients from the writings which
described their age. To learn this Way, one must follow these lessons and these

examples. Mencius believed he had cultivated himself properly. He knew the Way, he could bring others to it and lead them along it. But he himself had been shown the Way by others, specifically by Confucius. And he could never depart from the Way he had been shown.

Mencius accorded new *power* to individuals. Each and every person had the ability to become a sage; each had within him, a potentially perfect moral guide. But because human nature needed to mature, because it was quite fragile in its nascent stages, the sages and classics retained a prominent place in his thought. These provided the paradigms for moral self-cultivation, the ideal forms which were one's ultimate goal. One measured one's progress with these standards. As one matured, one gained the ability to weigh each situation one encountered. Exceptional circumstances occasionally required one to make adjustments in traditional modes of conduct. But this could only be done by a moral connoisseur. He would do so with a confidence born of accumulated study and practice, but his confidence would be tempered by *doubt*.

Sagehood:
Wang Yang-ming

W ang Yang-ming believed sagehood is the original state of every human being. Every person is endowed with a complete and perfect moral guide: the mind in itself. People lose sight of their moral minds and are led astray only because of the obscuration of selfish desires.

> In all the world, the mind of every person originally is no different from that of a sage. But being blocked by selfishness and obscured by physical desires, what was great becomes small and what was penetrating becomes stopped up...[53]

Sagehood is realized when the interference of selfish desires has been eliminated, and the mind is able to function freely. In this state, the mind responds effortlessly and flawlessly to every situation it encounters. For Wang, individuals had within their immediate grasp the source of complete and perfect moral knowledge. They were endowed with immense *power*. In an instant of insight, through the attainment of enlightenment, they could become the ultimate and unerring arbiters of right and wrong.

For Wang, the quest for sagehood became a task of constant self vigilance. The goal was to recognize and preserve one's innate knowing by eliminating and guarding against the interference of selfish desires. Anything which distracted one from this task became a source of trouble, and one of the greatest and most pernicious distractions was over-intellectualizing the task of moral self-cultivation. Wang's goal was to *pi yu shih yen* (always *have* a task): to stay constantly aware of the operation of pure knowing *in the concrete situations of one's own life*. Looking elsewhere for moral knowledge could only lead one astray. Because of this, in Wang's thought, the role of both the classics and the sages was greatly diminished. They were as great a threat as they were an aid in the task of self-cultivation.

Wang believed Confucius had edited and passed on to posterity all six of the Confucian classics.[54] But, in stark contrast to Mencius, Wang believed that the significance of Confucius' work was not in *what he had preserved*; it was in *what he had eliminated*. Confucius' contribution, his main achievement, was *editing*. He had eliminated a mountain of complicated and confused writings, writings that had interfered with the practice of the Way.

Wang pointed out that Confucius did not *write* the *Spring and Autumn Annals*; he merely *wrote down* selections from an existing collection of historical records. Wang believed Confucius did not want to teach in words at all. Wang did not value the written word; he went so far as to way that the burning of the books by the first emperor of the Ch'in dynasty was not a bad idea *per se*, only his motivation made it improper. And he condemned the burning of the classics almost as an after thought.[55]

> As for the *Spring and Autumn Annals*, although it is said "Confucius composed it,"[56] actually it is the old text of the history of the state of Lu. When it is said he *wrote* it, it means he wrote down the old text, and when it is said he *edited* it, it means he edited out whatever was complicated and confused. He reduced it; he didn't add a thing. In transmitting the six classics, Confucius feared complicated and confused writings would bring chaos to the world. All he did was simplify them, so they would not affect the people of the world. He wanted to get rid of the words in order to seek the meaning. He did not rely on words to teach.
>
> After the *Spring and Autumn* period, complicated and confused writings became more abundant and the world became more chaotic. The First Emperor of the Ch'in dynasty was wrong to burn the books because he was motivated by a selfish thought. And burning the six classics was improper. If at the time his intention had been to brighten the Way by burning all writings opposed to the classics or violating principle, this would have been correct. Unintentionally, his action conformed with (Confucius' idea) of editing and transmitting the classics. Since the time of the Ch'in and Han dynasties, such writings again have grown more numerous each day...
>
> Confucius said, "When I was young, a historian would still leave a blank in the text,"[57] and Mencius said, "It would better to be without the *Book of History* than to completely trust in it. In the chapter *The Completion of War*, I would take only one or two passages."[58] In editing the *Book of History*, Confucius kept only a few chapters to cover the four to five hundred years from the time Yao and Shun down through the Hsia dynasty. Surely other things occurred, but because he recorded only what he did, we can see his intention. The sage only wanted to eliminate complicated and confused writing; later scholars have only wanted to add to them.[59]

Wang describes Confucius' and Mencius' relationships to the classics, the Confucian written tradition, in the same way he describes the task of self-cultivation: in terms of a paring-away rather than a building-up. According to Wang, the sages never wanted to rely on texts at all. But realizing they could not do away with texts completely, they dedicated themselves to the task of eliminating anything that was unnecessary, preserving only a limited core of essential writings.

For Wang, the classics lost much of their prestige, because he believed the *power* to determine the Way was located completely in *liang chih*. The classics were merely records of the operation of *liang chih* in past contexts. Their main value was as a testament to the faith past sages had demonstrated in relying upon their pure knowing to show them the Way through the difficulties they had faced. The classics preserved traces of *liang chih*; they were histories of *liang chih* in action. But these examples were from a different place and time. One couldn't learn rules of behavior from them.

> If we talk about them from the perspective of events, we call them history. If we talk about them from the perspective of the Way, we call them classics. Events are the Way, and the Way is events. The *Spring and Autumn Annals* is also a classic; the other five classics are also histories. The *Book of Changes* contains the history of Fu Hsi, the *Book of History* is a history beginning with the time of Yao and Shun. The *Book of Rites* and the *Book of Music* are histories of the Three Dynasties. The events (recorded in all the Classics) are the same (in kind), their Way is the same. How can they be said to be different?[60]

Each person has within him the same knowledge which guided the sages in the past. My *liang chih* is the same as that of the sages. I can see their actions, in an important sense, as my own. Wang followed Lu Hsiang-shan in this view.

> If in learning I understand what is fundamental, all the Six Classics are my footnotes.[61]

Not only the classics, but the sages themselves diminished in importance. Their actions were traces of *liang chih*, but these traces were a bit faded with age. They were not vibrant and vital like one's own *liang chih*. And they could never replace it. This sentiment is expressed at the conclusion of one of Wang's many poems.

> The thousand sages are all passing shadows;
> *Liang chih* alone is my teacher.[62]

The classics and the sages were history—in more ways than one. They represented pure knowing in action, but they were not the focus of self-cultivation. The task of moral self-cultivation was to pay attention to the operation of *liang chih* here and now. The goal was to attain sagehood, and a sage was one whose *liang chih* operated effortlessly in response to the situation at hand. The sages of the past and the classics themselves could become obstacles to the attainment of this goal. If one neglected the "sage within" and sought for moral guidance only in the records of the past, one might fail to see the most important lesson they had to teach.

If we examine the examples Wang chose from the classics, we see he preferred to discuss cases in which tradition was breached rather than cases in which it was preserved. He demonstrated no interest in describing the rituals of the golden age. He emphasized examples which highlighted the creative, spontaneous aspect of *pure knowing*. Wang discusses this in detail in a letter to one of his students.[63]

> ...As for Shun taking a wife without first notifying his parents, was there someone before him who took a wife without notifying *his* parents who served as an example? Did Shun first have to consult some text or ask some person before he could act? Or did he search within his own mind and, in an instant of thought, pure knowing weighed all factors and determined what was proper, after which he could not have turned from acting as he did? And as for King Wu launching a military expedition before burying his father, was there someone before him who launched a military expedition without burying *his* father who served as an example? Did King Wu first have to consult some text or ask some person before he could act? Or did he search within his own mind and, in an instant of thought, pure knowing weighed all the factors and determined what was proper, after which he could not have turned from acting as he did?[64]

Wang's goal was to restore the mind to its original state. In its original state, the mind is like a mirror. *Liang chih* reflects each situation as it appears and answers with the correct response. The mind's ability to respond in this manner is not contingent upon any prior acquaintance with the classics or the sages. As Wang pointed out in the passage above, the sages didn't have any examples to show them the Way; they relied upon *liang chih*. Wang believed everyone was a sage; every person had within him his own perfect moral guide. The *power* for moral decision rested completely within the individual, and it was immediately accessible.

> I asked, "A sage can respond to an unlimited number of changing circumstances. Doesn't he have to study some things beforehand?"
>
> The Master said, "How could he study so many things? The mind of the sage is like a clean mirror. Since it is completely clean, it responds to each thing as it comes and leaves nothing unreflected. There is never a trace of an earlier image remaining which would interfere with an image yet to be reflected. This is something the scholars of later generations have taught people to do; they have turned their backs on the teachings of Confucius...
>
> ... a sage does a thing when its time has come. One should only worry about one's mirror being clean, not that it won't be able to reflect things as they come. The study of changing circumstances is something done as the mind reflects the things it encounters. A student must be engaged in cleaning his mirror. He should only worry that *tz'u hsin* (this mind)[65] is not clean, not about his ability to respond to changing circumstances.[66]

Wang's lack of regard for the study of the classics seems to be contradicted by his "commentary" on the five classics. Ch'ien Te-hung certainly gives the impression that Wang was interested in confirming his intuitions with the lessons of the classics. The following is from a preface Ch'ien wrote to some fragments allegedly from Wang's *Wu-ching yi-shuo* "Opinions on the Five Classics."

> When the master lived in Lung-ch'ang, in the course of his study he attained enlightenment and verified it in the five classics. He felt the commentaries of former scholars did not exhaust the issues and so he began to write down his own opinions as commentary. After nineteen months, he had completed a general work on the five classics which he called his *Yi-shuo* (Opinions).

> Subsequently, he realized learning was more refined and the task was more simple and easy. Therefore, he did not bring this work out to show his students. I took every opportunity to ask the master about this work, but he would just smile and say, "I committed *that* to the flames of Ch'in long ago." When I would ask about it, he would say, "Just extend your pure knowing. Through a thousand classics and ten thousand canons, heretical works and depraved learning, it will be like the scales of a balance. Without a single exception, it will reveal the light and heavy throughout the whole world. There is no need for you to present people with a fragmented and confused intellectual understanding."

> After the master had passed away, while putting his affairs in order, I came upon these items among some of his discarded manuscripts. I copied them down for myself, and upon reading them I sighed and said, "My master's Way is comprehended in its entirety in this one work. Throughout his life he never departed from this. With this as an example, all the classics can be understood.[67]

Wang wrote his *Opinions on the Five Classics* during the difficult years he spent in Lung-ch'ang. In Wang's *Nien-p'u* (Chronological Biography), Ch'ien again briefly describes the composition of the *Wu-ching yi-shuo*.

> ... (The Master) made an oath to himself, saying, "All I can do is "await my destiny."[68] Day and night he led a life of discipline, seeking to discover "absolute refinement and singleness of purpose."[69] After awhile his heart was cleansed, but his followers all became ill.[70] He personally *chopped wood and carried water*,[71] cooked rice and fed them. Worried they might become depressed, he chanted poems for them. And if they still were not happy, he would mix in some songs from Chekiang[72] in jest. Slowly, they began to forget their illness.

Living in great hardship among barbarians, moved the master to think, "What would a sage do if he were in this situation? " Suddenly in the middle of the night he experienced a great enlightenment into the principles of *ko wu* and the extension of knowledge. It was as if, in his sleep, someone had spoken this to him. Unconsciously, he began to jump about; his followers were all alarmed by this. He began to understand that the Way of the sages is (to realize) one's own nature; to seek for principles in events and things is wrong. He then sought to confirm this in the words of the classics which he had committed to memory— none of which did not agree with his insight. He then wrote the *Yi-shuo* (Opinions).[73]

But Ch'ien seems to be stretching the truth a bit. It is clear, from Ch'ien's preface, that Wang did not think this "commentary" was worth preserving. Based on Wang's own words about committing it "to the flames of Ch'in,"[74] it may be wise to question the authenticity of Ch'ien's "fragments", fragments he wrote down "in his own hand." Ch'ien's claim that Wang spent nineteen months verifying his intuitions with the words of the classics, "none of which did not agree," and the impression he gives, in his preface, that this work is a commentary on the classics are both quite suspect. Wang's *Yi-shuo* was not a commentary in the traditional sense. The *Nien-p'u* clearly states that Wang was writing down comments on passages from the classics which he had *committed to memory*. More importantly, when we look at Wang's preface to the *Yi-shuo*, the only reliable part of it still extant, we get a very different impression of this work. From the preface, we see Wang didn't spend nineteen months combing through the classics to verify his insights. His attitude toward the classics was much less devoted.

When one has captured the fish, he forgets the the trap.[75] When one has finished the wine, he casts away the dregs. But if before getting fish or wine, one says the trap is the fish and the dregs the wine, then he will never succeed in getting fish or wine. The Five Classics contain the complete learning of the sages. And yet, one who has experienced these teachings for himself says that, in regard to the Way, they are like the trap and the dregs.

I often wondered why the scholars of the world seek for the fish by looking at the trap and call the dregs the wine. Saying that the dregs are the wine comes close; the wine is *within* the dregs. But to seek for the fish by looking at the trap is indeed wide of the mark.

When I lived among the Southern barbarians in Lung-ch'ang, I could not carry my books among the endless mountains. Each day I would sit in a rock grotto, silently remembering passages from the books I had read long ago and writing them down. Whenever I had a thought, I would immediately comment on it. In seven months time, I had generally covered the principles of the Five Classics, and I called the work I had produced my *Opinions*. Now the work does not necessarily completely agree with what former worthies have said. My intention was to write about their heartfelt views and use these to gladden the spirit and nourish the nature.

What I did was to forget the fish and just fish. I concentrated on brewing (the wine) without worrying about how it might taste. Alas! Those who view my words without grasping my intention will look at them like the trap and the dregs. If they seek in these for fish and wine, they will surely lose them!

My remarks total forty-six sections. There are ten sections for each of the classics except for the *Classic on Rites*. Because it contains so many errors, I have only written six sections on it.[76]

Wang did not attain his spiritual awakening through careful study of the classics, and he did not rely upon his ability to explain the classics as proof of his spiritual achievement. As far as texts went, he was much more interested in the *Four Books*.[77] He commented extensively on the terms of art in all of these books—especially the *Mencius*, *Great Learning* and *Doctrine of the Mean*.[78] But even in this, it is clear he was not primarily concerned with explaining these texts. He did not produce comprehensive, systematic, line by line traditional commentaries to any text.[79] Wang really did "forget the fish and just fish;" he forgot the text and just went fishing around for confirmation of his own ideas. He was looking for textual support for his view that the mind was principle, that *liang chih* was the ultimate arbiter of right and wrong. Judging from the creative philology he employed in his interpretation of terms like *ko wu*—his pure knowing empowered him to be limited only by his own imagination.[80] The aim of his interest in these texts was to support the supremacy of *liang chih*, and these texts could mean whatever *liang chih* told him they mean.

On one critical issue, Ch'ien's two pieces on the *Yi-shuo* agree with Wang's own preface. They agree in describing Wang's search through the *Five Classics* as a quest for *confirmation*. Wang's enlightenment did not result from a study of the classics; his personal insight illuminated their true meaning.

But Wang wasn't some Ming Dynasty "new critic"—he didn't think there were other valid interpretations. *Pure knowing* wasn't just his private language. All the universe shared in this language and anyone who allowed it to speak to him would understand and see that Wang's interpretation was the unique solution.

This is an unsettling aspect of Wang's thought. His sage seemed to be completely without *doubt*. Perhaps this should come as no great surprise: doubt requires the kind of abstract consideration of alternate possibilities which Wang condemned. Doubt could only be an impediment to *liang chih*, a thought interposed by the intellect, adding to and interfering with the mind in itself. Wang had more than confidence, he had a frightening certainty. As he said in the poem translated above, the sages themselves were "passing shadows." *Liang chih* was Wang's one and only teacher. In another poem, he says:

> Each and every human mind has Confucius within,
> But afflicted by hearing and seeing,
>   they become confused and deluded;
> Now I point to your true original face,
> It is none other than *liang chih*—have no more doubts![81]

This attitude led Wang to commit the ultimate heresy. He felt comfortable acknowledging the possibility of rejecting the words of Confucius himself.

> In learning, the important thing is to *get it with the mind*.[82] Even words from the mouth of Confucius, if one seeks in his mind and finds them to be wrong, dare not be accepted as true. How much less (the words) of those inferior to Confucius! Even words from the mouth of an ordinary person, if one seeks in his mind and finds them to be correct, dare not be regarded as false. How much less those of Confucius![83]

Wang is in fact guilty of the very thing Hsün Tzu had accused Mencius of advocating. And what is more remarkable, Wang freely admits that the classics, the rites and the sages themselves are dispensable. *Pure knowing* was the teacher and life provided the lessons.

A version of Hsün Tzu's old argument was used by a prominent member of the Tung-lin Academy in his attack on Wang Yang-ming. Ku Hsien-ch'eng[84] acknowledged Wang's teaching had the beneficial effect of making an individual realize the task of self-cultivation required great personal effort and needed to be practiced in the actual affairs of one's daily life. Wang's teaching was a medicine for the malaise of the unmotivated student and the ineffectiveness of the purely academic "study" of morality. But Ku could not accept Wang's willingness to reject the words of Confucius. He realized that the potential danger of anarchy accompanied Wang's "cure."

> "I would not consider anything to be false if I seek within my heart and find it to be true, even though I find no authority for it in Confucius. I would not consider a thing to be right if I seek within my heart and find it to be false, even though I find an authority for it in Confucius." ... About these two sentences of Yang-ming I have grave doubts and am unable to comprehend them. In my opinion Yang-ming's contribution lies here, but his deficiency lies also here...
>
> ...This shows that the two sentences of Wang Yang-ming are a medicine, (yes, but) one that causes a (new) disease; that is why I said:

"Yang Ming's contribution lies here, but his deficiency lies also here!"[85]

Wang's attitude toward classical texts, more than any other aspect of his thought, threatened the Confucian tradition. It undermined one of the pillars of Confucianism, its textual/commentarial tradition. Wang's view did not recognize the classics as in any way central to the tradition. But the Confucian tradition has always been and remains today organized around a set of sacred texts and a growing list of commentaries. The sacred texts are their repository of Truth. Having such a shared repository of Truth, Truth which continually gets reinterpreted by successive generations, seems to be a necessary part of what it means to *belong to a tradition*. In the case of Confucianism, it has remained the single most important feature of the orthodox tradition.[86]

In the absence of a set of sacred texts, a tradition can only be held together by some sort of apostolic succession. The Zen tradition in East Asia is an example of this kind of phenomenon. But orthodox Confucianism has never accorded any living person this much authority. In this regard, the tradition has retained a characteristically Chinese reverence for their spiritual ancestors. Confucianism has always been "conservative" in this way, and this has given the tradition great stability and impressive longevity. But Wang's way of thinking ran counter to this tradition. He was a charismatic teacher, a kind of guru to his disciples. When he did appeal to traditional authority it was either to witness his own understanding by a very limited and selective reading of the classics or to trace a kind of apostolic tradition that verified his authority.[87]

The learning of the sages is the learning of *hsin* (heart/mind). This learning was passed from Yao to Shun and from Shun to Yü with the words, "*Jen hsin* (The human mind) is precarious. *Tao hsin* (The mind of the Way) is extremely subtle. Maintain absolute refinement and singleness of purpose. Hold fast to the Mean."[88] This is the origin of the learning of the mind. The "Mean" is called the "mind of the Way." The "absolute refinement and singleness of purpose" of the mind of the Way is called "benevolence." The learning of Confucius and Mencius exclusively worked on the search for benevolence; this was the tradition of "absolute refinement and singleness of purpose." But even in their time there were deluded individuals who looked to external things. Thus Tzu-kung suspected benevolence was to be found in "broad study and extensive memorization"[89] and "widely conferring benefits on the masses."[90] The master taught him to find "the single thread"[91] and taught him to "draw the analogy from himself."[92] Confucius was trying to get him to search for it in his own mind...

In Mencius' time, Mo Tzu taught benevolence was "to grind every hair off of one's body"[93] and Kao Tzu's disciples taught "benevolence is

internal and righteousness external."[94] These greatly injured the learning
of the mind.

Mencius refuted the teaching that righteousness is external and said
"benevolence is the human mind[95] and "learning consists solely of
seeking the lost mind."[96] He also said, "Benevolence, righteousness,
ritual and knowledge are not welded onto me from the outside. They
are an integral part of me; I only fail to think about this."[97]

Coming down to the Sung Dynasty, the two masters, Chou Tun-i and
Ch'eng Hao began to rediscover the school of Confucius and Yen
Hui.... They came close to the principle of "absolute refinement and
singleness of purpose." After them there was Master Lu Hsiang-shan.
Though his level of purity was not as great as these two earlier masters,
the ease and directness (of his teachings) were truly inherited from
the Mencian tradition. Though in discussing his teachings he occasionally has some different ideas, these are the result of his particular personality. But in holding that one must seek for it in one's
mind he is one (with Mencius). Thus, I have concluded that the
learning of Master Lu is the learning of Mencius.[98]

Wang sought to establish a new line of succession. He sought to replace the
tradition of Ch'eng Yi and Chu Hsi with Ch'eng Hao, Lu Hsiang-shan and
himself. He had completed a movement away from the authority of texts and
toward the authority of moral intuition. He bases his tradition exclusively on
his personal insight, his *liang chih*. The charismatic teacher had completely
replaced the Confucian classics as the authority for the tradition.

But this kind of tradition has an inherent instability. When so much authority
rests in a charismatic teacher, his passing often elicits a destructive struggle
among his disciples. At its worst, this kind of conflict is motivated by greed
and a lust for power. But frequent schisms and fragmentation are simply
endemic to this kind of tradition. The individual followers have all been taught
they each have a "sage within" and unless some mechanism for reconciling
their differences is put in place, disagreements among the leading disciples can
result in the disintegration of the school. When students disagree, their teacher
can decide, but when sages disagree, they form their own schools.

Wang's school experienced this kind of division, and in some cases
degenerated into a debauched caricature of his original vision.[99] It seems none
of his disciples had the ability to continue Wang's work and hold the school
together. This is the picture Huang Tsung-hsi[100] provides in his *Ming-ju
hsüeh-an* (Case Studies of Ming Dynasty Confucians).

Ming learning began with Ch'en Hsien-chang[101] but achieved greatness only with Wang Yang-ming. This is because during the early part
of the Ming, those well-schooled in the teachings of former sages did

not understand through self-reflection and did not extend what they knew in order to reach into the inner secrets. The expression "All *this* person does is repeat the words of Chu Hsi and all *that* person does is repeat the words of Chu Hsi" and Kao Chung-Hsien[102] saying, "There is no real insight in the works of Hsüeh Wen-ching[103] and Lu Ching-yeh"[104] both of these remarks show that this is true. Because Wang Yang-ming taught the doctrine of pure knowing, people today can each attain a personal realization through self-reflection; each person has the means to achieve sagehood. Therefore, were it not for Wang Yang-ming, the learning that had come down from ancient times would have been cut off.

However, he did not expound his teaching about the extension of pure knowing until late in life, and he had not fully explored its significance with his students. Afterwards his disciples each mixed in ideas of their own, engaging in wild speculation as to its true meaning. They were like gamblers guessing at a shell game; none was able to reproduce the original intention of this teaching.[105]

It is more likely that it was the very nature of Wang's teachings which led his students to "wild speculation." Believing all people are sages, that they have within themselves the *power* to immediately become the arbiters of right and wrong and that they can make these judgments without hesitation or the slightest trace of *doubt*, proved to be both the greatest strength and worst weakness of Wang's thought. It led to the disintegration of Wang's thought as a school. But perhaps this would have pleased him. Perhaps it is in the nature of his thought that it must always remain as a challenge to an established tradition. It has remained, and continues, as an inspiration for exceptional individuals ever since it first appeared.

Sagehood:
Conclusion

Mencius changed Confucius' original notion of sagehood. Sages were no longer semi-divine creators of the ideal world; their work had become the preservation and restoration of models discovered in the past. Thus Mencius regarded Confucius, one who *transmitted but did not create*,[106] as the greatest sage of all.

Mencius' sage was an imposing but accessible ideal. Sagehood was the developed and refined expression of human nature. Each and every person possessed the *power* to attain sagehood. But this goal could only be attained after long and arduous application. One needed to study and reflect upon the classics and the sages of the past in order to realize their ideal in the present. These examples provided the paradigms for one's moral self-cultivation. Studying and reflecting upon these lessons helped the mind to grow into the ideal patterns developed long ago.

The human mind was to guide one throughout the course of self-cultivation and the moral life. But its development and growth was aided by the lessons presented in the classics. One *grew into* an understanding of the Truths embodied in the classics. As one's understanding grew, one gained the ability to recognize how to follow the Way through the actual situations one encountered in life. On *rare* occasions, one's developed moral sense would compel one to suspend an established practice as inappropriate in a given situation. The developed moral mind could *ch'üan* (weigh) exceptional circumstances and make the proper adjustments.

But this ability—this *power*—was always regulated by the pressure of tradition. The mind did not simply react to every situation it encountered; it sought to understand each situation properly, in traditionally sanctioned terms. Traditional practices were an ideal language for Mencius. One needed to study this language and practice it in order to become proficient in its use. And this language was a closed system, nothing more was required and nothing included could be abandoned. It allowed for infinite variation within the system described; one could, under special circumstances, bend the syntax of his ideal language. But this was not a task for a beginner. It required an accomplished language user and was always to be undertaken with an attitude of fear and trembling. One kept both eyes on the Way, on those rare occasions one felt compelled to deviate from its established course. One could have great confidence in his ability to understand the Way, but this confidence was always tempered with *doubt*.

Wang Yang-ming granted each individual complete *power*. Every person not only could *become* Yao or Shun: every person *was* Yao or Shun. All that separated one from the realization of sagehood was the interference of selfish thoughts. Moral self-cultivation became the removal of selfish thoughts, and this activity was carried out in the events of one's own life. There was no special place, for the classics or the sages, in Wang's thought. *Liang chih* was his teacher, and his own actions provided the lessons he needed to learn. Wang's interest in the classics was as testaments to the necessity of relying on one's own pure knowing. He emphasized the creative and spontaneous aspects of the moral life.

The *power* accorded *liang chih* was free from the pressure of tradition. The moral mind simply responded to each and every situation, like a mirror reflecting things placed before it. Tradition had no place on the mirror of the mind; it could only be an impediment to the mind's spontaneous functioning.

Wang believed the *li* (principles) of Confucian thought were the ideal universal language. He believed in the same language as Mencius; this is what makes it so difficult to distinguish Wang's fully *discovered* sage from Mencius' fully *developed* sage. But Wang believed this language was innate, there was no need to learn it. The mind itself was this language; it only awaited a concrete situation to describe. An individual could awaken to this mind in an instant of insight. He would then speak this language fluently, without hesitation or *doubt*.

As one studies Wang's philosophy, traditional Confucian notions about the nature of morality, human nature, the origin of evil, self cultivation and sagehood slowly begin to disappear. Like Alice watching the Cheshire cat, one sees less and less of what once was there. Occasionally the image comes back, but there is no doubt that it is fading. However, as one delves deeply into his thought and pieces together its various aspects, the Confucian vision gradually reappears—vivid and vital. One knows that it is not quite what it once was, but there is no doubt about where it came from.

The differences between Mencius and Wang have at times led me to question the bond Wang felt united them. But the relationships among the various issues I have examined—the ways these issues fit together for each thinker—cast up two pictures that, when compared, leaves me without doubt as to Wang's heritage and his allegiance. The similarity between their two visions of how one should live one's life dispels my doubts and leaves me wondering how two thinkers so dissimilar can be so much alike.

Appendix I:
The Evolution of the *Ch'uan-hsi lu*

This appendix provides a history of the evolution of the text of the *Ch'uan-hsi lu*, from its inception to its present state. It discusses not only variations in the actual content of the text but also different attitudes individuals have had regarding the text and its application.[1]

The *Ch'uan-hsi lu* began as a modest effort, on the initiation of Wang's devout disciple, his brother-in-law, Hsü Ai.[2] Hsü has been likened to Confucius' disciple Yen Hui because of their common good fortune and common sad fate. Both were fortunate in being regarded as the favorite disciples of their respective masters, and both shared the misfortune of succumbing to illness early in life.[3]

Hsü Ai wrote down and collected significant parts of fourteen conversations he himself had had with the master—seeming to defy the explicit prohibition Wang had given his disciples against recording any of his teachings. Hsü had a clever way of circumventing this prohibition; he explained why he was the exception to Wang's rule in his preface:[4]

> Among the disciples, there was one who, on his own, had written down the master's teachings. Hearing of this, the master said. "Sages and worthies teach the way physicians prescribe medicine: always matching the treatment to the ailment, taking into consideration the various symptoms and, whenever appropriate, adjusting the dosage. Their sole aim is to eliminate the ailment. They have no predetermined course of action. Were they indiscriminately to stick to a single course (of treatment), rarely would they avoid killing their patients. Now with you gentlemen, I do nothing more than diagnose and polish away each of your particular prejudices or obsessions. But as soon as you manage to make these changes, my words become nothing but *useless tumors*.[5] If subsequently you preserve my words and regard them as dogma, you will one day *mislead yourselves and others. Could I ever atone for such an offense?*"[6]

> Since I had carefully written down some of the master's teachings, one of my fellow students remonstrated with me. I then said to him, "In taking your position, you are *indiscriminately sticking to a single course* and have lost the master's meaning. Confucius once said to Tzu-kung, 'I prefer not talking.'[7] Yet on another day he said, 'I have talked with Yen Hui all day long.'[8] Now why wasn't he consistent in what he said? Since Tzu-kung sought for sageliness only in words, Confucius used *not talking* as a warning to him: to help him feel for it with his heart and seek a personal attainment. Yen Hui *listened in silence*[9] to Confucius' words, and in his heart he understood. In him, there was nothing lacking. Therefore, Confucius talked to him all day

long—like a river bursting its banks and rushing to the sea. Thus, Confucius' *not talking* to Tzu-kung was not (speaking) too little, and his speaking to Yen Hui *all day long* was not (speaking) too much. Each received what was appropriate to him.

In our present situation, writing down what the master says, as I have done, is surely contrary to his wishes. Since we disciples are constantly with the master, what possible purpose could this serve? But we must, occasionally, be away from the master's side and *live apart from the group.*[10] At such times, the *inspiring example*[11] of the master is far away and we are unable to receive his admonitions. For one such as I, of limited abilities, if he did not receive the master's teachings and was unable, regularly, to receive the master's admonitions and instructions, it would be rare indeed if he were not overcome (by the task) and lost.

Regarding the master's teachings, if we disciples only let them *enter our ears and pass out our mouths*[12] and do not ourselves embody these teachings, then in writing them down I have indeed committed a crime against the teacher. But if from this record we can grasp the general idea of his teachings and sincerely realize them in concrete action, then this record is truly the mind of the master, which can *talk (to us) all day long.*[13] Surely then it is too short!"

Having completed my record, I wrote this down as a preface to the first section in order to inform my fellow students.

Hsü Ai took his selections from typical conversations and compiled his collection in consultation with his fellow students.[14] From his preface, we know he made his selections intending that they serve as a guide to Wang's teaching: a guide for students who had *already studied with the master* but who had to leave his side and continue their study alone. Because the *Ch'uan-hsi lu* was designed to fulfill this special need, Hsü Ai felt it did not contradict the master's earlier prohibition about recording his teachings. Wang had given the prohibition fearing those not familiar with his teachings would fail to appreciate that they are all context-sensitive. Since Hsü Ai's collection was not intended as a reader for the general public, it is easy to see why Hsü was not concerned about the danger of Wang's teachings being misinterpreted by the uninitiated. Realizing that the prohibition itself was tailored to a specific context, Hsü Ai was encouraged to disregard it; the prohibition did not apply to his context. Hsü Ai's *Ch'uan-hsi lu* was a collection of conversations typical of the discussions Wang had with beginning students, and it was for students—a record to remind them of their experiences with the master.

In addition to the description in the preface, we can see that Hsü Ai compiled the *Ch'uan-hsi lu* as a guide for beginning students, from the nature of the selections he made. The majority of the conversations directly concern aspects of Wang's teachings on the *Great Learning* or the *Doctrine of the Mean*.[15] In the opening paragraph of his introduction, Hsü Ai identifies the *Great Learning* as the central text he discussed with Wang and quotes the *Doctrine of the Mean*.[16] Hsü also quotes both works repeatedly in his short postscript.[17] We know, from Ch'ien Te-hung, that Wang relied upon these two texts when introducing new students to his thought.[18]

The conversations Hsü Ai collected were of a type familiar to beginning students, representative of conversations Wang had had with all of them on "typical days." These conversations were not a primer to Wang's thought, an introduction intended for the uninitiated, they were a case-book of important lessons for students who had studied with the master but who, from time to time, had to leave his side. It was anticipation of these periods of separation that motivated Hsü Ai to compile the *Ch'uan-hsi lu*. He was afraid that, separated from the teacher and the group, students would lose the will to practice the lessons they had learned. In the second appendix, I show that knowing Hsü Ai's motivation for compiling the *Ch'uan-hsi lu* is critical to understanding the meaning of the title he chose.

From the preface, we see Hsü Ai emphasized the need for students to apply these lessons in their own lives. He repeated this imperative in his short postscript to the collection.[19]

> Since the old interpretation was lost long ago,[20] when I first heard the master's teachings, I was startled and unsure. I did not know where to begin (to understand them). Later, after listening to them for a long time, I gradually came to see that I myself must realize them and apply them in concrete situations. After this, I began to believe that the master's teachings were the legitimate heritage of the Confucian school. If one departs from these, there are nothing but narrow paths, leading nowhere.

> (His teachings), for example, that *ko wu* (the rectification of things) is the task of *ch'eng yi* (making the will sincere),[21] that *ming shan* (displaying goodness) is the task of *ch'eng shen* (making the self sincere),[22] that *ch'iung li* (completely understanding principle) is the task of *chin hsing* (fulfilling the nature),[23] that *tao wen hsüeh* (pursuing inquiry and study) is the task of *tsun te hsing* (honoring the virtuous nature),[24] that *po hsüeh* (extensive study) is the task of *yüeh li* (restraining oneself through the rites),[25] and that *wei ching* (maintaining purity) is the task of *wei yi* (maintaining singleness)[26]—all such teachings were at first difficult to put into practice. But after having contemplated them for a long time, *unconsciously my hands began to dance and my feet began to move* (in harmony with them).[27]

Hsü Ai's collection was a case-book for Wang's beginning students: a selection of important lessons they were to put into concrete application. As a group, the collection he made is a clear and informative introduction to Wang's early thought, and Wang did not depart substantially from the positions represented in this corpus. It was intended for beginning students, and it was compiled many years before Wang's death. We can assume that he knew of its purpose and its contents and did not disapprove of either. This is not the case for almost half the material in what is now the *Ch'uan-hsi lu*.[28] Several of the later versions were compiled years after Wang's death, and none of the later compilers made a point of collaborating with their fellow students, as Hsü Ai had done.[29]

Hsü Ai named his collection the *Ch'uan-hsi lu*, and this name was retained as the title of every version of the text.[30] Though Hsü Ai's collection of conversations was never published as an independent work, it appears, along with his introduction and postscript, as the opening section of every subsequent version of the text. His preface also appears as the first preface among those included in the two most important versions of Wang's complete works.[31]

In the closing lines of his preface, Hsü Ai remarked that if the record he had compiled helped the students realize Wang's teachings in their own lives: "Surely then it is too short!" These words were to prove prophetic, for his collection was soon to begin a long period of evolution and expansion.

Hsü died before his collection was published, but it was not long after his death that his fellow student, Hsüeh K'an, published a much-expanded version of the text. Hsü Ai's original collection was one *chüan* in length, and to this Hsüeh K'an added one *chüan* of conversations recorded by the disciple Lu Ch'eng and another *chüan* of conversations he himself had recorded.[32] Hsüeh K'an compiled this collection and published it in Ch'ien-chou.[33] At the time, Wang was 46 years old.

Hsü Ai's work had already been expanded to more than three times its original length. The range of topics covered in the work had also been extended. It was still, for the most part,[34] a collection of conversations between Wang and his students, but the additional conversations it now contained differed from those selected by Hsü Ai. They now included conversations in which Wang gave specific instructions—instructions tailored to the individual needs of a given student, in a given situation.[35]

Six years after the publication of Hsüeh K'an's text, when Wang was 52 years old, another disciple, Nan Ta-chi, published a still larger version of the *Ch'uan-hsi lu*. Nan took Hsüeh K'an's three volumes and added several letters Wang had written to his students. In the *Nien-p'u*,[36] there is the following entry:

10th month: the disciple Nan Ta-chi publishes an enlarged *Ch'uan-hsi lu*.

Hsüeh K'an first published the *Ch' uan-hsi lu* in Ch'ien, a total of three *chüan*. This year, Nan Ta-chi selected letters in which the master discussed learning. He added these, in five *chüan*, and published an enlarged edition in Yüeh.[37]

Nan Ta-chi was an active proselytizer of Wang Yang-ming's thought and in 1525 was instrumental in the reconstruction of the *Chi-shan Academy* in Shao-hsing.[38] Nan was directly involved in the activities of the academy, and he invited Wang to lecture at the academy. It has been suggested that Nan used his recently published edition of the *Ch' uan-hsi lu* as a text in the Academy.[39] If this is true, it would be the first instance of the *Ch' uan-hsi lu* being used as a text independent of Wang's personal instruction.

This might explain, in part, how the inclusion of student-specific teachings, of the kind Wang had earlier prohibited, had become acceptable. Wang had begun to entrust his students with the responsibility for teaching others. These new teachers would have needed a text, and given Wang's approach to teaching, the best kind of text would be a collection of illustrations of Wang in action. By being there to explain the significance of each passage, these new teachers would have felt more at ease about including them. In the sections added by Hsüeh K'an, we may even have a case in which the explanation of the significance of a specific example used by Wang is included as part of the text itself.[40]

Nan's addition of letters stretched the initial format of having only *conversations* between the master and his disciples. This section of the *Ch' uan-hsi lu*, in its various redactions, is the only part that departs from the strict sense of *recorded conversations*.[41] No volumes of the original version of this text are extant today, but an amended version, printed in Te-an Fu in 1544, does exist.[42]

Ch'ien Te-hung refers to Nan's original version of the text and tells us that it contained eight of Wang's letters and was published in two volumes.[43] But Ch'ien gives us this information about Nan's text in the preface to his redaction of it. Ch'ien felt Nan's version had become obsolete. He removed what had been the two opening letters of Nan Ta-chi's collection and placed them in Wang's *Wen-lu*.[44] Ch'ien believed these two letters—both replies to Hsü Ch'eng-chih—represented a temporary, compromise position that Wang had consciously employed when the world was not quite ready for his full message. Ch'ien also credits Nan with this interpretation and says it explains not only why Nan included these letters but also why he placed them as the opening selections to his collection. When Ch'ien wrote his preface, Wang's teachings were much more popular, the world was "realizing" its past errors. These letters no longer had a place in the *Ch' uan-hsi lu*, and Ch'ien replaced them with a second letter from Wang to Nieh Wen-yu.

In the present version of the *Ch'uan-hsi lu*, at the end of this section, there are also two short pieces on education.[45] These do seem to indicate that the *Ch'uan-hsi lu* was being used as a textbook. It is generally accepted that these pieces were added by Ch'ien Te-hung, but I am not sure about this. Ch'ien doesn't mention adding the short pieces on education in his preface, and it seems strange that he would have neglected to mention them when he went into such detail concerning his other modifications of Nan's text.[46]

Two versions of the *Ch'uan-hsi lu* now included a section consisting of Wang's letters, and this shows that the nature of the text had changed. It was no longer a record of Wang's teaching to beginners, basic teachings most of them would have received personally from Wang at some point. This entire section is more like the kind of personal instruction that Hsüeh K'an first introduced into the text, precisely the kind of instructions Wang had warned his students not to write down.

But the redaction of Nan Ta-chi's version of the *Ch'uan-hsi lu* is not Ch'ien's only contribution to the present text. Soon after the master's death, Ch'ien solicited his fellow students for records of their conversations with Wang Yang-ming.[47] Several students responded to his request, and from this material, Ch'ien selected items that presented individual problems for Wang to solve. Ch'ien combined these with problems he himself had presented to Wang and was about to publish this collection of conversations together with Wang's *Wen-lu* (Literary Works).[48] However, the death of his mother prevented Ch'ien from completing this task.

In addition to Ch'ien's postscript, there is a preface, by Ch'ien, to a work that he describes as a *hsü* (supplement) to Nan Ta-chi's *Ch'uan-hsi lu*.[49] According to this preface, Ch'ien's supplement to the *Ch'uan-hsi lu*[50] was published by Liu Ch'i-tseng, in the summer of 1554, in Ning-kuo,[51] at the Shui-hsi Academy.[52]

This work circulated among Wang's disciples. One of the disciples, Tseng Ts'ai-han, augmented Ch'ien's work by adding selections of his own choosing and published the result in Ching-chou,[53] calling his work the *I-yen* (Surviving Words).[54]

Ch'ien was not pleased with this text; he described it as "not refined." He edited it, discarding two-thirds of the material, and published this shorter edition in Ning-kuo, at the Shui-hsi Academy. He called this work the *Ch'uan-hsi hsü-lu*.[55]

At the urging of Shen Ch'ung,[56] Ch'ien set out to produce a new, expanded version of the *Ch'uan-hsi hsü-lu*. First, Ch'ien reexamined the material he had received from Wang's students in response to his original appeal. He selected enough conversations from this material to form an additional *chüan*. He then changed the format of the middle part of his earlier *Ch'uan-hsi hsü-lu* into question and answer form.[57] Ch'ien then sent this new, expanded manuscript

to Mr. Chang,[58] the magistrate of Huang-mei,[59] for publication. This was 28 years after the death of Wang Yang-ming and is described in Ch'ien Te-hung's postscript.[60]

In Ch'ien's postscript, Shen Ch'ung describes the experience of reading Tseng's *I-Yen*: "as though it enabled the students to talk to the teacher himself." A vestige of Hsü Ai's original purpose—to capture the "mind of the master"— had remained, but it had been greatly changed. These new students had never experienced Wang's teaching directly. They were not using the text in conjunction with past experiences to inspire personal practice. They were not under the direction of former students. They were doing precisely what Wang hoped they would never do: studying his teachings on their own.

But there was nothing else they could do. Wang was dead, and his students began to disagree about the interpretation of his teachings: the written record was the only place to turn. Through his words, they hoped "to talk to the teacher himself." Ch'ien wanted to recapture "the mind of the teacher," the mind that could "talk to the students all day long."[61]

In order to recapture the mind of the master, Ch'ien had to downplay Wang's early pronouncements against the written word. After Wang had died, Ch'ien began to insist that the master had approved the recording of certain techniques. In a postscript to the *Questions on the Great Learning*, Ch'ien claims Wang granted approval of his request to write down this work.[62] And in one of his prefaces to Wang's *Wen-lu*, Ch'ien claims Wang not only approved of a proposal to collect and edit the letters he wrote in reply to student's inquiries, we are told Wang had been thinking about compiling such a collection himself.[63]

While largely responsible for Wang's written legacy, Ch'ien was not unaware of the difficulties inherent in the task of preparing a record of Wang's teachings. As is clear from the preface below, Ch'ien retained a certain distrust of the written word; words could not completely convey Wang's message. Ch'ien was too much a student of Wang's to completely abandon this distrust. In many places, Ch'ien's preface bears a striking resemblance to Hsü Ai's original preface to the *Ch'uan-hsi lu*. It reads almost as if it were Ch'ien's apology for what circumstances had forced him to do.[64] The preface says:

> Someone asked, "Master, what if we edit the instructions you have given to disciples, in response to letters they have sent to you, and compile several volumes of instructions to help future students?
>
> The Master said, "I have thought about that myself. But I feel that our present course of study never stops and that my endless interactions with others leaves me no leisure. Someday I must build a stove in the mountains and gather together the most gifted, in literary talents, among you. We will meet and talk. And from these discussions, we

will produce a book that demonstrates the most important words of the sages. Afterwards, we will take all (my) fragmented and worthless writings and burn them, so they will not trouble mankind."

I, (Ch'ien) Te-hung, served the master in Yüeh for seven years.[65] Except for times when I returned home, I served him without interruption. The various insights I had all occurred in that space between speech and silence, between action and passivity. Sometimes, when I heard someone slander (the master's) principles, it would disturb me deeply. I would then work even more ardently to rectify myself. Whenever I had a doubtful matter. I would approach the master and inquire as to the truth. Since I basked in the warmth of his presence, I did not record everything he said.

Whenever I compare the written instructions with the inspiration I received when I served the master, I always am saddened by their inadequacy. From this, I know that the ancients did not deceive us when they said, "Writing does not fully express speech and speech does not fully express meaning."[66] Unfortunately, since the master has passed away, we can not hear his admonitions; his *inspiring example*[67] recedes farther from us each day. We can not receive (his) confirmation of our every thought.

After (the master had passed away), I collected his surviving writings and read through them in order. All the things I wanted to say but could not, the master had already set forth for me! Though his words can not completely express his meaning, they "draw the bow but do not release the arrows—brimming with energy."[68] Therefore, since his time in Ch'u,[69] I have not dared to let even the smallest fragment of his writings be lost. In all the world, in a hundred generations, would there be another with such thoughts in his breast? If I have made a true record, those who read it, in its proper order, not seeking the meaning through words but through a spiritual understanding, surely will be like a flowing river, bursting its banks. No one will be able to stop them![70]

Some scholars have attempted to isolate "strata" in Wang's writings, seeking to describe an historical development in his thought.[71] This approach is not without merit, but perhaps of greater importance are the changes wrought first by his success and later by his death. Even an important "stage" such as when Wang began to teach about *the extension of pure knowing* does not mark a new development in his thought. This idea is central to his thought and can be seen in his earliest teachings. Its emergence as an important doctrine is better understood as a change in pedagogy, a call for his ever-increasing number of students to be more self-reliant. It was more a function of circumstance than a change in theory.

While Wang was alive, as his school spread, he was forced to rely, more and more, on the written word in order to reach his ever-growing number of students. He began to circulate important letters and essays among his disciples. He employed his most advanced students as his surrogates, and they ensured that his words would not be misinterpreted. When different interpretations did arise among the disciples, Wang was there to pass judgment.[72]

As his following grew, Wang was forced to abandon the one-on-one, master/disciple relationship he so cherished.[73] As he became more popular, he was forced to rely more on the written word as a vehicle for his thought. This change could not but influence the way he presented his teaching. When Wang died, his words took on even more importance. They were the only place one could hope to find the "mind of the master."[74]

This process culminated in the compilation of Wang's complete works.[75] In the 6th year of Lung-ch'ing (cyclical year *jen-shen*) (1572), Hsieh T'ing-chieh[76] published Wang Yang-ming's *Ch'üan-shu* (Complete Works), in 38 *chüan*. The first three *chüan* of the *Ch'üan-shu* are the *Ch'uan-hsi lu*. Hsieh asked Ch'ien to compile the *Ch'uan-hsi lu* and to include, as an appendix, Wang's *Chu-tzu wan-nien ting-lun* (The Final Conclusions of Master Chu's Mature Years).[77] Ch'ien added this work, Wang's preface to it, and a short postscript by Yüan Ch'ing-lin.[78]

Among the present versions of the *Ch'uan-hsi lu*, the one included in Hsieh's *Ch'üan-shu* is widely regarded as the standard edition. But Hsieh himself knew very little about this text. In his preface to the *Ch'üan-shu*, dated 1572 he says:

> The *Wang Wen-ch'eng-kung ch'üan-shu* (Complete Works of Wang Yang-ming) consists of 38 *chüan*. The first three *chüan* contain (his *yü-lu* (Recorded Conversations) and were compiled by Hsü Ai while the master was alive.

It is surprising that Hsieh could be so ill-informed about the nature and history of the *Ch'uan-hsi lu*. As we have seen, very little of the present text of the *Ch'uan-hsi lu* was recorded by Hsü Ai, and much of it was added after Wang had died. Though the *Ch'uan-hsi lu* is called the *Yü-lu* in Hsieh's version, its middle *chüan* consists entirely of letters written by Wang. The history of the text is much more complex than Hsieh realized. It is a multi-layered, many-faceted text; some aspects of its history will never be adequately understood.

Appendix II:
The Meaning of the Term *ch'uan-hsi*

This appendix is an analysis of the meaning of the term *ch'uan-hsi* in the title of Wang's most important work, the *Ch'uan-hsi lu*. It presents a history of the interpretation of the title in Western languages and concludes by presenting a new interpretation.

The first person to translate the *Ch'uan-hsi lu* into a Western language was Frederick Goodrich Henke.[1] Henke translated part of an edition of Shih Pang-yao's *Yang-Ming hsien-sheng chi-yao* (The Essential Works of Master Wang Yang-Ming).[2] In his review of Henke's translation, David S. Nivison reveals that Henke himself did not realize he had worked from the abridged *Yang-ming hsien-sheng chi-yao*, thinking his text was a copy of the *Yang-ming ch'üan-shu* (The Complete Works of Wang Yang-ming). Nivison notes that many years later Wing-tsit Chan made a similar error: not realizing Henke had used an abridged text caused him to misjudge Henke's work.

But Professor Chan was not alone, nor was Henke. In his valuable series of articles, "Wang Shou-jen as a Statesman,"[3] Chang Yü-ch'üan misidentified the text Henke used as the "Complete Works of Yang-ming" (Yang-ming ch'üan-shu) (see page 30). Chang also must have used an edition of the *Yang-ming hsien-sheng chi-yao* in his own work, without realizing it was an abridged text.

Alfred Forke in his *Geschichte der neueren chinesischen Philosophie*,[4] was the first person to see correctly that Henke had translated from the *Yang-ming hsien-sheng chi-yao* and not from Wang's complete works. Forke notes the edition Henke cited in his introduction and mentions that the *Yang-ming hsien-sheng chi-yao* also appears in the *Ssu-pu ts'ung-k'an* collection.[5] Derk Bodde also correctly identified the text Henke used in a note in Fung Yu-lan's *History of Chinese Philosophy*.[6]

In his review, Professor Nivison describes the contents of the *Ssu-pu ts'ung-k'an* edition of the *Yang-ming hsien-sheng chi-yao*:

> Shih's work consists of three main parts: (1) Philosophical materials, four *chüan*; (2) administrative and political papers, seven *chüan*; (3) literary pieces, four *chüan*. Henke has translated all of the first of these three parts as well as Shih's *Nien-p'u*.[7]

When we realize Henke translated the first four *chüan*, that these constitute a major division within the text he used and that they are collectively referred to as the *li-hsüeh p'ien* (Philosophical Writings), the title Henke chose for his work, "The Philosophy of Wang Yang-ming," can be appreciated as appropriate.[8]

The *Yang-ming hsien-sheng chi-yao* opens with an abridged version of Hsüeh K'an's original three-*chüan* edition of the *Ch'uan-hsi lu*, and this appears as *Book I* of Henke's work.[9] Henke translates the title *Ch'uan-hsi lu* as: *Instructions for Practical Life*, but unfortunately he does not provide his reasons for this interpretation.

The next scholar to produce a major study of Wang's thought was Wang Ch'ang-che.[10] His work is not a translation of the *Ch'uan-hsi lu*, but it translates many passages from it. And in the introductory chapter, Wang Ch'ang-che translates the title as: *Recueil des Lecons du Maitre* (Collected Lessons of the Master). He describes the *Ch'uan-hsi lu* as a work "...qui rapporte les entretiens du Maitre avec ses disciples sur la doctrine morale..." (which reports conversations, concerning moral philosophy, between the master and his disciples).[11] Again, there is no specific discussion of the title of the work.

The next translations of the title *Ch'uan-hsi lu* appeared in studies of Wang Yang-ming which were parts of general surveys on Chinese thought. Derk Bodde, translating Fung Yu-lan's *History of Chinese Philosophy*, renders the title *Ch'uan-hsi lu* as: *Record of Instruction*.[12] Carsun Chang, in his book *The Development of Neo-Confucian Thought*, translates it: *Records of Instructions and Practices*.[13]

Professor Wing-tsit Chan is the first translator to identify the passage in the *Analects* that inspired Hsü Ai to name his original work the *Ch'uan-hsi lu*.[14]

.... I have not translated the title literally. The term "ch'uan-hsi" comes from the *Analects* 1:4 and means "what has been transmitted [from the teacher] and is to be learned well [and to be practiced]" or, according to another interpretation. "to transmit those doctrines which one has already learned well or put into practice himself." Wang's pupil Hsü Ai used the term as the title for his records of conversations with his teacher. Most annotators have emphasized the idea of learning, especially through recitation. But Wang denounced book learning and advocated practice instead. I believe that the title *Instructions for Practical Living* expresses better the meaning and the spirit of the original. The word *lu* (records) has been omitted.

Professor Chan probably knew, but did not reveal to his readers, that the two interpretations of the expression *ch'uan-hsi* that he provides are found in the *Ssu-shu chi-chu* (Collected Commentaries on the Four Books)[15] and the *Lun-yü Ho-shih teng chi-chieh* (Collected Explanations on the *Analects* by Master Ho and Others)[16] respectively. The first is the well-known work by Chu Hsi. The second work is by far the older dating from the middle of the third century. It is worth examining the passage from the *Analects* and both commentaries in greater detail. Leaving the last line untranslated for the moment, *Analects* 1:4 says:

> Tseng-tzu said, "Each day, I examine myself on three points. In my dealings on behalf of others, have I been disloyal? In association with my friends, have I been unfaithful? *Ch'uan pu hsi hu*?

Chu Hsi's comment on this passage says:

> ...To apply oneself to the utmost is called *chung* (loyalty). To realize this (in concrete affairs) is called *hsin (faithfulness)*. *Ch'uan* (transmission) refers to what had been received from the teacher. *Hsi* (practice) refers to cultivating (lit. *shou* "ripening") it within oneself. Tseng-tzu daily examined himself in these three respects. If he had (shortcomings in regard to any of these), he corrected them. If he was without (shortcomings in regard to any of these), he applied himself even more diligently. If one can truly order himself in this way, it may be said of him that he has attained the root of learning. But as regards the order of these three, *chung* (loyalty) and *hsin* (faithfulness) are the root of *ch'uan-hsi*...

Regarding the final line of the passage, the commentary in the *Collected Explanations on the Analects* says:

> This refers to everything one *ch'uan* (transmits). One must not *ch'uan* (transmit) anything which one has not personally investigated and *hsi* (practiced).

Both of these are grammatically possible and philosophically viable interpretations. I believe the second is the better interpretation if one is translating the *Analects*. But in the present case, this is not necessarily an important issue. Since Hsü Ai is the one who selected the expression *ch'uan-hsi* as the title of his collection, we are interested in how *he* interpreted the line, and how he applied that interpretation in the title of his work.

Professor Chan is correct to point out that Wang advocated *concrete practice* over *book learning*, some would say Wang did so to a fault. And it is important to realize Wang's reason for doing this. He was reacting to followers of the Ch'eng-Chu orthodoxy who, in Wang's eyes, had abandoned the task of moral self-cultivation and lapsed into an inert formalism. Even more important, to the present inquiry, than the fact that Wang held this view is the fact that Hsü Ai appreciated how important this view was to his master. One can see this clearly in Hsü Ai's preface to the *Ch'uan-hsi lu*.[17]

The importance of Hsü Ai's preface for understanding the title of his work was first pointed out by David S. Nivison, in his review of Chan's and Henke's translations.[18]

I have one perhaps trivial complaint to make about both men's handling of the *Ch'uan-hsi lu*. Henke's rendering of the title, "Instructions for Practical Life" and Chan's almost identical "Instructions for Practical Living" seem to me equally incomprehensible (surely Wang was not inveighing against "impractical living"). As Hsü Ai explains clearly in his preface (not translated by either Henke or Chan), the book is a "record" (*lu*) of Wang's teachings "transmitted" (*ch'uan*) in writing for those who cannot talk with him themselves, but with the caution—since Wang was uneasy about having his teachings fixed in a lifeless text—that they are not merely to be read and cherished in thought, but constantly to be adapted and applied (*hsi*) in one's moral life. Professor Chan of course understands this fully (p. 314).

These remarks are helpful in several respects. Most importantly, they point out Hsü Ai's emphasis on practice, a major theme of his preface and a central aspect of Wang's thought. This theme, that one must personally appropriate and put into practice the lessons one has learned, is the gist of Chu Hsi's interpretation of *Analects* 1:4. It was also precisely what was wrong with Chu Hsi's followers and Chu Hsi's method of self-cultivation, according to Wang Yang-ming. Wang insisted repeatedly that Chu's method led in the wrong direction: that his followers had lost sight of the active, personal aspects of self-cultivation and had lapsed into the routinized, lifeless pursuit of repetition, memorization and mimicry.[19]

In Wang's eyes, Chu's later followers were like people desiring to learn how to paint but who never proceed beyond admiring and copying the paintings of the masters. To Wang, they had become wedded to repetition and bound by precedents. This inhibited their moral development and eventually led to their moral decay. They had become obsessed with following lifeless forms of behavior, and this had led to competitiveness, jealousy and greed. They had forgotten that the moral life is something one must lead, not something one is led through. Without constant reflection and application, one cannot develop morally. This unhappy situation was not due to the poor abilities of the students. It was the result of a misguided pedagogy, one that led students to *copy* rather than to *create* for themselves.

The master said, "The human mind and Heavenly principle are inseparable. The books sages and worthies have written are like a portrait painter conveying the spirit by painting the real. A painting can do no more than show the shape and general outline and allow people to use this in order to discover the real. There are things about a person's spirit, feelings, expressions and behavior which cannot be conveyed. The voluminous writings of later generations have mimicked and copied what the sages have painted and destroyed it. They have cut it up and added to it—as they have seen fit—in order to prove to the world how clever they are. They have grown farther and farther from the real.[20]

One way of describing the difference between Chu Hsi and Wang is in terms of the notion of practice. Essentially, Wang criticized the followers of the Ch'eng-Chu school for restricting the sense of practice to repetition, memorization and mimicry. In Wang's mind, the measure of one's learning, in his day, had come to be judged solely in terms of one's ability to parrot the classics and their commentaries and to compose essays conforming to the rigid *pa-ku wen* style. For Wang this was terribly wrong. Practice should never be mere mimicry; it should always be a personal performance. Knowledge, and Wang was concerned with moral knowledge, is never just information; it is wisdom acquired through a profound, personal insight.

We speak of practice in the sense of practicing scales in music or strokes in penmanship. We practice the pronunciation of foreign words, and we practice memorizing lists of new vocabulary items. But we also use the word *practice* to describe the way one lives one's life. When we say someone *practices* the teachings of Jesus Christ, Buddha or Mohammed, we mean much more than that he has memorized these teachings and often repeats them. We mean he has appropriated these teachings, made them a part of himself, that he exhibits them in every aspect of his life. This goes far beyond the most comprehensive knowledge of scripture or the most accurate repetition of actions. It implies these teachings guide one's actions, and that one can interpret and apply these teachings in novel and difficult situations.

In a similar sense, *carrying on* a tradition can mean much more than merely preserving and perpetuating its teachings. It can mean applying these teachings in real-life situations, *carrying out* the teachings *carries* them *forward*. Libraries and museums can preserve and perpetuate knowledge about traditions, but human beings must *practice* them if they are to survive as *living traditions*.

I believe that, to Wang, the expression *ch'uan-hsi* conveyed this sense of *practice*: individuals carrying on a living tradition. We can see this clearly by examining how he used the expression on other occasions and how those within his school adopted the special sense he gave it. In the *Ch'uan-hsi lu*, in a letter to Lo Cheng-an, Wang uses the expression *ch'uan-hsi* with precisely this sense.[21] Wang was criticizing the scholars of his day for having replaced the personal practice of the spirit of the classics with the academic discussion of the letter of the classics. Learning, and for Wang this means moral education, had become identified with one's mastery of the classics and their commentaries. Wang said:

...but scholars today, as soon as they gain some facility in the practice (*ch'uan-hsi*) of classical commentary (*shun ku*), all think they know what learning (*hsüeh*) is about.

We can see that, in this passage, Wang used the expression *ch'uan-hsi* in the sense I have described above: carrying on a type of *ch'uan* (learning) by carrying on a type of *hsi* (practice).

Wang was not criticizing the preservation or passing on of classical commentaries *per se*. He was objecting to those who would reduce moral learning to the study of philological and textual issues, those who failed to ever put the lessons of the classics into actual practice.

There is another occurrence of the term *ch'uan-hsi* in the *Ch'uan-hsi lu*. In Ch'ien Te-hung's postscript to what is now the third *chüan* of the *Ch'uan-hsi Lu*, he quotes Shen Ssu-wei:

> My only fear is that the practice (of the Way) (*ch'uan-hsi*) is not widespread; I have never thought that the repetitions (in the text) would prove confusing (to those who read it).[22]

This was written long after Hsü Ai had named his collection, but it serves as evidence that within Wang's school, the expression *ch'uan-hsi* was used as a term of art. Its meaning was derived from the passage in the *Analects* and roughly followed Chu Hsi's exposition. It meant: "to personally *hsi* (practice) the *ch'uan* (lessons) one has learned."[23]

In his preface, Hsü Ai describes his collection as a work students can take with them, when they leave the master's side, to serve as a guide in their study. Most importantly, as Professor Nivison has pointed out, they are to apply the lessons contained in the book in concrete situations. We can now see why Hsü Ai chose to name his collection the *Ch'uan-hsi lu*. It was a record (*lu*) for the personal practice (*hsi*) of the lessons (*ch'uan*) Wang's students had learned. Accordingly, we should translate the title: *A Record for Practice*.

There is another motivation for interpreting the title in this way. Wang and his followers saw themselves in competition with the followers of the Ch'eng-Chu school, and I believe this influenced Hsü Ai's choice of a title.

Those familiar with the history of Neo-Confucianism know that Chu Hsi, in collaboration with Lü Tsu-ch'ien, compiled an anthology, selected from the works of Chou Tun-i, Chang Tsai, Ch'eng Hao and Ch'eng Yi called the *Chin-ssu lu* (A Record for Reflection).[24] This work was designed as a primer to Confucian thought for isolated yet resolute scholars who were without a teacher or good friend to guide them through the voluminous works of these four masters. The *Chin-ssu lu* resembles the *Ch'uan-hsi lu* in several important respects. Both works are called records *lu*, both have two-character titles derived from passages in the *Analects*,[25] and both were designed for beginning students.[26]

We know that Wang believed Chu Hsi and his followers had placed too much emphasis on textual study and that Wang, in contrast, emphasized the need for practice. We also know, from his preface, that Hsü Ai appreciated this aspect of Wang's teachings; he too emphasized the need for concrete practice. I believe that when Hsü Ai chose the title for his record of Wang's discourses, he chose a title that resembled Chu Hsi's *Chin-ssu lu* (A Record for Reflection)—by being both a record (*lu*) of sayings and having a two-character title taken from a passage in the *Analects*. But his title also vividly illustrated a central difference between the thought of Wang and Chu: Chu emphasized study; Wang emphasized practice.

Chu Hsi's work was a *Record for Reflection*, a collection of writings any interested person could read, ponder and through this process begin to understand the Way. Wang rejected this approach and Hsü Ai appreciated the Master's position. Hsü Ai named Wang's work *A Record for Practice*—a representative collection of Wang's remarks to beginning students, which they could take with them, when apart from the teacher, to guide them in the concrete *practice* of Wang's teachings.

Appendix III:
A Finding List for the *Ch'uan-hsi lu*

This appendix is a finding list which correlates the section numbers employed by Professor Wing-tsit Chan, in his translation of the *Ch'uan-hsi lu*, with the *SPTK* edition (*WWCKCS* Taipei, 1965) of the text.

BEGIN BOOK I:

Section: 1
WWCKCS: 1:56a
Section: 2
WWCKCS: 1:56b
Section: 3
WWCKCS: 1:56b
Section: 4
WWCKCS: 1:57a
Section: 5
WWCKCS: 1:57b
Section: 6
WWCKCS: 1:59a
Section: 7
WWCKCS: 1:60a
Section: 8
WWCKCS: 1:60a
Section: 9
WWCKCS: 1:60a
Section: 10
WWCKCS: 1:60b
Section: 11
WWCKCS: 1:61a
Section: 12
WWCKCS: 1:63a
Section: 13
WWCKCS: 1:63a
Section: 14
WWCKCS: 1:63b
Section: 15
WWCKCS: 1:64a
Section: 16
WWCKCS: 1:64a

Section: 17
WWCKCS: 1:64b
Section: 18
WWCKCS: 1:64b
Section: 19
WWCKCS: 1:64b
Section: 20
WWCKCS: 1:64b
Section: 21
WWCKCS: 1:65a
Section: 22
WWCKCS: 1:65a
Section: 23
WWCKCS: 1:65b
Section: 24
WWCKCS: 1:65b
Section: 25
WWCKCS; 1:66a
Section: 26
WWCKCS: 1:66a
Section: 27
WWCKCS: 1:66a
Section: 28
WWCKCS: 1:66a
Section: 29
WWCKCS: 1:66b
Section: 30
WWCKCS: 1:66b
Section: 31
WWCKCS: 1:67a
Section: 32
WWCKCS: 1:67a
Section: 33
WWCKCS: 1:67b

Section: 34
WWCKCS: 1:67b
Section: 35
WWCKCS: 1:67b
Section: 36
WWCKCS: 1:67b
Section: 37
WWCKCS: 1:67b
Section: 38
WWCKCS: 1:67b
Section: 39
WWCKCS: 1:68a
Section: 40
WWCKCS: 1:68b
Section: 41
WWCKCS: 1:68b
Section: 42
WWCKCS: 1:68b
Section: 43
WWCKCS: 1:68b
Section: 44
WWCKCS: 1:69a
Section: 45
WWCKCS: 1:69b
Section: 46
WWCKCS: 1:69b
Section: 47
WWCKCS: 1:69b
Section: 48
WWCKCS: 1:69b
Section: 49
WWCKCS: 1:70a
Section: 50
WWCKCS: 1:70b
Section: 51
WWCKCS: 1:70b
Section: 52
WWCKCS: 1:70b
Section: 53
WWCKCS: 1:70b
Section: 54
WWCKCS: 1:71a

Section: 55
WWCKCS: 1:71a
Section: 56
WWCKCS: 1:71a
Section: 57
WWCKCS: 1:71a
Section: 58
WWCKCS: 1:71a
Section: 59
WWCKCS: 1:71a
Section: 60
WWCKCS: 1:71a
Section: 61
WWCKCS: 1:71a
Section: 62
WWCKCS: 1:71b
Section: 63
WWCKCS: 1:71b
Section: 64
WWCKCS: 1:71b
Section: 65
WWCKCS: 1:71b
Section: 66
WWCKCS: 1:72a
Section: 67
WWCKCS: 1:72b
Section: 68
WWCKCS: 1:72b
Section: 69
WWCKCS: 1:73a
Section: 70
WWCKCS: 1:73a
Section: 71
WWCKCS: 1:73a
Section: 72
WWCKCS: 1:73a
Section: 73
WWCKCS: 1:73b
Section: 74
WWCKCS: 1:73b
Section: 75
WWCKCS: 1:73b

Section: 76
WWCKCS: 1:74a
Section: 77
WWCKCS: 1:74b
Section: 78
WWCKCS: 1:74b
Section: 79
WWCKCS: 1:75a
Section: 80
WWCKCS: 1:75a
Section: 81
WWCKCS: 1:75a
Section: 82
WWCKCS: 1:75a
Section: 83
WWCKCS: 1:75a
Section: 84
WWCKCS: 1:75a
Section: 85
WWCKCS: 1:75b
Section: 86
WWCKCS: 1:75b
Section: 87
WWCKCS: 1:75b
Section: 88
WWCKCS: 1:75b
Section: 89
WWCKCS: 1:75b
Section: 90
WWCKCS: 1:75b
Section: 91
WWCKCS: 1:76a
Section: 92
WWCKCS: 1:76a
Section: 93
WWCKCS: 1:76a
Section: 94
WWCKCS: 1:76b
Section: 95
WWCKCS: 1:76b
Section: 96
WWCKCS: 1:77a

Section: 97
WWCKCS: 1:77a
Section: 98
WWCKCS: 1:77a
Section: 99
WWCKCS: 1:77b
Section: 100
WWCKCS: 1:78b
Section: 101
WWCKCS: 1:78b
Section: 102
WWCKCS: 1:79b
Section: 103
WWCKCS: 1:80a
Section: 104
WWCKCS: 1:80a
Section: 105
WWCKCS: 1:80a
Section: 106
WWCKCS: 1:80b
Section: 107
WWCKCS: 1:80b
Section: 108
WWCKCS: 1:81a
Section: 109
WWCKCS: 1:81a
Section: 110
WWCKCS: 1:81a
Section: 111
WWCKCS: 1:81a
Section: 112
WWCKCS: 1:81b
Section: 113
WWCKCS: 1:81b
Section: 114
WWCKCS: 1:81b
Section: 115
WWCKCS: 1:81b
Section: 116
WWCKCS: 1:82a
Section: 117
WWCKCS: 1:82a

Section: 118
WWCKCS: 1:83a
Section: 119
WWCKCS: 1:83a
Section: 120
WWCKCS: 1:83b
Section: 121
WWCKCS: 1:84a
Section: 122
WWCKCS: 1:84a
Section: 123
WWCKCS: 1:85b
Section: 124
WWCKCS: 1:85b
Section: 125
WWCKCS: 1:85b
Section: 126
WWCKCS: 1:85b
Section: 127
WWCKCS: 1:86a
Section: 128
WWCKCS: 1:86b
Section: 129
WWCKCS: 1:87a

BEGIN BOOK II:

Section: 130
WWCKCS: 2:88b
Section: 131
WWCKCS: 2:88b
Section: 132
WWCKCS: 2:89a
Section: 133
WWCKCS: 2:89b
Section: 134
WWCKCS: 2:90b
Section: 135
WWCKCS: 2:91b
Section: 136
WWCKCS: 2:92b

Section: 137
WWCKCS: 2:93b
Section: 138
WWCKCS: 2:95a
Section: 139
WWCKCS: 2:95b
Section: 140
WWCKCS: 2:97a
Section: 141
WWCKCS: 2:98a
Section: 142
WWCKCS: 2:99b
Section: 143
WWCKCS: 2:100b
Section: 144
WWCKCS: 2:102a
Section: 145
WWCKCS: 2:103a
Section: 146
WWCKCS: 2:103b
Section: 147
WWCKCS: 2:104a
Section: 148
WWCKCS: 2:104b
Section: 149
WWCKCS: 2:104b
Section: 150
WWCKCS: 2:105a
Section: 151
WWCKCS: 2:105b
Section: 152
WWCKCS: 2:105b
Section: 153
WWCKCS: 2:106a
Section: 154
WWCKCS: 2:106a
Section: 155
WWCKCS: 2:106b
Section: 156
WWCKCS: 2:107a
Section: 157
WWCKCS: 2:107a

Section: 158
WWCKCS: 2:108b
Section: 159
WWCKCS: 2:108b
Section: 160
WWCKCS: 2:108b
Section: 161
WWCKCS: 2:109a
Section: 162
WWCKCS: 2:109b
Section: 163
WWCKCS: 2:110b
Section: 164
WWCKCS: 2:111a
Section: 165
WWCKCS: 2:111a
Section: 166
WWCKCS: 2:112a
Section: 167
WWCKCS: 2:112b
Section: 168
WWCKCS: 2:113a
Section: 169
WWCKCS: 2:114a
Section: 170
WWCKCS: 2:114b
Section: 171
WWCKCS: 2:115b
Section: 172
WWCKCS: 2:116b
Section: 173
WWCKCS: 2:117a
Section: 174
WWCKCS: 2:117b
Section: 175
WWCKCS: 2:118a
Section: 176
WWCKCS: 2:118b
Section: 177
WWCKCS: 2:119b
Section: 178
WWCKCS: 2:119b

Section: 179
WWCKCS: 2:120a
Section: 180
WWCKCS: 2:120b
Section: 181
WWCKCS: 2:121a
Section: 182
WWCKCS: 2:121b
Section: 183
WWCKCS: 2:121b
Section: 184
WWCKCS: 2:122a
Section: 185
WWCKCS: 2:122b
Section: 186
WWCKCS: 2:122b
Section: 187
WWCKCS: 2:123b
Section: 188
WWCKCS: 2:123b
Section: 189
WWCKCS: 2:124a
Section: 190
WWCKCS: 2:125a
Section: 191
WWCKCS: 2:125a
Section: 192
WWCKCS: 2:125b
Section: 193
WWCKCS: 2:126b
Section: 194
WWCKCS: 2:126b
Section: 195
WWCKCS: 2:126b
Section: 196
WWCKCS: 2:127b
Section: 197
WWCKCS: 2:128a
Section: 198
WWCKCS: 2:128a
Section: 199
WWCKCS: 2:128a

Section: 200
WWCKCS: 2:128a

BEGIN BOOK III

Section: 201
WWCKCS: 3:129a
Section: 202
WWCKCS: 3:130a
Section: 203
WWCKCS: 3:130a
Section: 204
WWCKCS: 3:130b
Section: 205
WWCKCS: 3:130b
Section: 206
WWCKCS: 3:131a
Section: 207
WWCKCS: 3:131a
Section: 208
WWCKCS: 3:131b
Section: 209
WWCKCS: 3:131b
Section: 210
WWCKCS: 3:131b
Section: 211
WWCKCS: 3:131b
Section: 212
WWCKCS: 3:132a
Section: 213
WWCKCS: 3:132a
Section: 214
WWCKCS: 3:132a
Section: 215
WWCKCS: 3:132a
Section: 216
WWCKCS: 3:132b
Section: 217
WWCKCS: 3:132b
Section: 218
WWCKCS: 3:132b

Section: 219
WWCKCS: 3:133a
Section: 220
WWCKCS: 3:133a
Section: 221
WWCKCS: 3:133a
Section: 222
WWCKCS: 3:133b
Section: 223
WWCKCS: 3:134a
Section: 224
WWCKCS: 3:134a
Section: 225
WWCKCS: 3:134a
Section: 226
WWCKCS: 3:134a
Section: 227
WWCKCS: 3:134b
Section: 228
WWCKCS: 3:134b
Section: 229
WWCKCS: 3:135a
Section: 230
WWCKCS: 3:135a
Section: 231
WWCKCS: 3:135b
Section: 232
WWCKCS: 3:135b
Section: 233
WWCKCS: 3:135b
Section: 234
WWCKCS: 3:136a
Section: 235
WWCKCS: 3:136a
Section: 236
WWCKCS: 3:136a
Section: 237
WWCKCS: 3:136b
Section: 238
WWCKCS: 3:136b
Section: 239
WWCKCS: 3:136b

Section: 240
WWCKCS: 3:137a
Section: 241
WWCKCS: 3:137a
Section: 242
WWCKCS: 3:137b
Section: 243
WWCKCS: 3:138a
Section: 244
WWCKCS: 3:138a
Section: 245
WWCKCS: 3:138b
Section: 246
WWCKCS: 3:138b
Section: 247
WWCKCS: 3:138b
Section: 248
WWCKCS: 3:139a
Section: 249
WWCKCS: 3:139a
Section: 250
WWCKCS: 3:139a
Section: 251
WWCKCS: 3:139b
Section: 252
WWCKCS: 3:139b
Section: 253
WWCKCS: 3:139b
Section: 254
WWCKCS: 3:139b
Section: 255
WWCKCS: 3:140a
Section: 256
WWCKCS: 3:140a
Section: 257
WWCKCS: 3:140a
Section: 258
WWCKCS: 3:140b
Section: 259
WWCKCS: 3:140b
Section: 260
WWCKCS: 3:140b

Section: 261
WWCKCS: 3:141a
Section: 262
WWCKCS: 3:141a
Section: 263
WWCKCS: 3:141a
Section: 264
WWCKCS: 3:141b
Section: 265
WWCKCS: 3:141b
Section: 266
WWCKCS: 3:141b
Section: 267
WWCKCS: 3:141b
Section: 268
WWCKCS: 3:142a
Section: 269
WWCKCS: 3:142a
Section: 270
WWCKCS: 3:142b
Section: 271
WWCKCS: 3:142b
Section: 272
WWCKCS: 3:142b
Section: 273
WWCKCS: 3:143a
Section: 274
WWCKCS: 3:143a
Section: 275
WWCKCS: 3:143b
Section: 276
WWCKCS: 3:143b
Section: 277
WWCKCS: 3:144a
Section: 278
WWCKCS: 3:144a
Section: 279
WWCKCS: 3:144a
Section: 280
WWCKCS: 3:144b
Section: 281
WWCKCS: 3:144b

Section: 282
WWCKCS: 3:145a
Section: 283
WWCKCS: 3:145a
Section: 284
WWCKCS: 3:145a
Section: 285
WWCKCS: 3:145b
Section: 286
WWCKCS: 3:145b
Section: 287
WWCKCS: 3:146a
Section: 288
WWCKCS: 3:146a
Section: 289
WWCKCS: 3:146a
Section: 290
WWCKCS: 3:146a
Section: 291
WWCKCS: 3:146b
Section: 292
WWCKCS: 3:146b
Section: 293
WWCKCS: 3:147a
Section: 294
WWCKCS: 3:147a
Section: 295
WWCKCS: 3:147b
Section: 296
WWCKCS: 3:147b
Section: 297
WWCKCS: 3:148a
Section: 298
WWCKCS: 3:148b
Section: 299
WWCKCS: 3:148b
Section: 300
WWCKCS: 3:149a
Section: 301
WWCKCS: 3:149a
Section: 302
WWCKCS: 3:149a

Section: 303
WWCKCS: 3:149a
Section: 304
WWCKCS: 3:149a
Section: 305
WWCKCS: 3:149a
Section: 306
WWCKCS: 3:149a
Section: 307
WWCKCS: 3:149a
Section: 308
WWCKCS: 3:149b
Section: 309
WWCKCS: 3:150a
Section: 310
WWCKCS: 3:150a
Section: 311
WWCKCS: 3:150a
Section: 312
WWCKCS: 3:150a
Section: 313
WWCKCS: 3:150b
Section: 314
WWCKCS: 3:151a
Section: 315
WWCKCS: 3:151a
Section: 316
WWCKCS: 3:152a
Section: 317
WWCKCS: 3:152b
Section: 318
WWCKCS: 3:153a
Section: 319
WWCKCS: 3:153b
Section: 320
WWCKCS: 3:154a
Section: 321
WWCKCS: 3:154b
Section: 322
WWCKCS: 3:154b
Section: 323
WWCKCS: 3:155a

Section: 324
WWCKCS: 3:155a
Section: 325
WWCKCS: 3:155b
Section: 326
WWCKCS: 3:155b
Section: 327
WWCKCS: 3:155b
Section: 328
WWCKCS: 3:156a
Section: 329
WWCKCS: 3:156a
Section: 330
WWCKCS: 3:156a
Section: 331
WWCKCS: 3:156b
Section: 332
WWCKCS: 3:156b
Section: 333
WWCKCS: 3:156b

Section: 334
WWCKCS: 3:156b
Section: 335
WWCKCS: 3:157a
Section: 336
WWCKCS: 3:157a
Section: 337
WWCKCS: 3:157a
Section: 338
WWCKCS: 3:157b
Section: 339
WWCKCS: 3:158a
Section: 340
WWCKCS: 3:158a
Section: 341
WWCKCS: 3:158a
Section: 342
WWCKCS: 3:158b
Section: 343
WWCKCS: 3:158b

Notes

Introduction

1. For a concise biography of Wang Yang-ming, see L. Carrington Goodrich and Chaoying Fang, *Dictionary of Ming Biography*, (New York: Columbia University Press, 1976), Vol. 2, pp. 1408-1416. For a detailed study of Wang's early life, see Tu Wei-ming, *Neo-Confucian Thought in Action*, (Berkeley: University of California Press, 1976).

2. For a thorough account of Wang's career as an official, see Chang Yü-ch'üan, "Wang Shou-jen as a Statesman," *Chinese Social and Political Science Review*, Vol. 23, pp. 30-99, 155-257, 319-375, 473-517.

3. Lo Ch'in-shun was one well-know contemporary critic of Wang. For a study of his thought, which includes a thorough discussion of his criticisms of Wang, see Irene T. Bloom, *Knowledge Painfully Acquired* (New York: Columbia University Press, 1987). For a letter from Wang to Lo, see Wing-tsit Chan, *Instructions for Practical Living and Other Neo-Confucian Writings by Wang Yang-ming*, (New York: Columbia University Press, 1963), pp. 157-165.

4. Among Wang's later critics, two of the harshest were members of the Tung-lin Academy: Ku Hsien-ch'eng and Kao P'an-lung. For a thorough account of the academy and Wang's critics within it, see Heinrich Bush, "The Tung-lin Academy and Its Political and Philosophical Significance," *Monumenta Serica*, XIV, 1949-55, pp. 1-163. See also Charles O. Hucker, "The Tung-lin Movement of the Late Ming Period," in John K. Fairbank, ed., *Chinese Thought and Institutions*, (Chicago: University of Chicago Press, 1959, pp. 132-62.

5. For studies of Wang's thought in Korea, see: Ch'ong In-bo, *Yangmy'onghak y'ollon*, (Seoul: Sams'ong munhwa chaedan, 1975); Kim Kir-hwan, *Han'guk Yangmy'onghak y'on'gu*, (Seoul: Ilchisa, 1984); Yun Nam-han, *Choso'n sidae ui Yangmy'onghak y'on'gu*, (Seoul: Chimmundang, 1982). For Japanese studies of Wang, see the monumental twelve-volume compendium on Wang, commemorating the 500th anniversary of his birth: Yōmeigaku Taikei compiled by Araki Kengo and others (Tokyo: Meitoku shuppansha, 1972). In particular, see volumes 8, 9 and 10 of this work, edited by Yamazaki Michio entitled, *Nihon no Yōmeigaku*.

6. Wang's influence can also be seen in the modern literature of Japan. His doctrine of "the unity of knowledge and action" fascinates Isao, the tragic hero of Yukio Mishima's *Runaway Horses*. See Michael Gallagher, (trans.), *Runaway Horses*, (New York: Pocket Books, 1975), pp. 353-354. Wang's thought fascinated Mishima himself, who saw it as a "philosophy of revolution." See Mishima's article: "Kakumei tetsugaku to shite no Yōmeigaku", *Shokun*, (Sept. 1970), pp. 22-45.

7. See Wang's *Questions on the Great Learning* (*WWCKCS* 26:736a,b). For a translation, see Chan, *Instructions*, p. 272.

8. Part of Wang's general orders on military conduct. See Chang, *Wang Shou-jen*, pp. 346, 358.

9. For Wang's view of his relationship to Mencius, see his preface to the collected works of Lu Chiu-yüan (translated by Julia Ching in *To Acquire Wisdom: The Way of Wang Yang-ming*, (New York: Columbia University Press, 1976), pp. 206-208). See also Wang's letter to Lo Ch'in-shun (Chan, *Instructions*, section 176).

10. For Mencius' view of his relationship to Confucius and his place in the Confucian tradition, see *Mencius* 3B9.

11. There is evidence that both Mencius and Wang were aware that their historical situations influenced the presentation of their thought (For Mencius, see *Mencius* 3B9. For Wang, see Chan, *Instructions*, section 176.) But because of their underlying belief concerning the uniqueness of the Way, neither could imagine he had fundamentally changed the tradition.

12. See *Mencius* 3A5, 3B9, 7A26. Mencius also attacked other foes of Confucianism, among them the philosopher Kao Tzu (see *Mencius* 2A2 and 6A1-6), the philosopher Tzu-mo (see *Mencius* 7A26) and the so-called Agriculturalists (see *Mencius* 3A4). For a discussion of the Agriculturalists, see A. C. Graham, "The Nung-chia 'School of the Tillers' and the Origins of Peasant Utopianism in China," *BOAS*, Vol. 42; No. 1, 1979, pp. 66-100.

13. Confucius claimed to be a transmitter—not a maker (*Analects HYIS* #16: 11/7/1). I cannot here argue for my account of what this line means—commentators offer a variety of different explanations—I take it at face value. Confucius was a traditionalist who thought he was preserving the Way to live: a way discovered by the ancient sage-kings.

14. An important example—one I examine later in this study—is the incorporation of the notion of an innate and wholly good Buddha nature with the traditional Chinese (specifically Mencian) notion of an innate and fundamentally good human nature. See Chapter 2: *Human Nature*.

15. To understand the interaction solely in terms of Buddhism's "conquest" of China is equally inaccurate and no less widespread a practice. For balanced and revealing studies of Buddhism's influence on Chinese thought, see Arthur F. Wright, *Buddhism in Chinese History*, (Stanford: Stanford University Press, 1959) and Wm. Theodore De Bary, "Buddhism and the Chinese Tradition," *Diogenes*, #47 (Fall 1964), pp. 102-24.

Chapter 1: The Nature of Morality

1. For an example of familial obligations taking precedence over social obligations, see the *Analects* (*HYIS* #16: 26/13/18).

2. *Analects* (*HYIS* #16: 4/3/11). (cf. the *Doctrine of the Mean* 19:6). Confucius regarded these obligations and practices, and the family and social structures within which they existed, as fundamental features of the universe, a system decreed by Heaven. They were the given structure within which human life was to be lived. See the *Analects* (*HYIS* #16: 2/2/4, 16/9/5, 22/12/1, 42/20/3).

3. This is an important distinction to remember, and I will relate it specifically to Mencius later in this chapter. For examples, see the *Analects* (*HYIS* #16: 7/4/16, 28/14/12, 34/16/10, 39/19/1).

4. This internal aspect of *li* is critical to Confucius' vision. For examples, see the *Analects* (*HYIS* #16: 5/3/15, 5/3/26/ 22/12/2, 22/15/5, 26/13/20, 36/17/9, 39/19/1) et al.

5. *Analects* (*HYIS* #16: 2/2/7. See also 2/2/6 and 3/2/8.

6. The Confucian version of the *Golden Rule* has a long and varied history. The most complete discussion of this topic is an as yet unpublished paper by David S. Nivison, *Golden Rule Arguments in Chinese Moral Philosophy*, presented as the annual Evans-Wentz lecture at Stanford University in 1984. See also Herbert Fingarette, "Following the 'One Thread' of the Analects," *Journal of the American Academy of Religion: Thematic Issue*, Vol. XLVII, 3s (Sept. 1979) pp. 373-405. For my understanding of the Confucian Golden Rule, see my "Reweaving the 'one thread' of the *Analects*," *Philosophy East and West*, 40.1 (January 1990).

7. See the *Analects* (*HYIS* #16: 11/6/30, 32/15/24/ et al.

8. *Analects* (*HYIS* #16: 1/1/2).

9. Confucius first drew a distinction—between the Way and profit—that became central to Confucian moral philosophy. See the *Analects* (*HYIS* #16: 7/4/16. 11/6/22, 28/14/12, 34/16/10, 39/19/1).

10. Herbert Fingarette aptly describes Confucianism as "A Way without a Crossroads." See Herbert Fingarette, *Confucius—the Secular as Sacred*, (New York: Harper and Row, 1972), pp. 18-36.

11. Every major thinker in early China made an appeal to an earlier, golden age. But they disagreed over when this age occurred, what kind of society it was and who were the most important sages.

12. This era was the beginning of philosophical debate in China, but one cannot ignore the essentially religious tone of this debate. Confucius saw his Way as the *decree of Heaven*. Mo Tzu argued that his policy of benefitting all with partiality to none was the *Will of Heaven*. Taoists argued that their Way is *Natural, Heavenly*.

13. See Chapter 2: *Human Nature* and Chapter 4: *Self Cultivation* for detailed accounts of these aspects of Mencius' thought.

14. See the *Mencius* (*HYIS* #17: 1/1A/1, 14/2B/1, 27/4A3, 27/4A/9).

15. See the *Mencius* (*HYIS* #17: 1/1A/2, 12/2A/8, 51/7A/4).

16. For examples of Heaven as a force that acts on the side of the righteous, see *Mencius* (*HYIS* #17: 7/4A/7, 36/5A/5, 50/6B/15).

17. See *Analects* (*HYIS* #16: 2/2/1) for an example of Confucius invoking a celestial/terrestrial analogy. This was a very old belief in China. It is reflected in the design of early Chinese cities, which like those of many early peoples, recreated celestial patterns on earth. See Paul Wheatley, *The Pivot of the Four Quarters: A Preliminary Enquiry into the Origins and Character of the Ancient Chinese City*, (Chicago: Aldine Publishing Co., 1971).

18. See Mencius' discussion with King Hui of Liang in the *Mencius* (*HYIS* #17: 1/1A/2.

19. See the *Analects* (*HYIS* #16: 6/4/8, 6/4/9, 10/6/11, 14/8/7, 30/15/2 and the *Mencius* (*HYIS* #17: 22/3B/1, 33/4B/29, 44-45/6A/10).

20. *Analects* (*HYIS* #16: 6/4/8).

21. It is appropriate that the opening dialogue of the *Mencius*, between Mencius and King Hui of Liang, is dedicated to this distinction. For additional examples, see *Mencius* (*HYIS* #17: 14/2B/1, 22/3B/1, 27/4A/9, 47/6B/4, 53/7A/25 and 55/7B/10).
22. See above, note #9.
23. *Mencius* (*HYIS* #17: 53/7A/26). Mencius' characterization of Yang Chu is not accurate or fair. Yang Chu taught that one should not injure oneself for material gain; *one should not sacrifice a single hair even to gain an empire.* See A. C. Graham, *The Book of Lieh Tzu,* (London: John Murray, 1973), pp. 148-49.
24. *Mencius* (*HYIS* #17: 53/7A/26).
25. See *Mencius* (*HYIS* #17: 25/3B/9 and 57/7B/26). Yang and Mo were also criticized, as a pair, in the *Chuang Tzu.* a work composed soon after the *Mencius.* See *Chuang Tzu* (*HYIS* #20: 21/8/7, 24/10/26-27, 33/12/98, 66/24/40, 45). For a translation, see Burton Watson, *The Complete Works of Chuang Tzu,* (New York: Columbia University Press, 1968), pp. 99, 111, 141.
26. For examples, see the *Mencius* (*HYIS* #17: 1/1A/1, 22/3B/1, 27/4A/9, 47/6B/4, 53/7A/25, 55/7B/10).
27. Chuang Tzu rejected the utility of both Yang and Mo, but for a different reason: both thinkers relied on the human perspective in their calculation of utility. Chuang Tzu's argument of the "usefulness of the useless" was an all-out attack against the viability of such utilitarian standards. From the perspective of Heaven, *all things are equal.*
28. Perhaps Mencius singled them out because they represented these two extremes.
29. The Kao Tzu of the *Mencius* may be the same Kao Tzu as is mentioned in the closing sections of *Mo Tzu* chapter 48 (*HYIS* #21: 88/48/81-86). The chapter, like much of the book, was compiled long after Mo Tzu's death. (For a translation, see Y. P. Mei, *The Ethical and Political Works of Motse,* (London: Arthur Probsthain, 1929), pp. 241-42). A. C. Graham believes there are extant writings of what he describes as "the school of Kao Tzu," in the *Kuan Tzu.* See A. C. Graham, "The Background of the Mencian Theory of Human Nature," *Tsing Hua Journal of Chinese Studies,* N.S., 6, 1-2 (1967), pp. 227-231.
30. For their debate, see *Mencius* (*HYIS* #17: 42-43/6A/1-6). For Mencius' earlier criticism, see (*HYIS* #17: 11/2A/2).
31. *Mencius* (*HYIS* #17: 11/2A/2).
32. *Mencius* (*HYIS* #17: 21-22/3A/5).
33. For this analysis of Mencius' criticisms of Kao Tzu and I-chih, see David S. Nivison, "Two Roots or One?", *Proceedings and Addresses of the American Philosophical Association,* 53, 6, pp. 739-761.
34. See *Mencius* (*HYIS* #17: 25/3B/9).
35. See *Mencius* (*HYIS* #17: 25/3B/9).
36. If I understand Mencius correctly, in offering these two criticisms, he is defending a version of Confucius' view that society is a strict and unique hierarchy. See the *Analects* (*HYIS* #16: 23/12/11).
37. See *Mencius* (*HYIS* #17: 19-21/3A/4).
38. *Mencius* (*HYIS* #17: 20/3A/4). I discuss this aspect of Mencius' position more fully in the following chapter *Human Nature.*

39. The most elegant and sophisticated attack on this aspect of Mencius' position is chapter two of the *Chuang Tzu* . Its title, *Ch'i wu lun* (A Discussion of the Equality of All Things), is quite possibly a pun on this line from the Mencius: *Fu wu chih pu ch'i wu chih ch'ing yeh.*
40. See *Mencius* (*HYIS* #17: 21/3A/4).
41. See *Mencius* (*HYIS* #17: 53/7A/26).
42. See *Mencius* (*HYIS* #17: 58-59/7B/37). In his description of *the paragon of the village,* Mencius quotes Confucius: "The paragon of the village is *te chih tse yeh* (the thief of virtue)." See *Analects* (*HYIS* #16: 36/17/11).
43. There is a tension, in Mencius' thought, between the need to follow the traditional rules defined by *li* (the rites) and the urge to follow one's moral intuition. In part, this tension can be seen as arising from his desire to preserve Confucius' original vision while still following the implications of his own thinking. I discuss this aspect of Mencius' thought in the final chapter: *Sagehood.*
44. See *Mencius* (*HYIS* #17: 42/5B/9).
45. See *Mencius* (*HYIS* #17: 7/1B/8).
46. See *Analects* (*HYIS* #16: 5/3/17, 19/10/11).
47. In *Mencius* (*HYIS* #17: 2-4/1A/7), Mencius uses the display of compassion King Hsüan spontaneously exhibited toward an ox being led to slaughter as the beginning of his discussion on the moral life. Ironically, the King's act of compassion involves *transgressing the rite* of consecrating a bell.
48. *Mencius* (*HYIS* #17: 54/7A/45).
49. For examples of Wang's use of the family image to describe the ideal society, see Chan, *Instructions,* sections 142, 179.
50. Ch'eng Hao is generally recognized as the first thinker to develop the notion of *forming one body with Heaven, Earth and all things.* (see *HNCSYS,* (*SPPY* ed.), 2A:2a.) This was an extremely important metaphor for Wang. For examples, see Chan, *Instructions,* sections 89, 142, 143, 179, 180, 182, 267, 274, 276, 285.
51. See Chan, *Instructions,* section 274. Wang often supported his notion of an underlying unity by pointing to cases in which a single principle governed a diverse variety of everyday phenomena. See the discussions of Wang's notions of *the alternation of day and night, forming one body* and *the principle of unceasing production and reproduction* below.
52. One of the distinctive features of early Confucianism—the feature that most clearly distinguished it from philosophical Taoism—was that it took human values as its moral standard.
53. It is interesting to note that Wang—like Chu Hsi—did not fully approve of Shao Yung. (See Chan, *Instructions,* section 281). Nevertheless, Wang was influenced by his thought and even appears to have adopted some of his metaphysical terminology (see Chan, *Instructions,* sections 69, 157.)
54. For a discussion of the early stages of Neo-Confucian thought, see "Chou Tun-yi and the beginnings of Neo-Confucianism," A.C. Graham, *Two Chinese Philosophers: Ch'eng Ming-tao and Ch'eng Yi-ch'uan,* (London: Lund Humphries, 1958), Appendix II; pp. 8-22. See also the description in J. Percy Bruce, *Chu Hsi and His Masters,* (London: Probsthain, 1923).

55. Neither the character nor the concept is found in the *Analects*. In the *Mencius*, the character occurs only once in anything like the sense it assumed in Neo-Confucian thought (see *Mencius*, *HYIS* #17: 4/6A/7).

56. For a discussion of the evolution of the concept, see Wing-tsit Chan, "The Evolution of the Neo-Confucian Concept *Li* as Principle," *Tsing Hua Journal of Chinese Studies*, Vol. 4, no. 2, (1964), pp. 123-49. For a study of the concept in the thought of the Ch'eng brothers, see A.C. Graham, *Two Chinese Philosophers*, pp. 8-22.

57. This point was first observed by Joseph Needham. See Joseph Needham, *Science and Civilization in Ancient China*, (Cambridge: Cambridge University Press, 1956), pp. 473-474.

58. This account of the operation of principle helps us to understand other notions that were prominent in Neo-Confucian thought. For example, the explanation of causality in terms of influence and response (instead of necessary causes and effects) and the view of change as alternating cycles of order and disorder. It also provides some explanation for the marked absence of discussion on problems such as free will and theodicy. But this picture of the world tends to obscure rather than resolve such questions. For example, describing the choices available to human beings as a vast array of major and minor principles appears to remove the immediate problem of whether or not we are free to make more than one choice. But it doesn't answer the question of whether or not the particular choice one makes is in any way free.

59. It is strange that Wang did not attach more importance to the family as the basis of his moral theory. He believed principles were the mind in itself; that all people possessed a complete and perfect moral intuition: *liang chih*. He adopted this term from *Mencius* 7A15, and in this passage Mencius uses *family relationships* as the paradigm cases of *liang chih*.

60. I believe it is this aspect of Wang's thought—and Neo-Confucian thought in general—that results in their apparent obsession with attaining sagehood. Early Confucians were deeply concerned with moral self-cultivation, but they did not exhibit the all-consuming dedication to the goal of attaining sagehood characteristic of Neo-Confucians. For Neo-Confucians, the task of self-cultivation was to become *aware* of what we already knew—to undo our own self-deception and embrace our true selves. Their task took on a frenetic quality that is not evident in early Confucianism.

61. Chan, *Instructions*, sections 142-143.

62. The notion that one's relationships to others are critical parts of one's identity has always been an important feature of Confucian thought. But Wang, along with most other Neo-Confucians, took this in new directions. Any sense of separateness from others became a "selfish thought,"—a source of evil. One was to act, motivated by the transpersonal *liang chih*. The closer one came to this ideal, the less one's actions were one's own. In the process, the self was effaced in a way unknown in early Confucianism.

63. Chan, *Instructions*, section 276.

64. Professor Mou Tsung-san was the first to suggest this excellent translation for *hsin chih pen t'i*. See Mou Tsung-san, "The Immediate Successor of Wang Yang-ming: Wang lung-hsi and His Theory of *ssu-wu*," *Philosophy East and West*, Vol. 23, no. 1 and 2 (January and April, 1973), p. 104, note 2. For his analysis of this term see his "Wang-hsüeh te fen-hua yü fa-chan'" *Hsin-ya Shu-Yüan hsüeh-shu nien-k'an*, Vol. 14, (1972), pp. 93-94.

65. See Chan, *Instructions*, section 277.

66. I use the translation "pure knowing" for *liang chih*—a translation first suggested by David S. Nivison—because it captures these two crucial aspects of the concept. The *locus classicus* of the expression is in the *Mencius* (*HYIS* #17: 51/7A/15). There it referred to the nascent sprouts of moral intuition, which are both *innate* and *good*. For Wang, the character *liang* always means both "innate" and "good." In different contexts one or the other of these two senses will be more pronounced, but they are always both present.

67. For Wang's use of the mirror metaphor, see (Chan, *Instructions*, sections 21, 76. See also Hsü Ai's remark in section 62. For a study of this metaphor in Eastern and Western thought, see Paul Demieville, "Le miroir spirituel," *Sinologica*, 1:2 (1947), pp. 112-137.

68. Lee H. Yearley argues that Wang presents an anomalous case for the general distinction he draws by developing Kierkegaard's categories of *teachers* and *saviors*. As is the case in the mirror metaphor, part of the difficulty arises from attempting to attribute the agency of certain actions within Wang's system of thought. Professor Yearley is correct to point to Wang's unique metaphysical perspective as the key to understanding this anomaly. See Lee H. Yearley, "Teachers and Saviors," *The Journal of Religion*, Vol. 65, no. 2; (April 1985), pp. 225-243.

69. The one notable exception being the Chittamatra School. For a discussion of this school and how it differs, see Jeffrey Hopkins, *Meditation on Emptiness*, (London: Wisdom Publications, 1983), pp. 365-397.

70. See Chan, *Instructions*, section 276.

71. See Chan, *Instructions*, sections 274, 337

72. See Chan, *Instructions*, sections 275, 337.

73. Chan, *Instructions*, section 337. See also the *Ta Hsüeh Wen*, Chan, *Instructions* p. 272.

74. Chan, *Instructions*, section 122.

75. For a discussion of Wang's views on self-cultivation and how they compare with Mencius', see Chapter 4: *Self-Cultivation.*

76. The following discussion is based on a passage from the *Ch'uan-hsi lu*. For a translation, see Chan, *Instructions*, section 267.

77. For a translation, see James Legge, trans., *The Chinese Classics*, Vol. III: *The Shoo-King*, reprint, (Hong Kong: Hong Kong University Press, 1960), pp. 61-62.

78. For a discussion of this aspect of Wang's thought see Chapter 3: *The Origin of Evil.*

79. See *Analects* (*HYIS* #16: 11/6/30).

80. A reference to the *Analects* (*HYIS* #16: 11/6/30).

81. See *Analects* (*HYIS* #16: 11/6/30).
82. *HNCSYS*, (*SPPY* ed.), 2A.2a,b. (cf. 2A:15b).
83. See Chan, *Instructions*, section 207.
84. For this example, see Chan, *Instructions*, p. 194. The example of the blushing thief is taken from the *Mencius* (*HYIS* #17: 35/5A/2). There the "thief" is Hsiang—evil elder-brother of the sage Shun. Hsiang had plotted with Shun's father to kill Shun and falsely believing they had succeeded, he divided up Shun's possessions between his parents and himself. Hsiang "blushed" upon finding Shun alive and well. Cf. the story in the *Mencius* with *Shu Ching* III, 3; 2:9 (Legge, *The Shoo King*, p. 161). See Legge's note on this passage, concerning the origin of Mencius' story.
85. The most complete statement of this idea is Wang's essay: *Questions on the Great Learning*. (*WWCKCS* 26:736a-740a). For a translation, see Chan, *Instructions*, pp. 272-80. See also Chan, *Instructions*, sections 179, 276.
86. *Mencius* 7A4 may appear to be an exception. But Mencius' claim concerns the scope of human nature's potential, not its connection with the external world.
87. We see ideas something like this in the *Mencius*. For example, "He so cared for the people of the world that if there were a single man or woman who did not enjoy the benefit of the rule of Yao and Shun, Yi Yin felt as if he himself had pushed that man or woman into a ditch. To this degree, he took upon himself responsibility for the world." *Mencius* (*HYIS* #17: 37/5A/7). (See 38/5B/1 for an identical passage and 33/4B/29 for the same idea). Mencius' sage took responsibility for relieving the suffering of others, but Wang's sage felt this suffering himself. This is because, for Wang, the universe is united by principle.
88. Fung Yu-lan described the goal of Neo-Confucians as creating "Confucian Buddhas"—"Confucian Bodhisattvas" would have been more accurate. See Fung Yu-lan, *Chung-kuo che-hsüeh shih*, (Shanghai: Chung-kuo shu-chu, 1939), p. 812.
89. For Fan Chung-yen's dictum see *Fan Wen-ch'eng-kung chi*, (*SPPY* ed.), 7:4a. For a discussion of its significance, see De Bary, "Buddhism and the Chinese Tradition" p. 121-122. For a concise study of Fan's political thought and career, see James T. C. Liu, "An Early Sung Reformer: Fan Chung-yen," in John K. Fairbank, ed., *Chinese Thought and Institutions*, (Chicago, 1957), pp. 105-131. For Chang Tsai's *Western Inscription*, see *Chang-tzu ch'üan-shu*, (*SPPY* ed.), 1:1a-6b. For a translation see Wing-tsit Chan, *A Source Book In Chinese Philosophy*, (Princeton: Princeton University Press, 1963), pp. 497-498.
90. Chinese Buddhists and Neo-Confucians both owe their great love of nature to early Taoist thinkers such as Chuang Tzu.
91. An early example of this type of thinking is the well-known story, told by one of the Ch'eng brothers (probably Ch'eng Hao), of Chou Tun-Yi refusing to cut the grass in front of his house. See *HNCSYS* (*SPPY* ed.) 3:2a. Wang refers to this episode in one of the most interesting passages in the *Ch'uan-hsi lu*. See Chan, *Instructions*, section 101.
92. See Chan, *Instructions*, section 179.

93. For a more thorough discussion of this aspect of Wang's thought, see Chapter 3: *The Origin of Evil*.

94. Mencius did say that "for nourishing the mind there is nothing better than making the desires few" *Mencius* (*HYIS* #17: 58/7B/35). He also said, "following the desires of one's eyes and ears so as to bring disgrace to one's mother and father" is one of the five common types of unfilial behavior. *Mencius* (*HYIS* #17: 33/4B/30). But, Mencius never advocated the *elimination* of desires. See Chapter 3: *Human Nature*.

95. For Mo Tzu's criticisms of the Confucians and his arguments for his position, see *Mo Tzu* (*HYIS* #21: chapters 16, 25, 39 et al.) For a translation, see Burton Watson, *Mo Tzu: Basic Writings*, (New York & London: Columbia University Press, 1963), pp. 39-49, 65-77, 124-136.

96. These four are central doctrines of Mo Tzu's philosophy and the names of chapters 11, 16, 8 and 31 respectively, in the *Mo Tzu*. For a translation, see Watson, *Mo Tzu: Basic Writings*, pp. 34-38, 39-49, 18-33 and 94-109.

97. A reference to the *Analects*. See (*HYIS* #16: 34/16/8).

98. This line is not found in the *Analects*. However, it is a teaching attributed to Confucius in the 29th chapter of the *Hsün Tzu* (*HYIS* #22: 105/29/23).

99. Confucius is traditionally credited with compiling the *Ch'un-ch'iu* and using it as a vehicle to judge the moral performance of past government officials. Mencius was the first to propagate this myth. See *Mencius* (*HYIS* #17: 25/3B/9).

100. A reference to the *Analects*. See (*HYIS* #16: 1/1/6).

101. A reference to the *Analects*. See (*HYIS* #16: 11/6/30).

102. A reference to the *Analects*. See (*HYIS* #16: 1/1/7).

103. The four courses of study were: literature, conduct, loyalty and faithfulness. See *Analects* (*HYIS* #16: 1/1/6).

104. A reference to the *Analects*. See (*HYIS* #16: 31/15/20).

105. References to the *Analects*. See (*HYIS* #16: 4/3/12).

106. *Li Chi*, (*SPPY* ed.), 7:17a. For a translation, see Legge, *Li Ki*, Vol. 1, p. 403.

107. *Han Ch'ang-li Ch'üan-chi*, (*SPPY* ed.), 11:16a, b.

108. Ch'eng Yi is referring to a conversation Mencius had with a follower of Mo Tzu, named I-chih (see *Mencius* (*HYIS* #17: 21/3A/5). But Mencius never ascribed this belief to Mo Tzu; it was part of his argument against I-chih.

109. This expression *pa pen sai yüan* originally came from the *Tso Chuan* (Duke Chao, 9th year). (For a translation, see James Legge, "The Ch'un Ts'ew with the Tso Chuen," (reprint), *The Chinese Classics*, Vol. 5, (Hong Kong: Hong Kong University Press, 1970), p. 625.) But there it meant to cast off something good. Over time, the expression came to mean exactly the opposite: to rid oneself of evil influences. Wang's well-known essay in the *Ch'uan-hsi lu* took this expression as its theme and is often referred to by this title. (See Chan, *Instructions*, sections 142-143.) Perhaps this passage by Ch'eng Yi provided the theme for Wang's essay.

110. Referring to Mencius' characterization of Mo Tzu and Yang Chu respectively. See *Mencius* (*HYIS* #17: 25/3B/9).

111. *HNCSYS*, (*SPPY* ed.), 18:36b-37a.

112. *HNCSYS*, (*SPPY* ed.), 1.2b.

113. *HNCSYS*, (*SPPY* ed.), 2A.8a.

114. See *Chang-tzu ch'üan-shu*, (*SPPY* ed.), 2:17b. For a translation of this passage, see Wing-tsit Chan, *A Source Book in Chinese Philosophy*, (Princeton: Princeton University Press, 1963), p. 508. Other selections from the *Cheng Meng* can be found on pp. 500-514.

115. *HNCSYS*, (*SPPY* ed.), 2A.lb.

116. David S. Nivison was the first to point this out to me.

117. Wang condemned those who looked for morality outside of the mind. His criticisms of Chu Hsi and his followers are essentially all of this nature. Wang even likens them to Kao Tzu on this account. For examples, see Chan, *Instructions*, sections 133, 135.

118. The following discussion is based on a passage from the *Ch'uan-hsi lu*. See Chan, *Instructions*, section 93.

119. Here again we see Wang supporting his moral position with his metaphysical belief in the unity of the universe and offering empirical "evidence" for his belief: the "fact" that a variety of phenomena follow the *principle of unceasing production and reproduction*.

120 See *Mencius* (*HYIS* #17: 21-22/3A/5). David S. Nivison has suggested—and it seems plausible—that Wang had this section of the *Mencius* in mind when he offered this criticism of Mo Tzu's doctrine.

Chapter 2: Human Nature

1. The one notable exception is Li Ao of the T'ang dynasty. For more on Chinese theories of human nature, see: D. C. Lau, "Theories of Human Nature in Mencius and Shyuntzyy," *BOAS*, London, 15 (1953): 541-65; A. C. Graham, "The Background of the Mencian Theory," and A. C. Graham, *Two Chinese Philosophers* pp. 44-60, 131-137.

2. See Graham, *The Background of the Mencian Theory*.

3. These are two of Mencius' examples. See *Mencius* (*HYIS* #17: 51/7A/15) and (*HYIS* #17: 13/2A/6). Today, we might see these examples differently. I might understand Mencius' example of *the child and the well* as a manifestation of an instinct for species preservation—an instinct that has helped socially-conscious humans to survive in greater numbers and which, over time, has become characteristic of human behavior. Though we may question Mencius' reading of such examples, his insistence of their significance remains a profound and provocative observation.

4. *Mencius* (*HYIS* #17: 13/2A/6).

5. See *Mencius* (*HYIS* #17: 44/6A/8) and (*HYIS* #17: 45/6A/10).

6. *Mencius* (*HYIS* #17: 31/4B/12).

7. For examples, see *Tao-te Ching* chapters 10, 20, 28, 55.

8. This is an important part of the message in the famous "Ox Mountain Parable" (*Mencius* 6A8). As I understand him, Mencius believed that everyone was *theoretically* capable of moral self-cultivation, though he clearly decided there

were cases which *practically* were beyond hope. An example of the later type would be King Hsüan of Ch'i (*Mencius* 1A7 and 6A9).

9. King Hsüan's sparing of the ox is an example of this type of action. The king failed to see the moral significance of his action until Mencius pointed it out to him. See Mencius (*HYIS* #17: 3/1A/7).

10. For an example of the "testimonial" type, see *Mencius* (*HYIS* #17: 44-45/6A/10).

11. See *Mencius* (*HYIS* #17: 13/2A/6 and 21/3A/5).

12. David S. Nivison first described this example to me as a "thought experiment."

13. *Mencius* (*HYIS* #17: 45/6A/14).

14. This line of argument seems, in part, to be directed against followers of the school of Yang Chu who maintained that every part of the body—even a single hair—was equally precious and not to be sacrificed at any cost.

15. *Mencius* (*HYIS* #17: 45-46/6A/15). The state in which the "lower" faculties are led blindly to pursue their objects is the starting point of self-cultivation. If one develops one's moral mind, it grows to influence and shape the lower faculties. They are trainable and, under the direction of the mind, eventually will learn to pursue only suitable objects. At advanced stages of cultivation the mind is no longer in conflict with the "lower" faculties. One achieves the *pu tung hsin* (unmoved mind) described in Mencius 2A2. See also Confucius' spiritual autobiography in the *Analects* (*HYIS* #16: 2/2/4).

16. This position—and perhaps Mencius himself—is criticized in chapter 2 of the *Chuang Tzu*. Chuang Tzu rejects the notion of a natural hierarchy within the self. According to him there is no *chen chün* (true ruler) to be found. In truth, we are rather loose confederations of different parts, none of which has ultimate authority over the others. See *Chuang Tzu* (*HYIS* #20: 4/2/17). For a translation, see Burton Watson, *The Complete Works of Chuang Tzu*, p. 38.

17. *Mencius* (*HYIS* #17: 20/3A/4).

18. See *Mencius* 6A/15 above. See also Mencius' conversation with King Hsüan of Ch'i in Book I of the Mencius (*HYIS* #17: 3/1A/7).

19. See *Mencius* (*HYIS* #17: 50/7A/1).

20. To the best of my knowledge, A. C. Graham is the first person to see this critical aspect of Mencius' notion of human nature. See A. C. Graham, *The Background of the Mencian Theory*.

21. For examples, see Mencius (*HYIS* #17: 13/2A/6, 43-44/6A/7, 44/6A/8, 44/6A/9) et al.

22. Mencius draws the analogy between the need for grain to ripen and the need for benevolence to ripen. See *Mencius* (*HYIS* #17: 46/6A/19).

23. See *Mencius* (*HYIS* #17: 43/6A/6).

24. See *Mencius* (*HYIS* #17: 44/6A/7).

25. See *Mencius* (*HYIS* #17: 29-30/4A/27).

26. See *Mencius* (*HYIS* #17: 1/1A/2).

27. See *Mencius* (*HYIS* #17: 51/7A/4).

28. See *Mencius* (*HYIS* #17: 12/2A/5). Mencius thus explains—*demystifies*—the magical power of *te* (virtue) which Confucius so dramatically described in the Analects. See (*HYIS* #16: 2/2/1 and 24/12/19).

29. *Mencius (HYIS* #17: 28/4A/16).
30. *Mencius (HYIS* #17: 52/7A/21).
31. *Mencius (HYIS* #17: 54/7A/38). Lee H. Yearley has pointed out to me the important contrast between Mencius' ideal of moral and physical perfection and the ideal described by Chuang Tzu. Chuang Tzu's "perfected people" do not follow a set of conventional virtues or accept conventional standards of physical beauty. They are the lowly, the deformed, and yet they have perfected their personal *te* (virtue). For examples, see chapter five of the *Chuang Tzu: The Sign of Virtue Complete*. The title of this chapter—*te ch'ung fu* (virtue, filled-out, sign)—may be a conscious parody of Mencius' notion of the ideal man. The character *ch'ung* (to complete, fill-out) is an important term of art in the *Mencius*. It describes the process of developing and completing the nascent moral sense. (See page 39 for a discussion of its meaning and significance for Mencius). For examples, see *Mencius (HYIS* #17: 13/2A/6, 57/7B/25, 57/7B/31).
32. There is a tension, in Mencius' thought, between following precedents established by the sages and following one's moral intuition. Which of these describes the Way and how each functions in the process of self-cultivation is a difficult problem.
33. For a discussion of Buddhism's influence on Wang's thought, see *YMGTK*, Vol. 1; pp. 291-320. For an analysis which discusses Buddhism's influence on Wang yet defends him as a Confucian, see Wing-tsit Chan, "How Buddhistic is Wang Yang-ming," *Philosophy East and West*, Volume 12, no. 3, (1962), pp. 203-215.
34. Chan, *Instructions*, section 174.
35. Chan, *Instructions*, section 38. cf. *Mencius* 7A1 (see above pages 33-34). For Mencius, developing the nature, guided by the moral mind, led to an understanding of Heaven. For Wang, the mind itself was Heavenly principle; it was a "god within." To understand one's own nature was to awaken to this "god within."
36. Paraphrasing *Mencius* 7A15.
37. Chan, *Instructions*, section 118. The characters which I have translated as "extend"— *ch'ung t'o*—occur only once in the *Ch'uan-hsi lu*. But they are synonymous with the characters *k'uo ch'ung* (to expand and fill-out)—a term of art in the *Mencius*. See the discussion of this term and its significance on page 39.
38. *Mencius (HYIS* #17: 51/7A/15).
39. For Mencius' use of this expression see *Mencius (HYIS* #17: 13/2A/6). For related uses of *ch'ung*, see 26/3B/10, 40/5B/4, 57/7B/25, 57/7B/31. For Wang's use of *k'uo ch'ung*, see Chan, *Instructions*, sections 16, 107, 136, 189, 225, 318.
40. This is the position of the Ch'eng-Chu school. For a classic statement of this position, see Chu Hsi's commentary on the fifth chapter of the *Great Learning*. For a translation, see Legge, *The Chinese Classics*, Vol. 1, pp. 365-366.
41. References to chapter twenty of the *Doctrine of the Mean*. For a translation, see Legge, *The Chinese Classics*, Vol. 1, pp. 413-414.
42. A reference to *Mencius* 7A15.
43. Chan, *Instructions*, section 136.
44. In order to keep track of these terms in Wang's argument, I have marked the second "chih" with an apostrophe ('). The characters are etymologically related,

but Wang claims they are exactly the same in meaning. He relies upon the two lines he cites in this passage, in which he uses each of the characters in two distinct senses, to make his case.

45. In the first quote, Wang combines the meaning of two passages in the *Analects* (*HYIS* #16: 40/19/14 and 40/19/17) (cf. chapter 10 of the *Hsiao Ching* (The Classic of Filial Piety). For a translation, see Sister Mary Lelia Makra. *The Hsiao Ching*, (New York: St. John's University Press, 1961, p. 23.) The second quote is from one of the commentaries on the *I Ching* (The Classic of Changes). The line appears in the first section of the seventh of the *Shih Yi* (Ten Wings). For a translation, see James Legge, trans., *The Sacred Books of the East*, (Oxford: Clarendon Press, 1882), Vol. XVI, p. 410.

46. *Mencius* (*HYIS* #17: 12-13/2A/6 and 43/6A/6).

47. *Ta Hsüeh Wen* (Questions on the *Great Learning*), *WWCKCS*, 26:739a. (cf. Chan, *Instructions*, p. 278).

48. Chan, *Instructions*, section 117.

49. Chan, *Instructions*, section 91. Wang's position is very clear in this passage. The nature is perfect and fully formed; the task is to "return to its original state." For some other passages concerning the Heavenly endowed, perfect and fully-formed nature, see sections: 127, 134, and 155. See also the *Ta Hsüeh Wen* (Questions on the *Great Learning*); Chan, *Instructions*, pp. 271-80.

50. For examples, see Chan, *Instructions*, sections 207, 237, 289.

51. For examples, see Chan, *Instructions*, sections 99, 107.

52. The metaphor of the sun and clouds appears in *The Platform Sūtra*, a work which Wang had read and which he frequently cited. (See *TSD* 2008). For a translation, see Charles Luk, "The Dharma Treasure of the Alter Sutra of the Sixth Patriarch," *Ch'an and Zen Teaching*, Series Three, (Berkeley: Shambala Publications, 1973), pp. 19-102. Both the metaphor of gold—for the innate nature—and of refining gold—for the process of self-cultivation—are found in the *Nirvana Sūtra*, another text Wang had read (See *TSD* 375).

53. Mencius uses the image of the "lost heart" (See *Mencius* (*HYIS* #17: 44/6A/8, 45/6A/11)). But Mencius' "lost heart" is a *sprout*, while Wang's is the full and perfect moral mind.

54. Part of the force of this metaphor is to draw a distinction between *tao hsin* (the mind of the Way), perfectly pure mind, and *jen hsin* (the human mind), defiled mind. I discuss this distinction and the issues that surround it in the following chapter: *The Origin of Evil.*

55. See Chapter 1, page 20 note #84 for the *locus classicus* of the blushing thief.

56. Chan, *Instructions*, section 207.

57. Exactly how one loses sight of this innate endowment is a difficult problem for Wang. I discuss this question in the following chapter: *The Origin of Evil.*

58. Chan, *Instructions*, section 99. The italicized line is from *Mencius* 6B2. This is perhaps Wang's worst philosophical moment. He has just argued that Yao and Shun had more natural endowment than anyone else, and that this is why they achieved such greatness. And yet he goes on to assert that *anyone can become a Yao or Shun.*

59. It is important to note Mencius never argued that such ability was in any way hereditary. Also, because he believed in the development of the moral nature, Mencius could accept a natural diversity and still argue for the possibility of attaining equality.

60. This translation is no longer extant, though two later versions survive. See *TSD* 666 and 667.

61. Two versions of this work are still extant. See *TSD* 310 and 353. For a translation, see Alex and Hideko Wayman, tr., *The Lion's Roar of Queen Srīmālā*, (New York: Columbia University Press, 1974). For a study of the notion of the *tathāgatagarbha* and an annotated translation of the older Chinese version of the *sūtra*, see Diana Paul, *The Buddhist Feminine Ideal: Queen Srīmālā and the Tathāgatagarbha*, (Missoula: Scholars Press, 1980).

62. *TSD* 670. For a translation, see D. T. Suzuki, *The Lankāvatāra Sūtra*, (London: Routledge and Kegan, 1978).

63. *TSD* 1666. For a translation, see Yoshita S. Hakeda, *The Awakening of Faith*, (New York: Columbia University Press, 1967).

64. For a discussion of the specific texts with which Wang was acquainted, see Julia Ching, *To Acquire Wisdom*, pp. 159-161. See also Chan, *How Buddhistic is Wang Yang-ming?*.

65. For a discussion of Ch'eng Yi's view and Chu Hsi's contribution, see A. C. Graham, *Two Chinese Philosophers*, pp. 44-60.

66. *HNCSYS*, (*SPPY* ed.), 6:2a.

67. Quoting *HNCSYS*, (*SPPY* ed.), 1:7b.

68. Paraphrasing *Chu Tzu Wen-chi*, (*SPPY* ed.), 61:22b).

69. Quoting Kao Tzu's remark in *Mencius* (*HYIS* #17: 42/6A/3).

70. Quoting part of Ch'eng Hao's remark which in turn is a quote of the "Record of Music" chapter of the *Book of Rites*. See Legge, (reprint), *Li Ki*, (New York: University Books, 1967), Vol. 2, p. 96.

71. Paraphrasing Ch'eng Yi. *HNCSYS*, (*SPPY* ed.), 1:7b.

72. Chan, *Instructions*, section 150. Wang quotes Ch'eng Yi's earlier remark (*HNCSYS*, (*SPPY* ed.), 6:2a) again in the *Ch'uan-hsi lu* (see Chan, *Instructions*, section 242), making the same point.

73. Chan, *Instructions*, section 308.

74. *HNCSYS*, (*SPPY* ed.), 1:7b.

75. Chan, *Instructions*, section 101.

76. For examples of Wang's use of the original nature/physical nature distinction, see Chan, *Instructions*, sections 99, 150, 242, 164, 335.

77. *Analects* (*HYIS* #16: 35/17/2.

78. Wang is referring to Chou Tun-i's description of the physical nature as containing firmly good/firmly bad and weakly good/weakly bad aspects. See Graham, *Two Chinese Philosophers*, p. 46.

79. Chan, *Instructions*, section #335.

80. Wang criticized Hsün Tzu's pedagogy but did not reject his analysis of human nature as completely wrong. Wang believed that, like Kao Tzu, Hsün Tzu had hold of only half the truth. He overlooked the original moral nature, the mind

itself, and was concerned exclusively with the physical nature. His teaching was one-sided, and thus led to error.

81. Chan, *Instructions*, section 308.
82. *Mencius* (*HYIS* #17: 54/7A/38).
83. Chan, *Instructions*, section 242.
84. See *Hsün Tzu*, chapter 33.
85. See *Mencius* (*HYIS* #17: 42-43/6A/4).
86. Above, I have discussed the difference between Wang and Chu Hsi on the issue of *chih chih* (the extension of knowledge). For a discussion of Wang's understanding of the notion of *ko wu* and how it differed from that of Chu Hsi, see the fourth chapter: *Self Cultivation*.
87. Chan, *Instructions*, section 133. See also section 135.
88. For a more complete discussion of this issue, see Chapter 5: *Sagehood*.

Chapter 3: The Origin of Evil

1. To my mind, this is one of the most interesting features of early Confucian thought. Perhaps the most important example occurs in the *Analects*: Confucius' favorite disciple Yen Hui—a man without the slightest moral deficiency—contracts a disease and dies at an early age. See *Analects* (*HYIS* 20/11/8-11). Another poignant example is the death of the disciple Po Niu. See *Analects* (*HYIS* 10/6/10).
2. *Mencius* (*HYIS* #17: 50/7A/1). Cf. *Mencius* (*HYIS* #17: 58/7B/33): "The superior person follows the proper way and simply awaits his destiny."
3. See *Mencius* (*HYIS* #17: 37/5A/6).
4. See *Mencius* (*HYIS* #17: 50/7A/2). "To die in fetters and handcuffs," implies one has committed some crime.
5. *Mencius* (*HYIS* #17: 52/7A/18).
6. *Mencius* (*HYIS* #17: 50/6B/15).
7. *Mencius* (*HYIS* #17: 50-51/7A/3). The "it" which one gets or loses is the moral heart/mind, cf. *Mencius* 6A6.
8. Some commentators claim this parable referred to a mountain located outside the capital city of the state of Ch'i.
9. Mencius believed the world was permeated throughout by a lively, psycho-physical energy called *ch'i*. Cultivating this energy was an important aspect of moral self-cultivation. Mencius had a special expression—*hao jan chih ch'i* (flood-like ch'i)—for the energy of moral courage which accompanies the growth of the moral sprouts (see the following chapter, pages 76-77 for a discussion of this idea). In the *Ox Mountain* parable, we see Mencius believed the *ch'i* of the early morning had a salubrious effect on one's moral sprouts. It energized and revived the moral sprouts. Jeffrey Riegel has studied Mencius' concept of *ch'i* and identified important examples of the use of the term in the literature of the time. His analysis of this concept in Mencius' thought differs from my own, but his study should be read by anyone interested in this problem. See Jeffrey Riegel, "Reflections on an Unmoved Mind: An Analysis of Mencius 2A2," *Journal of the American Academy of Religion Thematic Issue*, x1vii, 3s, (1979), pp. 433-458.
10. This remark is not found in the present version of the *Analects*.

11. *Mencius* (*HYIS* #17: 44/6A/8).
12. Lee H. Yearley has pointed out that the parable has another, characteristically Mencian, dimension. It is a claim about human nature, and if one entertains it seriously it causes one to look for signs—in oneself as well as in others—of the claim it makes. It *engages* one in the task of self-cultivation.
13. The *Ox Mountain* parable also implies that only unnatural, improper, human activity can harm the moral life. In this regard, its message is related to Mencius' famous *Farmer of Sung* parable. See the following chapter: *Self Cultivation*.
14. *Mencius* (*HYIS* #17: 44/6A/9).
15. This distinction is not critical to the main point of the *Ox Mountain* parable. However, it is an important and controversial feature of Mencius' position. I examine this issue in the following chapter: *Self Cultivation*.
16. *Mencius* (*HYIS* #17: 4/1A/7). See also, *Mencius* (*HYIS* #17: 44/6A/9).
17. *Mencius* (*HYIS* #17: 20/3A/4). Translation by James Legge, "The Works of Mencius," *The Chinese Classics*, (reprint), (Hong Kong: Hong Kong University Press, 1970), Vol. II; pp. 251-52. Because Mencius believed human nature had a tendency for goodness, he emphasized the need *to provide the proper environment* for the growth of human nature. He believed goodness arises from human nature. His harshest critic, Hsün Tzu, argued human nature had a tendency for strife and disorder. He emphasized the need *for restraints* on human nature. For Hsün Tzu's views, see chapter 23 of the *Hsün Tzu: Hsing O* (Human Nature is Evil). For a translation, see Burton Watson, *Hsün Tzu Basic Writings* , pp. 157-171.
18. Not until the period of Neo-Confucianism, do we find individuals who sought to make Confucianism a popular movement. (One such person was Wang Ken, a follower of Wang Yang-ming.) This kind of action occurred only after Confucianism had undergone radical changes—after it had incorporated a view of human nature which was essentially Buddhist in character. For a discussion of the popularization of Confucian thought in the Ming dynasty, see Wm. Theodore De Bary, "Individualism and Humanitarianism in Late Ming Thought," and Tadao Sakai, "Confucianism and Popular Educational Works," in *Self and Society in Ming Thought*, (New York: Columbia University Press, 1970), pp. 145-245 and 331-336.
19. See *Mencius* (*HYIS* #17: 43-44/6A/7).
20. For examples of Mencius' view of the sages, see *Mencius* (*HYIS* #17: 20/3A/4, 24-25/3B/9, 33/4B/29.)
21. See *Mencius* (*HYIS* #17: 13/2A/9).
22. See *Mencius* (*HYIS* #17: 35/5A/2).
23. *Mencius* (*HYIS* #17: 44/6A/7).
24. See *Mencius* (*HYIS* #17: 44/6A/7).
25. *Mencius* (*HYIS* #17: 12/2A/2).
26. Mencius' description of the succession of the sage-emperors does nothing to relieve this difficulty. According to his account, the sages proposed successors, and their succession was confirmed *by Heaven*, which manifested its desire through the will of the people. See *Mencius* (*HYIS* #17: 36/5A/5, 36-37/5A/6).

27. *Mencius* (*HYIS* #17: 24-25/3B/9) see also 33/4B/29.
28. *Mencius* (*HYIS* #17: 17/2B/13).
29. For the concept of *te*, see David S. Nivison, "Royal 'Virtue' in Shang Oracle Inscriptions," *Early China*, no. 4, (Berkeley), (1978-79); Donald J. Munro, "The Origin of the Concept of te," *The Concept of Man in Early China*, (Stanford: Stanford University Press, 1969), pp. 185-197.
30. But for Confucius, *te* was still a paranormal power. For him the *te* of the gentleman moved humanity like the wind moves the grass (*Analects* (*HYIS* #16: 24/12/19)). (Mencius quotes this saying. See *Mencius* (*HYIS* #17: 18/3A/2).) And he compared the gentlemen's *te* with the power governing celestial motion. One who ruled by *te* held subordinates around him as the pole star holds the lesser stars around it (*Analects* (*HYIS* #16: 2/2/1)). Confucius was prone to draw terrestrial/celestial analogies—between the gentleman and the Heavens—because both the gentleman and celestial objects followed Heavenly patterns. Another example is Confucius' description of a gentleman's mistakes. These were *like an eclipse of the sun or moon* (*Analects* (*HYIS* #16: 40/19/21)).
31. It is easy to see a relationship between this idea and Mencius' notion of innate moral sprouts—an endowment which must be preserved and nourished by proper conduct.
32. *Mencius* (*HYIS* #17: 31/4B/22).
33. Confucius and his early followers were attacked by their main rivals—the Mohists— for being fatalistic. In the *Mo Tzu*, chapters 35—37 are three versions of a chapter entitled *Fei Ming* (Against Fatalism) (chapter 35 is translated by Burton Watson in *Mo Tzu: Basic Writings*, pp. 117-123 and all three versions appear in Y. P. Mei's *The Ethical and Political Works of Motse*, pp. 182-199). Chapter 39 of the *Mo Tzu*, entitled *Fei Ju* (Against Confucians), contains specific attacks linking Confucianism and fatalism (for a translation, see Watson, pp. 124-136 or Mei, pp. 201-211).
34. Chan, *Instructions*, section 34. Cf. the conversation between Kung-tu Tzu and Mencius (Chapter 2, pp. 32-33 above).
35. Chan, *Instructions*, section, 336.
36. Chan, *Instructions*, section, 309.
37. Chan, *Instructions*, section, 44.
38. Chan, *Instructions*, section, 215.
39. A dramatic example of this attitude, reminiscent of the first example above, is Ch'eng Hao's reaction to the death, by illness, of his own son. See Graham, *Two Chinese Philosophers*, p. 128.
40. See pages 55-56 above, for Mencius' view on this incident.
41. Quoting the *Mencius*, (*HYIS* #17: 50/6B/15).
42. Chan, *Instructions*, section, 296.
43. For Mencius' view, see above page 51.
44. Chan, *Instructions*, p. 265.
45. The *Five Classics* were: The *Book of Poetry*, the *Book of History*, the *Book of Changes*, the *Spring and Autumn Annals* and the *Book of Rites*. The *Four Books* were: the *Analects*, the *Mencius*, the *Great Learning* and the *Doctrine of the Mean*.

46. This criticism was made by many Neo-Confucians (e.g. Ch'eng Yi, see Graham, *Two Chinese Philosophers*, pp. 85-86. Mahāyāna Buddhists had earlier criticized Therevādins in a strikingly similar way. They argued the Therevāda ideal of the *Arhant* was selfish and offered the Bodhisattva as an alternative.

47. Chan, *Instructions*, section, 269.

48. Chan, *Instructions*, section, 162.

49. *Liu-tsu ta-shih fa-pao t'an-ching*, *TSD*, 2008:353b. The criticism, within Buddhism, that purity itself can be an attachment is much older than the *Platform Sūtra*. But the particular form this criticism took in this sutra seems to be what influenced Wang.

50. This distinguishes Wang from many other Neo-Confucians who held Buddhism and Taoism primarily responsible for the decline of Confucianism. For example, Han Yü was one of the earliest and harshest critics of Buddhism and Taoism (see his *Lun Fo-ku piao* (Memorial on the Buddha's Bone), *Han Ch'ang-li ch'üan-shu* (*SPPY* ed.), 39:3a-5b and *Yüan Tao* (On the Tao), 11:1a-5b). Ch'eng Yi-ch'uan singled out Buddhism as the single most pernicious doctrine (see Graham, *Two Chinese Philosophers*, pp. 83-91).

51. Chan, *Instructions*, section, 49.

52. Wang's descriptions of these four errors resemble Mencius' criticisms of the *hsiang yüan* (paragon of the village—see above page 12). Wang used this expression to describe himself in the time before he had complete faith in his *liang chih*. See Chan, *Instructions*, section 312. See also section 141.

53. See above, pp. 7-10.

54. Though there is a tension, in Mencius' thought, between the individual's moral intuition and the letter of classical writings, he never rejected what he considered to be authentic classical writings. Not only did Wang fail to emphasize study of the classics, he displayed a certain animosity for intellectual pursuits in general. I discuss this issue in greater detail in the final chapter: *Sagehood*.

55. Chan, *Instructions*, section, 5.

56. Chan, *Instructions*, sections, 5, 125, 133, 134.

57. Chan, *Instructions*, section, 5.

58. *HNCSYS*, (*SPPY* ed.), 2A:2b-3a. For other examples of this story with additional flourishes, see 15:4a and 18:5a.

59. The *Four Sentence Teaching* and the conversation in which it occurred are found in the *Ch'uan-hsi lu* (see Chan, *Instructions*, section 315). Chan discusses some aspects of the controversy surrounding this teaching in his introduction to this section (pp. 241-243).

60. See *Ho-nan Ch'eng-shih wai-shu* (*SPPY* ed.), 2:4a.

61. Chan, *Instructions*, section, 10.

62. Chan, *Instructions*, section, 290. See also section 241.

63. See above, pp. 42-44.

64. Chan, *Instructions*, section, 155.

65. Wang described these as the "qualitative" and "quantitative" differences respectively. See above, pp. 41.

66. See the discussion of this issue on pages 41-42.

67. For Mencius' view of history, see above, pp. 56-60.
68. Chan, *Instructions*, section, 143.
69. Literally: "Increased the hegemon's *fan li* (fence)." Their efforts only served to raise a wall—a screen—around the way of the hegemon and this made it increasingly difficult to see the Way of the sage. In the following line: "the gate and wall of the sagely Way" is a reference to Confucius' teachings (see *Analects* (*HYIS* #16: 40/19/23)).
70. Chan, *Instructions*, section, 143.
71. Chan, *Instructions*, section, 143.
72. At this time, in China, the notion of the age of the degenerate *dharma* was widespread. It was a central teaching of the popular *Pure Land* sect of Buddhism and recognized by most other sects.
73. Buddhists had no explanation for the appearance of *avidyā* (ignorance) and this was the beginning of *pratītya-samutpāda* (The Twelve-fold Chain of Dependent Co-arising). But the Buddha had explicitly ruled out such inquiries; they did not tend to enlightenment. The point is illustrated by the well known parable of the man wounded by a poisonous arrow of unknown provenance who wanted to know all the details surrounding the arrow and the man who shot it instead of seeking to have it removed. For a translation of this story, see Henry Clarke Warren, *Buddhism in Translations*, (reprint) (New York: Atheneum, 1979), pp. 120-122.
74 This aspect of Wang's thought gives it an "existential" air. But without recognizing the source of this aspect of his thought, describing it as "existential" can mislead more than enlighten. Several scholars have offered their views on this subject. The following three are well worth consulting: Hwa Yol Jung, "Wang Yang-ming and Existential Phenomenology," *International Philosophical Quarterly*, Vol. 5; No. 4, (December, 1965), pp. 612-636. Takehiko Okada, "Wang Chi and the Rise of Existentialism," *Self and Society*, pp. 121-144. David S. Nivison, "Moral Decision in Wang Yang-ming: The problem of Chinese "existentialism," *Philosophy East and West*, 23; (1973), pp. 121-138.

Chapter 4: Self-Cultivation

1. These two models developed out of discussions with Lee H. Yearley and Kwong-loi Shun. The distinction was originally drawn, by A. C. Graham, to distinguish between Mencius' and Chu Hsi's notions of the "four sprouts." (See Graham, *Two Chinese Philosophers*, p. 54).
2. See *Mencius*, (*HYIS* #17: 12-13/2A/6, 43/6A/6).
3. For a description of these four types, see above, pp. 30-31.
4. *Mencius*, (*HYIS* #17: 12-13/2A/6).
5. For the context of this remark, see below page 76.
6. See below page 77, for the *locus classicus* of this teaching. For Wang's interpretation, see below pp. 83-84.
7. For an analysis of Mencius' notion of *extension* see David S. Nivison, "Mencius and Motivation," *Journal of the American Academy of Religion Thematic Issue* xlvii, 3s (September, 1979), pp. 418-432.
8. *Mencius*, (*HYIS* #17: 57/7B/31).

9. *Mencius*, (*HYIS* #17: 3/1A/7) translation by David S. Nivison "Mencius and Motivation," p. 420).

10. *Mencius*, (*HYIS* #17: 43-44/6A/7).

11. *Analects*, (*HYIS* #16: 2/2/4).

12. *Mencius*, (*HYIS* #17: 31/4B/17).

13. *Mencius*, (*HYIS* #17: 52-53/7A/24).

14. Mencius draws on the notion of *ch'i*—a kind of psycho-physical energy. (See Chapter 3, page 52, note #9 for a brief discussion of this notion in Mencius' thought). But he uses this term—in the expression *hao jan chih ch'i* (flood-like energy)—in the sense of moral strength or moral courage. In one way, it is like the early concept of *te* (virtue)—a moral power one augments through the performance of righteous acts. Mencius' flood-like energy is the power which motivates one to moral action. It grows naturally in the properly cultivated individual just as the "energy" of any creature increases as it matures.

15. *Mencius*, (*HYIS* #17: 11/2A/2).

16. *Mencius*, (*HYIS* #17: ll/6A/8).

17. *Mencius*, (*HYIS* #17: 24/3B/8).

18. I believe this is the proper description of the effect of Mencius' advice on the king. I am indebted to Professor Alison H. Black for making this clear to me in her response to my paper, "One Vision Two Views: Mencius and Wang Yang-ming on Human Nature and Self-Cultivation." Presented at the 37th annual meeting of the *Association for Asian Studies*, Philadelphia, (24 March 1985).

19. *Mencius*, (*HYIS* #17: 3/1A/7).

20. In two senses: the king should have tempered his compassion with a firm commitment to perform the sacrifice as prescribed by ritual, and he should have directed his compassion to the more deserving recipients, his people.

21. It is tempting to interpret this as the beginning of the natural extension of the king's compassion for suffering, from the case of the ox to the case of the people or as evidence that a deeper but yet to be revealed commitment lies with the people.

22. The case of King Hsüan seems to present the worst possible scenario. It is not clear the king sensed any corresponding feelings of compassion for his subjects. It wasn't just that his other desires were *stronger* than his desire for benevolence, it seems they completely prevented him from feeling compassion for his people.

23. For an example of this use of *tzu tsei*, see *Mencius* (*HYIS* #17: 13/2A/6).

24. *Mencius*, (*HYIS* #17: 28/4A/11) Translation by James Legge, *The Chinese Classics*, Vol. 2, *The Works of Mencius*, trans., (Hong Kong: Hong Kong University Press, 1960), pp. 301-302.

25. *Mencius* (*HYIS* #17: 58/7B/35).

26. This expression appears 21 times in Wang's *Ch'uan-hsi lu* along with related expressions such as: *ssu hsin* (selfish heart/mind) (appears 8 times), *ssu i* (selfish idea) (appears 17 times) and *ssu nien* (selfish thought) (appears twice).

27. For a discussion of the term, see A. C. Graham, *Two Chinese Philosophers*, pp. 74-82; D. C. Lau, "A Note on *ko wu*," *BOAS*, Vol. 30, (1967), pp. 353-57.

28. James Legge, "The Great Learning," *The Chinese Classics*, Vol. 1, p. 358. Leggge's note on the term *ko wu* is helpful and interesting. His preference would lead him to interpret the term close to the spirit of Wang Yang-ming.

29. *Ssu-shu chi-chu*, (*SPPY* ed.), *Ta Hsüeh*, 1:2a.

30. *Ho-nan Ch'eng-shih wai-shu*, (*SPPY* ed.), 2:4a.

31. *HNCSYS*, (*SPPY* ed.), 25:1a.

32. *Mencius* (*HYIS* #17: 29/4A/21).

33. Chan, *Instructions*, section, 7. In this passage, Wang explains several key terms of art in the *Great Learning*. See also sections: 6, 85, 137 and *Questions on the Great Learning*, Chan, *Instructions*, p. 279 et al.

34. For a discussion of his aspect of Wang's teaching, see David S. Nivison, *Moral Decision in Wang Yang-ming*.

35. These are two of Wang's paradigm illustrations of the *unity of knowledge and action*. The question of Wang's identification of affections as actions was first raised by David S. Nivison. See his review of Chan and Henke in *JAOS*, 84, no. 4, (1964), p. 437.

36. Chan, *Instructions*, section, 5.

37. Chan, *Instructions*, section, 290. See also section, 241.

38. *Mencius* (*HYIS* #17: 11/2A/2). This brief passage serves as the introduction to the well known *Farmer of Sung* parable (see above page 77 for a translation and discussion of the parable).

39. Parodoxically, by holding this view, Wang seems to disallow some of Mencius' most important self-cultivation devices, such as the "thought experiment" of the child and the well. It also seems to argue against the study of the Confucian Classics.

40. Chan, *Instructions*, section, 186.

41. *Liu-tsu ta-shih fa-pao t'an-ching*, *TSD*, 2008: 350b.

42. Chan, *Instructions*, section, 39.

43. *Mencius*, (*HYIS* #17: 46/6B/2).

44. See Chan, *Instructions*, section, 313 et al.

45. For examples, see Chan, *Instructions*, sections, 30, 115, 225.

46. Chan, *Instructions*, section, 30.

47. Chan, *Instructions*, section, 150.

48. *Ssu-shu chi-chu*, (*SPPY* ed.), *Meng Tzu*, 2:12a.

49. Chan, *Instructions*, section, 91. Again, Wang is explicating terms of art in the *Great Learning*.

50. There is one passage in the *Mencius* (*HYIS* #17: 13/2A/6) which uses this kind of imagery to describe the development of the four sprouts: "All men have these four sprouts in themselves. If any man develops them fully they will be like a *fire that has begun to burn or a spring that has begun to find vent*." But Mencius used these images to describe the irrepressible nature of the growth of the moral sprouts when they are properly cultivated.

51. Chan, *Instructions*, section, 115.

Chapter 5: Sagehood

1. Mencius wanted everyone to regard sagehood as the ultimate goal, and he believed everyone was capable of attaining the goal. But whether or not he believed everyone would, in the best of societies, become sages is not clear. Wang clearly believed everyone in the ideal society of the golden age was in fact a sage—though their sagehood was manifested in many different ways. Even in his own decadent time, "The streets were filled with sages."

2. *Mencius*, (*HYIS* #17: 46-47/6B/2).

3. Three of Confucius' closest disciples.

4. I follow D. C. Lau's interpretation of Tzu Kung's remarks. See D. C. Lau, *Mencius*, (Penguin Classics, 1983), p. 80.

5. *Mencius*, (*HYIS* #17: 13/2A/2).

6. *Analects*, (*HYIS* #16: 32/15/31). See also *Analects*, (*HYIS* #16: 3/2/15): "Study without thought is wasted; thought without study is dangerous." Waley takes this in a novel way. He believes the first line is a "proverbial saying" to which Confucius offers a rejoinder. See Arthur Waley, *The Analects of Confucius*, (reprint) (New York: Vintage Books, 1938), p. 91, note 3. This is perhaps too clever. I take the point to be: thought without studying *is worse than* studying without thought.

7. *Mencius*, (*HYIS* #17: 45-46/6A/15). For a translation of the entire passage, see above pages 32-33. Another passage of importance is Mencius' conversation with King Hsüan of Ch'i, in which the heart/mind is identified as the measure of right and wrong: "Ch'üan (by weighing) we know what is light and heavy. By measuring we know what is long and short. This is how it is with all things, and, most importantly, with the heart/mind. I ask your majesty to measure your heart/mind." *Mencius*, (*HYIS* #17: 3/1A/7).

8. The 23rd *p'ien* (chapter) of the *Hsün Tzu*— entitled *Hsing O* (Human Nature is Evil)—is an explicit refutation of Mencius' position. For a translation, see Burton Watson, *Hsün Tzu: Basic Writings*, (New York: Columbia University Press, 1963), pp. 157-171.

9. *Hsün Tzu*, (*HYIS* #22: 88/23/36-39, 46-47).

10. Watson, *Hsün Tzu*, p. 158. (*HYIS* #22, 87/23/11).

11. Quoting the *Li Chi* (The Book of Rites), chapter one. For a translation, see Legge, *Li Ki*, Vol. 1; p. 77.

12. *Mencius*, (*HYIS* #17: 29/4A/18). For another example of "weighing the circumstances," see 53/7A/26. The character *ch'üan*, which I translate as "weighing the circumstances," appears in the quote translated in note seven above. There it means literally to weigh something with a balance. But the passage goes on to draw an analogy between this kind of weighing and the weighing of events, which is the proper function the mind.

13. We have no evidence to conclude Mencius ever believed a given rite was *wrong* and should be abandoned. He was searching for interpretations that would show every rite was correct. Only our understanding of the rites or our ability to apply them properly could be mistaken.

14. Mencius' balance between the personal power of moral intuition and the traditional pressure of the rites must not be confused with the modern Western view of justice by laws established through precedents. I mean, by the latter, the notion that a given law is interpreted and its meaning set through the establishment of precedents. Mencius' view could not accommodate the radical change in interpretation characteristic of the latter view. The world could not change to such a degree that a traditional rite should be abandoned or fundamentally changed.

15. *Mencius, (HYIS* #17: 55/7B/3).

16. Mencius quotes approvingly from the *Book of History,* a total of 18 times. Eleven times he introduces the quote with *shu yüeh* (the book says) (see *Mencius, (HYIS* #17: 6/1B/3, 8/1B/11 (2x), 18/3A/1, 23/3B/5 (2x), 24/3B/9, 25/3B/9, 36/5A/4, 48/6B/5, 55/7B/3). He also quotes specific parts of the present *Book of History* by name (see *Mencius* 35/5A/4). This quote is now found in the canon of Yao not—as Mencius says—the Canon of Shun. See Legge, *The Shoo King,* p. 40, 1/1A/2, 12/2A/4 (seen again in 27/4A/9, 24/3B/5 (2x), 36/5A/5). There is also one case of a line, in the present *Book of History,* quoted to Mencius. The person speaking was the Mohist I-chih (see *Mencius* 21/3A/5). It is significant that in all of these cases, the passages quoted can be found, occasionally with slight variations, in the present version of the *Book of History.* And except for the case noted, all citations which name a section within the *Book of History* agree with the present version. (I am indebted to Legge's work on the *Book of History*—see the prolegomena to his translation, pp. 1-15. I owe the passage quoted by I-chih to Professor David S. Nivison).

17. See *Mencius, (HYIS* #17: 6/1B/3, 12/2A/4).

18. See *Mencius, (HYIS* #17: 25/3B/9 and 31/4B/21).

19. As I shall argue in what follows, it is not at all clear that in Confucius' time there was a single text called the *Book of History.* (Legge makes this point in the prolegomena to his translation, p. 3). But there is strong evidence for the claim that a text called the *Book of Poetry* existed in Confucius' time and was central to his school.

20. Confucius quotes the *Book of History* in *Analects (HYIS* #16: 3/2/21) and answers a question posed by a student in 30/14/40.

21. The beginning of the last chapter in the *Analects (HYIS* #16: 41/20/1) is probably not authentic. It is a patchwork of passages. Close correlates are found to several sections in the present *Book of History* (see Legge's note on this section in his translation of the *Analects* page 350). Neither here, nor in the two cases cited in the previous note are the passages found in the *Analects* exactly as they appear in the present version of the *Book of History.*

22. See *Analects (HYIS* #16: 12/7/18).

23. See note #19 above.

24. Confucius quotes from the *Book of Poetry* in *Analects, (HYIS* #16: 2/2/2, 17/9/27, 23/12/10). He paraphrases from it in 12/7/11 cf. *Mao Shih, (HYIS* #9: 45/195/6), and his criticisms of *ch'iao yen* (clever talk) in 1/1/3, 9/2/25, 32/15/27 and 36/17/15 find precedents in *Mao Shih,* 45/194/5 and 47/198/5. In 1/1/3, 9/2/25 and 36/17/15 "clever talk" is coupled with *ling se* (a pleasant manner). The latter

expression also is found in the *Book of Poetry* (*Mao Shih*, 71/260/2) but there it lacks the negative connotation Confucius gave it.

25. For examples, see *Analects* (*HYIS* #16: 4/3/2, 5/3/20, 15/8/15, 36/17/8).

26. See *Analects* (*HYIS* #16: 2/2/2, 25/13/5). The present version of the *Book of Poetry* contains 305 selections.

27. See *Analects* (*HYIS* #16: 5/3/20, 14/8/8, 15/8/15, 36/17/8).

28. *Analects* (*HYIS* #16: 36/17/8). Translation by Legge, *Confucian Analects*, p. 323.

29. *Analects* (*HYIS* #16: 36/17/8).

30. *Analects* (*HYIS* #16: 34/16/13).

31. *Analects* (*HYIS* #16: 4/3/8). Confucius was challenged by Tzu-hsia's questions. As a teacher, this pleased him. Compare his comment about his favorite disciple, Yen Hui, in 19/11/4. Yen Hui was so gifted, he posed no challenge to Confucius.

32. *Mencius*, (*HYIS* #17: 2/1/15).

33. See *Analects* (*HYIS* #16: 25/13/5).

34. See *Analects* (*HYIS* #16: 17/9/27).

35. See *Analects* (*HYIS* #16: 20/11/5). The lines are from *Mao Shih* (*HYIS* #9: 68/256/5). "A flaw in the white-jade scepter may be ground away, but nothing can be done for a flaw in speech." The sentiment is like that expressed in the lines quoted earlier by Tzu-kung and also captures Confucius' characteristic caution about glib speaking. As for Confucius giving his elder brother's daughter to Nan Jung as a wife, an earlier passage tells us Confucius gave him his own daughter (See *Analects*, 7/5/1). He must have been very pleased with Nan Jung!

36. Mencius quoted from the *Book of Poetry* a total of 26 times (See *Mencius*, (*HYIS* #17: 1/1A/2, 3/1A/7, 5/1B/3, 6/1B/3, 7/1B/5 (3x), 12/2A/3, 12/2A/4 (2x), 18/3A/3, 19/3A/3 (2x), 22/3B/1, 25/3B/9, 26/4A/1, 26/4A/2, 27/4A/4, 27/4A/8 (2x), 28/4A/10, 34/5A/2, 35/5A/4, 41/5B/7, 46/6A/17, 56/7B/19).

37. *Mencius*, (*HYIS* #17: 47/6B/3). The ode referred to is *Mao Shih* (HYIS #9: 46/197).

38. *Mencius*, (*HYIS* #17: 43/6A/6) (see also 12/2A/4).

39. The vast, long and rich commentarial tradition of China is chiefly the legacy of Mencius' early efforts.

40. *Mencius*, (*HYIS* #17: 7/1B/8).

41. This question is raised in regard to a passage in the *Analects*. See *Analects* (*HYIS* #16: 19/10/14).

42. *Mencius*, (*HYIS* #17: 42/5B/7).

43. *Mencius*, (*HYIS* #17: 35-36/5A/4). Translation adapted from that of James Legge, *Mencius*, pp. 352-353. Another important example is 47/6B/3 (Legge, *Mencius*, pp. 426-428).

44. Mencius' need to understand and explain the texts of his own tradition is not unlike the need many Christians have felt to understand and explain the Bible. This need continued down through the Confucian tradition. And like the history of Biblical interpretation, it generated a staggering array of interpretations. This continuing process of interpretation is part of what it means *to be in a tradition*.

45. *Mencius*, (*HYIS* #17: 30/4B/1).

46. See *Mencius*, (*HYIS* #17: 24/3B/9).

47. *Mencius, (HYIS* #17: 25/3B/9). For an almost identical case of Mencius making this type claim, see 11/2A/2.
48. *Mencius, (HYIS* #17: 32/4B/24).
49. *Mencius, (HYIS* #17: 37-38/5A/8).
50. I am indebted to the work of W.A.C.H. Dobson and follow his interpretation in both of these passages. He first pointed out the significance of these passages in the introduction to a section of his translation of the *Mencius* (W.A.C.H. Dobson *Mencius*), (Buffalo: University of Toronto Press, 1974), pp. 170-171). In this introduction he also points out that in quoting Confucius, Mencius cites many passages not in the present *Analects*. In fact, the passages Mencius cites that do appear in the present version of the *Analects* are far fewer than those that do not. But for my argument the critical fact is Mencius never *contradicts* a saying he believed came from Confucius.
51. Mencius HYIS #17: 35/5A/4). Translation adapted from that of W.A.C.H. Dobson.
52. Dobson also points out, in the introduction mentioned above, how and in what ways Mencius began the apotheosis of Confucius. This process continued throughout the tradition and led to the "dehumanization" of the Confucius of the *Analects*. For a brief discussion, with examples, of this phenomenon, see Appendix I in Arthur Waley's translation of the *Analects* (Arthur Waley, *The Analects of Confucius*, (New York: Vintage Books, 1938), pp. 71-79.
53. Chan, *Instructions*, section 142. See also sections 179, 313 et al.
54. See Chan, *Instructions*, section 11. The six classics were: the *Book of Changes, Book of History, Book of Poetry, Spring and Autumn Annals, Book of Rites* and the *Book of Music*. The last was lost at the beginning of the Han dynasty—long before Wang's time.
55. Wang did not regard his own thoughts on the classics with any great respect. His disciple, Ch'ien Te-hung, in his preface to Wang's now lost *Opinions on the Five Classics* asked Wang for a copy of the work. Wang responded by saying, "I committed *that* to the flames of Ch'in long ago." See below, p. 106.
56. Quoting Mencius. See above p. 95, note #18.
57. *Analects (HYIS* #16: 32/15/26).
58. *Mencius (HYIS* #17: 55/7B/3).
59. Chan, *Instructions*, section 11.
60. Chan, *Instructions*, section 14.
61. *Hsiang-shan ch'üan-chi* (SPPY ed.) 34:1b. Wang saw Lu as part of the true transmission of the Confucian Way. See below pp. 110-111. For more on Lu, see Siu-chi Huang, *Lu Hsiang-shan: A Twelfth Century Chinese Idealist Philosopher*, (New Haven, 1944).
62. *WWCKCS* 20:632b.
63. The letter begins with six examples, from the classics, in which traditional taboos or rituals were violated and yet the action commended. Two of the cases—Shun's marriage and King Wu's military expedition—are discussed in that part of the passage which I have translated. For the entire letter, See Chan, *Instructions*, section 139.

64. Chan, *Instructions*, section 139.
65. *Tz'u hsin* (this mind): one of Wang's names for the mind in itself.
66. Chan, *Instructions*, section 21.
67. *WWCKCS* 26:742a.
68. Quoting the *Mencius* (*HYIS* #17: 58/7B/33).
69. Quoting the *Shu Ching*. See Wang's preface to Lu Chiu-yüan's collected works, below p. 110, note #88.
70. Cf. the similar situation of Confucius and his disciples described in the *Analects* (*HYIS* #16: 30/15/2).
71. Cf. the well-known gatha of the layman P'ang Yün: "Spiritual understanding and marvelous application are found in carrying water and hauling firewood." *P'ang Yün chü-shih yü-lu* in the *Hsü-tsang ching*: 1 *chi*, 2 *p'ien*, 25 *t'ao*, 1 *ts'e*. The verse can also be found in the *Ching-te Ch'uan-teng lu, TSD* 2076:263b. (I am indebted to Professor Irene T. Bloom for directing me to the original source of this quote. For Lo Ch'in-shun's comments on the verse from P'ang Yün, see Irene T. Bloom, *Knowledge Painfully Acquired* p. 153-154.) Wang's sudden enlightenment occurred in the midst of the mundane chores of everyday life. This is another manifestation of Wang's belief in finding salvation in the here and now.
72. This was their native province.
73. *Nien-p'u, sui* 37, (Spring). *WWCKCS* 32:909b.
74. See the preface above. Wang's reference to the "flames of Ch'in" recalls his earlier discussion of the burning of the books—see above pp. 102-103.
75. A reference to a story in the twenty-sixth chapter of the *Chuang Tzu*. (*HYIS* #20: 75/26/48). For a translation see Burton Watson, *Chuang Tzu*, p. 302.
76. *WWCKCS* 22:668a. Wang believed many of the passages in the *Book of Rites* were "added by later scholars and are not the original text of Confucius." See Chan, *Instructions*, section 11.
77. The *Four Books* were: The *Analects, Mencius, Great Learning* and *Doctrine of the Mean*.
78. The *Great Learning* and *Doctrine of the Mean* were particularly well-suited to Wang's purposes. They did not provide precedents for action—they were not history in his sense of *liang chih's* responses to actual circumstances. In this regard, much of the *Mencius* was also well suited to Wang's task. Mencius' main concern was with the theoretical justification of morality.
79. The significance of this cannot be underestimated. Wang felt no great need to witness his insight by producing traditional commentaries on the classics. When he did comment on the classics, it was always in the context of responding to a particular student's question on some passage from the classics. It was almost as if the classics provided *koans* for Wang's students. This is true of Wang's short essay on the *Great Learning*. It was not composed as a critique of the *Great Learning*; it evolved as responses to particular questions about the text were raised by Wang's students. That is why it is called *Questions on the Great Learning*.
80. This is of course true of every interpreter and dramatically clear to anyone who examines Neo-Confucian commentators. But the genius of Chu Hsi was his ability to produce a *comprehensive interpretation*. He was able to carry the

Confucian tradition in a new direction because his interpretation preserved so much of the tradition. Wang's interpretation was not grounded in the classics. It did not account explicitly for as much of the tradition, and hence it was regarded as unorthodox.

81. This is one of four poems entitled, *Four Hymns to Liang Chih Shown to My Students. WWCKCS* 20:629a.

82. Here, Wang is using Mencius' language: i.e. "get it with the mind." Cf. *Mencius*, (*HYIS* #17: 11/2A/2, 44/6A/7, 46/6A/15).

83. Part of one of Wang's letters to Lo Ch'in-shun. See Chan, *Instructions*, section 173.

84. Ku Hsien-ch'eng (1550-1612). For his biography see L. Carrington Goodrich and Chaoying Fang, (eds.), *Dictionary of Ming Biography*, (New York: Columbia University Press, 1976) Vol. 1, pp. 736-744. For a more detailed study of his thought, which includes a discussion of his criticisms of Wang Yang-ming, see Heinrich Busch, *The Tung-lin Academy*, pp. 97-120.

85. Translation by Heinrich Busch. (*The Tung-lin Academy*, pp. 100-103). Earlier in the same work, (translated by Busch on p. 99) Ku commends the liberating spirit of Wang's teachings, but he warns that such "opening up" can have serious side-effects. At one point, he illustrates the danger by comparing the effects of Wang's teachings with the "opening up" of Hun-tun. The friends of Hun-tun (Primordial Chaos) wanted to show their friendship by "opening up" Hun-tun— providing him apertures through which he could perceive the world. Each day they drilled another hole in him, and on the seventh day he died. For the story, see *Chuang Tzu* (*HYIS* #20: 21/7/33). For a translation, see Burton Watson, *Chuang Tzu*, p. 97.

86. In note 80, above, I suggest this ultimately decided the issue of orthodoxy in favor of the Ch'eng-Chu School over the Lu-Wang School.

87. In the following preface to the complete works of Lu Hsiang-shan, Wang traces a new succession of what he calls "the teaching of the mind." This new orthodoxy establishes Wang as the inheritor of the true transmission of the Way. It opposes the lineage which recognizes the Ch'eng-Chu orthodoxy as the legitimate heir of Confucius' Way. The issue of *tao-t'ung* (the transmission of the Way) came to the fore of Confucian thinking when Chu Hsi first used the term to define a Confucian orthodoxy. For a discussion of Chu Hsi's ideas on this issue, see Wing-tsit Chan, "Chu Hsi's Completion of Neo-Confucianism," *Sung Studies*, 2; no. 1 (1973), pp. 59-90. For a general study, see Julia Ching, "The Confucian Way (Tao) and (Tao-t'ung)," *Journal of the History of Ideas*, 35 (1974), pp. 371-388. Wang's attempt to establish a new transmission—a transmission of the mind—is strikingly similar to the claims in the Ch'an/Zen tradition of a mind-to-mind transmission. It is also similar to the attempt—in the *Platform Sūtra*—to unseat the orthodox, "Northern Ch'an," and establish a new line, "Southern Ch'an," as the true transmission.

88. Quoting the "Counsels of the Great Yü chapter of the *Book of History*. See Legge, *The Chinese Classics*, Vol. 3, pp. 61-62.

89. *Analects* (*HYIS* #16: 30/15/3).

90. *Analects* (*HYIS* #16: 11/6/30).
91. *Analects* (*HYIS* #16: 30/15/3).
92. *Analects* (*HYIS* #16: 11/6/30).
93. *Mencius*, (*HYIS* #17: 53/7A/26).
94. *Mencius*, (*HYIS* #17: 42/6A/4).
95. *Mencius*, (*HYIS* #17: 45/6A/11).
96. *Mencius*, (*HYIS* #17: 45/6a/11).
97. *Mencius*, (*HYIS* #17: 43/6A/6).
98. *WWCKCS* 7:242b-243b. For a complete translation, see Julia Ching, *To Acquire Wisdom*, pp. 206-208.
99. The traditional division of Wang Yang-ming's school into three branches—Che Chung, Chiang Yu and T'ai Chou—represent a geographic rather than a philosophical grouping. This is clear from the fact that Ch'ien Te-hung and Wang Chi are given as the representatives of the Che Chung school. Wang's disciples each went their own separate way after the master's death. One can see them at their best and their worst in the following two articles in *Self and Society*: Takehiko Okada, "Wang Chi and Rise of Existentialism," pp. 121-144; Wm. Theodore De Bary, "Individualism and Humanitarianism in Late Ming Thought," pp. 145-247.
100. Huang Tsung-hsi (1610-1695), the great intellectual historian. For his biography, see Arthur W. Hummel, ed., *Eminent Chinese of the Ch'ing Period*, (Washington: United States Printing Office, 1943), Vol. 1, pp. 351-354.
101. Ch'en Hsien-chang (1428-1500). For his biography, see Goodrich and Fang, *Dictionary*, Vol. 2, pp. 153-156. For his thought, see Jen Yu-wen, "Ch'en Hsien-chang's Philosophy of the Natural," *Self and Society*, pp. 53-92.
102. Kao Chung-hsien (1562-1626). (*tzu*: P'an-lung) of the *Tung-lin Academy*. See Goodrich and Fang, *Dictionary*, Vol. 1, pp. 701-710. See also Busch, *The Tung-lin Academy*, pp. 121-133.
103. Hsüeh Wen-ching (1389-1464). A scholar of the Ch'eng-Chu School. See Goodrich and Fang, *Dictionary*, Vol. 1, pp. 616-619.
104. Lu Ching-yeh (1479-1542). Disciple (twice removed) of Hsüeh Wen-ching. See Goodrich and Fang, *Dictionary*, Vol. 1, pp. 1010-1013.
105. *MJHA*, (*SPPY* ed.), 10:1a.
106. See *Analects* (*HYIS* #16: 11/7/1). See also note 13 of the introduction.

Appendix 1

1. For brief histories of the text, see *YMGTK*, Vol. 2, pp. 13-14, 24-25 and Chan, *Instructions*, pp. 311-316
2. Hsü Ai (1487-1518) *tzu*: Yüeh-jen; *hao*: Heng-shan. For his biography, see *MJHA* 11:3a-4b. The *MJHA* indicates he died in 1517, but according to Wang's *Nien-p'u* (sui 47, 8th month), Hsü died in September of 1518 (see *WWCKCS* 32:932a). Hsü is commonly regarded as Wang's first student, but as Chang Yü-ch'üan has pointed out, Wang formally accepted students as early as 1505—two years before he accepted Hsü (See Chang Yü-ch'üan), "Wang Shou-jen as a Statesman," *Chinese Social and Political Science Review*, Vol. 23, p. 191, n. 107.

3. Yen Hui died in in 32nd year (see the *Analects* (*HYIS* #16: 10/6/3, 20/11/7, 20/11/8, 20/11/9 et al.) Hsü Ai succumbed at the age of 31, awaiting Wang's return from a campaign to suppress bandits (see *WWCKCS* 32:932a).
4. For Hsü's preface, see *WWCKCS* 7a,b.
5. An illusion to a metaphor that appears twice in the *Chuang Tzu*: "a protruding tumor, a dangling wen." See *Chuang Tzu*, chapters 6 and 8 (*HYIS* #20: 18/6/68. 21/8/1).
6. In his preface to his *Chu-tzu wan-nien ting-lun*, Wang quotes a line from a letter Chu wrote in which Chu expressed his regret for early doctrinal mistakes: "I can not atone for the crime of having deceived myself and others." For the preface, see *WWCKCS* 3:160a,b. For a translation, see Chan, *Instructions*, pp. 264-267. For Chu Hsi's letter, see *Chu-tzu wen-chi*, 40:27a.
7. A reference to the *Analects* (*HYIS* #16: 36/17/17).
8. A reference to the *Analects* (*HYIS* #16: 3/2/9).
9. A reference to the *Analects* (*HYIS* #16: 11/7/2).
10. *Li chün su chu*—a reference to the words of Confucius' disciple Tzu-hsia. See the *T'an Kung* chapter of the *Li Chi*; SPPY 2:10b. For a translation, see James Legge, trans., *Li Ki*, reprint, (New York: University Books, 1967), Vol. 1: p. 136. Wang himself used this allusion in a poem. For a translation of the poem, see Julia Ching, *To Acquire Wisdom*, p. 222.
11. *Yi hsing*—said of Wen Wang. See *Shih Ching*, Mao #235.
12. Quoting the *Encouraging Learning* chapter of the *Hsün Tzu* (*HYIS* #22: 1/2/30). For a translation, see Burton Watson, *Hsün Tzu: Basic Writings*, (New York: Columbia University Press, 1963), p. 20.
13. See the above quote of *Analects* 2:9.
14. In his introduction, Hsü says: "...I have prepared this record from things which I have heard on typical days. I have privately shown it to like-minded friends, compared it (with their impressions) and made corrections.." *WWCKCS* 1:56a. For a complete translation of the introduction and a different interpretation of this line, see Chan, *Instructions*, pp. 3-5.
15. The exceptions being the last four items. These concern the status of the classics and their application in study—again topics important for beginning students.
16. See Chan, *Instructions*, pp. 3, 4.
17. See the notes to the translation below.
18. In his introduction to Wang's *Ta Hsüeh Wen*, Ch'ien says: "My teacher, when meeting students for the first time, would always quote the opening chapters of the *Great Learning* and the *Doctrine of the Mean*— in order to illustrate the entire task of sagely learning and to help them enter its path." See *WWCKCS* 26:736a.
19. See *WWCKCS* 1:64a. For Chan's translation, see Chan, *Instructions*, pp. 24-25.
20. Literally, "long ago sank". The line refers to the fact that the "old interpretation" of the *Great Learning*—which Wang claimed to revive—had passed from view with the ascendence of the Ch'eng-Chu school's interpretation (cf. the opening line of Hsü's introduction).
21. See *Great Learning*, chapter 1.
22. See *Doctrine of the Mean*, chapter 20.

23. See *I Ching*, *Shuo-kua chüan*, chapter 1.
24. See *Doctrine of the Mean*, chapter 20.
25. See the *Analects* (*HYIS* #16: 11/6/27 and 16/9/11).
26. From the *Ta-yü mo* chapter of the *Shu Ching*. See James Legge, *The Chinese Classics*, Vol. III: *The Shoo-King*, reprint, (Hong Kong: Hong Kong University Press, 1960), pp. 61-62.
27. The reference is to the *Mencius* (*HYIS* #17: 30/4A/27), where Mencius relates the spontaneous inclination human beings have for moral action to their spontaneous inclination to dance when they hear music: both types of action *are* motivated by joy. (Cf. the *Yüeh-chi* chapter of the *Li Chi*. For a translation, see Legge, *Li Ki*, Vol. II; p. 131.)
28. The last version of the text Wang could have seen was the two-volume version published by Nan Ta-chi in 1524. Unfortunately, no copies of this version are extant today.
29. This is especially true in the case of Ch'ien Te-hung; a man who had a tremendous influence on the form and content of the present text of the *Ch'uan-hsi lu*.
30. As we shall see below, in some versions the title was modified: e.g. *Supplement to the Ch'uan-hsi lu*.
31. See *WWCKCS* 1:7a,b and the second preface in the *YMCS* (*SPPY* ed.).
32. Hsü Ai's original text (including his preface, introduction and postscript) is the shortest *chüan* of the three: Hsüeh K'an's section is about 25% longer than Hsü Ai's and Lu Ch'eng's is almost 50% longer.
33. An old name for Kan-chou in southern Kiangsi Province. The date of the publication (the date when the blocks were cut) is given as: 8th month of the 13th year of Cheng-te (cyclical year *wu-yin*) (sometime between 5 September and 4 October, 1518). For details on Hsüeh K'an's compilation, see Wang's *Nien-p'u*, 47th *sui*; *WWCKCS* 32:932a.
34. As Professor Chan points out, this section includes the only passage that records the words of a disciple. Appropriately—or perhaps ironically—the disciple is Hsü Ai. (See Chan, *Instructions*, p. 45.)
35. For examples, see the following sections in Chan, *Instructions*: 19, 40, 44, 49, 101, 103, 105, 107, 117, 122, 123, 124, 126.
36. 53rd *sui*, 10th month of the 3rd year of Chia-ch'ing (cyclical year *chia-shen*) (between 27 October and 24 November, 1524). *WWCKCS* 34:962b.
37. Yüeh—the name of an ancient state in what is now Chekiang Province—is the literary name for Chekiang. Here it refers specifically to Yüeh-ch'eng—the capital of the ancient state— the modern city of Shao-hsing.
38. For a memorial Wang wrote commemorating the construction of a pavilion at the academy, see *WWCKCS* 7:250a-251b. For a translation, see Ching, *To acquire Wisdom*, pp. 212-214.
39. This view is attributed to Yamamoto Shōichi. See *YMGTK*, Vol. 2, p. 13.
40. This may even be a note that became part of the text. See Chan, *Instructions*, section 68.

41. In wang's *Ch'üan Shu* (Complete Works), the *Ch'uan-hsi lu* appears as Wang's *yü-lu* (Recorded Conversations), but this part of it, strictly speaking, belongs in his *Wen-lu* (Literary Works).
42. See *YMGTK*, Vol. II; p. 17. See Vol. 13, pp. 26-30 for Satō Issai's discussion of the two versions of Nan's work and the relationship between these and Ch'ien's redaction.
43. See Ch'ien's preface to his redaction of Nan's work, *WWCKCS* 2:88a. For a translation, see Chan, *Instructions*, pp. 88-90. Ch'ien wrote this in 1535.
44. Where, strictly speaking, all the letters belong. See the above note.
45. See *WWCKCS* 2:126b-128b. For a translation, see Chan, *Instructions*, pp. 182-186.
46. Whether these passages on education, as well as other material in this part of the *Ch'uan-hsi lu*, were added by Ch'ien or someone else is still a matter of debate. For a brief discussion, see *YMGTK*, Vol. 13, p. 24.
47. This fact, and most of the account that follows, is based on Ch'ien's postscript. See *WWCKCS* 3:158b-159b. For a translation, with a slightly different interpretation, see Chan, *Instructions*, pp. 261-263.
48. The *Wen-lu* was published in 1536. See *WWCKCS* 35:996b.
49. This preface appears in two lesser-known versions of the *Ch'uan-hsi lu*. See *YMGTK* (see Vol. 5, pp. 95-97).
50. Professor Chan claims that Nan Ta-chi's version "came to be known as the *Hsü-k'o Ch'uan-hsi lu*" (see Chan, *Instructions*, p. 314). I assume he bases this remark on the reference to Nan's publication in the *Nien-p'u* (see *WWCKCS* 34:962b). But exactly the same working appears in Ch'ien's preface. In both cases, the words *hsü-k'o* are not part of the title of the work. In any event, the two works should not be confused.
51. Capital of a Prefecture in modern Anhui Province.
52. The academy was founded by Liu Ch'i-tseng (see Wang's *Nien-p'u*, *WWCKCS* 35:1009b). For a discussion of the academy, See *YMGTK* Vol. 2, p. 23.
53. A city in modern Hupei Province.
54. According to Ch'ien's postscript, this was sometime in 1555.
55. According to the postscript, this was sometime between the publication of the *I-yen* (sometime in 1555) and the summer of 1556.
56. He was a student of Wang Yang-ming's thought. His *tzu* was Ssu-wei and his *hao*: Ku-lin.
57. I assume that this was the material that Tseng had added to Ch'ien's original manuscript and that Ch'ien had retained when he edited Tseng's *I-yen*. Since the other selections in the original manuscript were "questions put to the master for correction," there would have been no need to alter any of this material.
58. Nothing more is known about him.
59. A county in present day Hopei Province.
60. The postscript is dated: summer of the 35th year of Chia-ch'ing (cyclical year *ping-ch'en* (1556), fourth month (sometime between 9 May and 6 June).
61. In his use of these metaphors, Ch'ien's postscript clearly echoes Hsü Ai's original preface to the *Ch'uan-hsi lu*,

62. See *WWCKCS* 26:740a.
63. This is included among the prefaces in the *Complete Works* (see *WWCKCS* 15a,b). A complete translation is provided below.
64. Wang's teachings have an uncanny ability to accommodate this kind of revisionism. Hsü Ai's claim that Wang's original prohibition must be interpreted as the response to a particular set of circumstances applies with equal force to Ch'ien's situation.
65. The time Ch'ien was with master in Chekiang, up until Wang left for his final campaign.
66. Quoting the Great Appendix to the *I Ching*, Part I, chapter 12.
67. See note number 11 above.
68. Quoting the *Mencius* (*HYIS* #27: 54/7a/41).
69. A place near Nanking, located on and taking its name from a tributary of the Yangtze. Wang held a minor post there. According to the *Nien-p'u* (*sui* 42), it was during his stay in Ch'u that Wang first began to attract a large following. (see, *WWCKCS* 32:916a).
70. Quoting the *Mencius* (*HYIS* #17: 51/7A/16). Cf. the similar remark made by Hsü Ai in his preface, translated on page 116 above.
71. For example, see Yamashita Ryūji, *Yōmeigaku no kenkyū*, (Tokyo, 1971), Vol. 2, pp. 108-115.
72. Wang's discussion with Ch'ien Te-hung and Wang Chi over the meaning of the *Four-Sentence Teaching* is a famous example of Wang adjudicating such a disagreement. (see Chan, *Instructions*, pp. 241-245).
73. Not coincidentally, his insistence on this approach is most prominent in his early writings and fades as his school grew in popularity.
74. Ch'ien's early concern with a "true record" was quite perceptive. The major schism in Wang's school occurred shortly after his death. It concerned the different interpretations of Ch'ien and Wang Chi concerning the famous *Four-Sentence Teaching*. An important part of their debate revolved around the issue of what Wang had said. Ironically, it became a *textual* as much as an interpretive matter.
75. Actually the process continues. Shih Pang-yao's collection *Yang-ming hsien-sheng chi-yao* (The Essential Works of Wang Yang-ming) (see appendix 2, page 124) is a later attempt, by an admirer of Wang's thought, to isolate his most important works. And modern translations such as Wing-tsit Chan's *Instructions for Practical Living and Other Neo-Confucian Writings by Wang Yang-ming* and Julia Ching's *The Philosophical Letters of Wang Yang-ming* also present selections of Wang's works which reflect the particular interests of the compiler.
76. A later follower of Wang. He compiled the first and most authoritative edition of Wang's complete works.
77. Originally written in 1518. For a discussion of this work, a translation of Wang's preface and Ch'ien's preface to the appendix, see Chan, *Instructions*, pp. 265-267. For the appendix, see *WWCKCS* 3:159b-170a.
78. A later follower of Wang. I assume he was chosen for this honor because he had turned—as Wang claimed Chu Hsi himself had—away from Chu Hsi's early thought and embraced Wang's position in his "mature years."

Appendix 2

1. Frederick Goodrich Henke, trans., *The Philosophy of Wang Yang-ming*, (London and Chicago: The Open Court Publishing Co., 1916); reprint, (New York: Paragon Book Corporation, 1964).

2. For more on the text Henke used, see David S. Nivison, review of *Instructions for Practical Living and Other Neo-Confucian Writings by Wang Yang-ming* by Wing-tsit Chan and *Instructions for Practical Life* by Frederick Goodrich Henke, *Journal of the American Oriental Society* 84, no. 4 (1964), pp. 440-41. Also see the references to Forke and Fung in the following paragraph.

3. Chang Yü-ch'üan, "Wang Shou-jen as a Statesman," *Chinese Social and Political Science Review*, Vol. XXIII, pp. 30-99, 155-257, 319-375, 473-517.

4. Alfred Forke, *Geschichte der neueren chinesischen Philosophie*, (Hamburg: Friederichsen, de Gruyter & Co., 1938), p. 383.

5. Forke did not point out, as Professor Nivison has, that the pagination of the *Ssu-pu ts'ung-k'an* edition differs from the edition Henke used. (It also differs from the edition Chang used which in all probability was the same as that used by Henke.)

6. See Fung Yu-lan, (trans.) Derk Bodde, (Princeton: Princeton University Press, 1953); Vol. II, p. 597, note 1.

7. Nivison, review, p. 440.

8. Chang Yü-ch'üan intended his series of articles to serve as a compliment to Henke's work (see Chang's introduction pages 30-31). He took the next major section of Wang's writing contained in the *Yang-ming hsien-sheng chi-yao*, which bear the title *ching-chi p'ien* (Administrative Writings), as his topic. This explains the title he chose: "Wang Shou-jen as a Statesman."

9. See Henke, *Philosophy*, pp. 47-140.

10. See Wang Tch'ang-tche, *La Philosophie Morale de Wang Yang-ming*, (Shanghai: T'ou-se-we, 1936).

11. See Wang, *La Philosophie*, p. 25.

12. See Fung, *History*, Vol. II, p. 602, note 1.

13. Carsun Chang, *The Development of Neo-Confucian Thought*, (New York: Bookman Associates, 1962); Vol. II, p. 54.

14. See the *Translator's Note* in Chan, *Instructions*, p. xiii.

15. See the *SPPY* edition: 1:2b.

16. See *Lun-yü Ho-shih teng chi-chieh*, (*SPPY* ed.), 1:2a.

17. See the translation on pages 115-116 in Appendix I.

18. See Nivison, review, pp. 440-41.

19. This is the gist of Wang's most famous attack on the evil tendencies of his time: the essay *Pa pen sai yüan* (Pulling up the Root and Stopping up the Source). For a translation, see Chan, *Instructions*, pp. 117-124. See chapter 1 page 23 note 109 for the origin of the title of this essay.

20. Chan, *Instructions*, section 20.

21. See *WWCKCS* 2:116b—2:117a.

22. See the *WWCKCS*, 3:159a.

23. The same idea is expressed in the opening line of the *Analects*: "To *hsi* (practice) what one has *hsüeh* (learned)—is this not a joy!"

24. The title of this work is taken from *Analects* 9:16, Tzu-hsia said, "To study widely, to be resolute of will, to ask pertinent questions and to be self-reflective (chin-ssu)—benevolence lies within this." The passage serves as a succinct description of Chu Hsi's method of self-cultivation: the personal appropriation of moral principles through study and reflection. I have discussed the history of the interpretation of the title of this work and offered a new translation of it in my "Reflections on the *Chin-ssu lu*," *Journal of the American Oriental Society*, 108.2 (1988), pp. 269-275.

25. For the term *chin-ssu*, see the *Analects* (*HYIS* #16: 39/19/6 and 11/6/30). James Legge's translation of and note on the first passage are worth consulting. See Legge, *Confucian Analects* p. 341. For the term *ch'uan-hsi*, see *Analects* 1/1/4.

26. There is one important difference, characteristic of the difference between these two schools. Chu Hsi and Lü Tsu-ch'ien intended their text to be used by isolated individuals for independent study. Hsü Ai compiled his text as a practice manual, for students who has *already studied with Wang*.

Works Cited

Works in Western Languages

Bloom, Irene T. *Knowledge Painfully Acquired*, New York: Columbia University Press, 1987.

Bruce, J. Percy. *Chu Hsi and His Masters*. London: Probsthain, 1923.

Busch, Heinrich. "The Tung-lin Academy and Its Political and Philosophical Significance." *Monumenta Serica* 14 (1949-55): 1-163.

Chan Wing-tsit. "How Buddhistic is Wang Yang-ming?" *Philosophy East and West* 12, no. 3 (1962): 203-215.

———. *Source Book in Chinese Philosophy*. Princeton: Princeton University Press, 1963.

———. trans., *Instructions for Practical Living and Other Neo-Confucian Writings by Wang Yang-ming*. New York: Columbia University Press, 1963.

———. "The Evolution of the Neo-Confucian Concept of *li* as Principle." *Tsing Hua Journal of Chinese Studies* n.s. 4, no. 2 (1964): 123-149.

———. "Chu Hsi's Completion of Neo-Confucianism." *Sung Studies* 2, no. 1 (1973): 59-90.

Chang, Carsun. *The Development of Neo-Confucian Thought*. New York: Bookman Associates, 1962. Vol. 2.

Chang, Yü-ch'üan. "Wang Shou-jen as a Statesman." *Chinese Social and Political Science Review* 23: 30-99, 155-257, 319-375, 473-517. Reprint. Arlington, Va.: University Publications of America, 1975.

Ch'en, Kenneth. *Buddhism in China*. Princeton: Princeton University Press. 1964.

Ching, Julia. trans., *The Philosophical Letters of Wang Yang-ming*. Columbia: University of South Carolina Press, 1973.

———. "The Confucian Way (Tao) and *Tao-t'ung*." *Journal of the History of Ideas* 35 (1974): 371-388.

———. *To Acquire Wisdom: The Way of Wang Yang-ming*. New York: Columbia University Press, 1976.

De Bary, Wm. Theodore. "Buddhism and the Chinese Tradition." *Diogenes*. (Montreal) no. 47 (Fall, 1964): 102-124.

———. "Individualism and Humanitarianism in Late Ming Thought." in Wm. Theodore De Bary. ed., *Self and Society in Ming Thought*. New York: Columbia University Press, 1970: 145-245.

Demieville, Paul. "Le Miroir Spiritual." *Sinologica* 1, no. 2 (1947): 112-137.

Dobson, W.A.C.H. trans., *Mencius*. Buffalo: University of Toronto Press, 1974.

Dubs, Homer H. "Han Yü and the Buddha's Relic: an Episode in Medieval Chinese Religion." *The Review of Religion.* Vol. xi, no. 1 (November 1946): 5-17.

Fingarette, Herbert. *Confucius—the Secular as Sacred.* New York: Harper and Row, 1972.

————. "Following the 'One Thread' of the Analects," *Journal of the American Academy of Religion: Thematic Issue.* Vol. 47, 3s (Sept. 1979): 373-405.

Forke, Alfred. *Geschichte der neueren chinesischen Philosophie.* Hamburg: Friederichsen, de Gruyter & Co., 1938.

Fung Yu-lan (English translation by Derk Bodde). *History of Chinese Philosophy.* Princeton: Princeton University Press, 1953. 2 Vols.

Gallagher, Michael, trans., *Runaway Horses.* New York: Pocket Books, 1975.

Goodrich, L. Carrington and Fang Chao-ying. *Dictionary of Ming Biography.* New York: Columbia University Press, 1976. 2 Vols.

Graham, A.C. *Two Chinese Philosophers*: Ch'eng Ming-tao and Ch'eng Yi-ch'uan. London: Lund Humphries, 1958.

————. "The Background of the Mencian Theory of Human Nature." *Tsing Hua Journal of Chinese Studies.* n.s. 6, 1-2 (1967): 215-274.

————. trans., *The Book of Lieh Tzu.* London: John Murray, 1973.

————. "The *Nung-chia* 'School of the Tillers' and the Origins of Peasant Utopianism in China." *Bulletin of the School of Oriental and African Studies* 42, no. 1 (1979): 66-100.

Hakeda, Yoshita S. trans., *The Awakening of Faith.* New York: Columbia University Press, 1967.

Henke, Frederick Goodrich. trans., *The Philosophy of Wang Yang-ming.* London and Chicago: The Open Court Publishing Co., 1916. Reprint. New York: Paragon Book Corporation, 1964.

Hopkins, Jeffrey. *Meditation on Emptiness.* London: Wisdom Publications, 1983.

Huang, Siu-chi. *Lu Hsiang-shan*: *A Twelfth Century Chinese Idealist Philosopher.* New Haven, 1944.

Hucker, Charles O. "The Tung-lin Movement of the Late Ming Period." in John K. Fairbank. ed., *Chinese Thought and Institutions.* Chicago: University of Chicago Press, 1957.

Hummel, Arthur W. ed., *Eminent Chinese of the Ch'ing Dynasty.* Washington: United States Printing Office, 1943-1944. 2 Vols. Reprint. Taiwan, 1970. 1 Vol.

Ivanhoe, Philip J. "One Vision Two Views: Mencius and Wang Yang-ming on Human Nature and Self-Cultivation." Paper presented at the 37th annual meeting of the *Association for Asian Studies*, Philadelphia (24 March 1985).

———. "Reflections on the *Chin-ssu lu*." *Journal of the American Oriental Society*. 108.2 (1988): 269-275.

———. "Reweaving the 'one thread' of the *Analects*". *Philosophy East and West* 40.1 (January 1990): 17-33.

Jayatilleke, K. N. *Early Buddhist Theory of Knowledge*. London: George Allen and Unwin Ltd., 1963.

Jen, Yu-wen. "Ch'en Hsien-chang's Philosophy of the Natural." in Wm. Theodore De Bary. ed., *Self and Society in Ming Thought*. New York: Columbia University Press, 1970: 53-92.

Jung, Hwa Yol. "Wang Yang-ming and Existential Phenomenology." *International Philosophical Quarterly*. Vol. 5, no. 4 (December 1965): 612-636.

Lau, D. C. "Theories of Human Nature in Mencius and Shyuntzyy." *Bulletin of the School of Oriental and African Studies*. 15 (1953): 541-565.

———. "A Note on *ko wu*." *Bulletin of the School of Oriental and African Studies*. Vol. 30 (1967): 353-357.

———. trans., *Mencius*. Baltimore: Penguin Books, 1970.

Legge, James. trans., *Yi King*. In F. Max Müller. ed., *The Sacred Books of the East*. Oxford: Clarendon Press, 1882. Vol. xvi.

———. trans., *Li Ki*. Reprint. New York: University Books, 1967. 2 Vols.

———. trans., *Confucian Analects. The Chinese Classics*. Vol. I. Reprint. Hong Kong: Hong Kong University Press, 1970.

———. trans., *The Great Learning. The Chinese Classics*. Vol. I. Reprint. Hong Kong: Hong Kong University Press, 1970.

———. trans., *The Doctrine of the Mean. The Chinese Classics*. Vol. I. Reprint. Hong Kong: Hong Kong University Press, 1970.

———. trans., *The Works of Mencius. The Chinese Classics*. Vol. II. Reprint. Hong Kong: Hong Kong University Press, 1970.

———, trans., *The Shoo King. The Chinese Classics*. Vol. III. Reprint. Hong Kong: Hong Kong University Press, 1970.

Liu, James T. C. "An Early Sung Reformer: Fan Chung-yen." in John K. Fairbank. ed., *Chinese Thought and Institutions*. Chicago: University of Chicago Press, 1957.

Makra, Sister Mary Lelia. trans., *The Hsiao Ching*. Reprint. New York: St. John's University Press, 1961.

Mei, Y. P. trans., *The Ethical and Political Works of Motse*. London: Arthur Probsthain, 1929.

Monroe, Donald J. "The Origin of the Concept of *Te*." in *The Concept of Man in Early China*. Stanford: Stanford University Press, 1969): 185-197.

Mou Tsung-san. "The Immediate Successor of Wang Yang-ming: Wang Lung-hsi and his Theory of *ssu-wu*." *Philosophy East and West* 23, no. 1 & 2 (January and April, 1973).

Needham, Joseph. *Science and Civilization in China*. Vol. 2. Cambridge: Cambridge University Press, 1956.

Nivison, David S. Review of *Instructions for Practical Living and Other Neo-Confucian Writings by Wang Yang-ming* by Wing-tsit Chan and *Instructions for Practical Life* by Frederick Goodrich Henke. *Journal of the American Oriental Society* 84, no. 4 (1964): 440-41.

————. "Moral Decision in Wang Yang-ming: The Problem of Chinese 'existentialism'." *Philosophy East and West*. 23 (1973): 121-138.

————. "Royal 'Virtue' in Shang Oracle Inscriptions." *Early China*. no. 4 (1978-79): 52-55.

————. "Mencius and Motivation." *Journal of the American Academy of Religion Thematic Issue*. xlvii, 3s (September 1979): 418-432.

————. "Two Roots or One?" *Proceedings and Addresses of the American Philosophical Association*. 53, 6 (1980): 739-761.

————. *Golden Rule Arguments in Chinese Moral Philosophy*. 1984. Paper presented as the annual Evans-Wentz lecture, Stanford University, Stanford, CA.

Okada, Takehiko. "Wang Chi and the Rise of Existentialism." in Wm. Theodore de Bary. ed., *Self and Society in Ming Thought*. New York: Columbia University Press, 1970: 121-144.

Paul, Diana. *The Buddhist Feminine Ideal: Queen Śrīmālā and the Tathāgatagarbha*. Missoula: Scholar's Press, 1980.

Riegel, Jeffrey. "Reflections on an Unmoved Mind: An Analysis of Mencius 2A2." *Journal of the American Academy of Religion Thematic Issue*. xlvii, 3s (1979): 433-458.

Sakai, Tadao. "Confucianism and Popular Educational Works." in Wm. Theodore De Bary. ed., *Self and Society in Ming Thought*. New York: Columbia University Press, 1970: 331-336.

Suzuki, D. T. trans., *The Lankāvatāra Sūtra*. London: Routledge and Kegan, 1978.

Tu Wei-ming. *Neo-Confucian Thought in Action*. Berkeley: University of California Press, 1976.

Waley, Arthur. trans., *The Analects of Confucius*. New York: Vintage Books, 1938.

Wang Tch'ang-tche. *La Philosophie Morale de Wang Yang-ming*. Shanghai: T'ou-se-we, 1936.

Warren, Henry Clarke. trans., *Buddhism in Translations*. Reprint. New York: Atheneum, 1979.

Watson, Burton. trans., *Hsün Tzu: Basic Writings*. New York: Columbia University Press, 1963.

————. trans., *Mo Tzu: Basic Writings*. New York: Columbia University Press, 1963.

————. trans., *The Complete Works of Chuang Tzu*. New York: Columbia University Press, 1968.

Wayman, Alex and Hideko. trans., *The Lion's Roar of Queen Srīmālā*. New York: Columbia University Press, 1974.

Wheately, Paul. *The Pivot of the Four Quarters: A Preliminary Enquiry into the Origins and Character of the Ancient Chinese City*. Chicago: Aldine Publishing Co., 1971.

Wright, Arthur F. *Buddhism in Chinese History*. Stanford: Stanford University Press, 1959.

————. ed., *Confucianism and Chinese Civilization*. Stanford: Stanford University Press, 1964.

Yearley, Lee H. "Teachers and Saviors." *The Journal of Religion* 65, no. 2 (April 1985): 225-243.

Works in Chinese, Japanese or Korean

Analects. HYIS. Supplement No. 16. *A Concordance to the Analects of Confucius*. Reprint. Taipei: Ch'eng-wen Publishing Company, 1972.

Araki Kengo, Okada Takehiko, Yamashita Ryūji, Yamanoi Yū, eds. *Yōmeigaku Taikei* (An Outline of Wang Yang-ming Learning). Tokyo: Meitoku shuppansha,1972. 12 Vols.

Chang-tzu ch'üan-shu (Complete works of Chang Tsai). Reprint. (*SPPY* ed.).

Ching-te Ch'uan-teng lu (The Ching-te Record of the Transmission of the Lamp). Reprint. *TSD*. 2076.

Ch'ong, In-bo. *Yangmy'onghak y'ollon* (A Survey of Wang Yang-ming Learning). Seoul: Sams'ong munhwa chaedan, 1975.

Chu Hsi. *Lun-yü chi-chu* (Collected Commentaries on the Analects). In *Ssu-shu chi-chu* (Collected Commentaries on the Four books). Reprint. (*SPPY* ed.).

————. *Chu Tzu wen-chi* (The Collected Works of Chu Hsi). Reprint. (*SPPY* ed.).

Chuang-tzu. HYIS. Supplement No. 20. *A Concordance to the Chuang Tzu*. Cambridge Massachusetts: Harvard University Press, 1956.

Fan Wen-ch'eng kung chi (Collected Works of Fan Chung-yen). Reprint. (*SPTK* ed.).

Fung Yu-lan. *Chung-kuo che-hsüeh shih* (A History of Chinese Philosophy). (Shanghai: Chung-kuo shu-chü, 1939).

Han Ch'ang-li chi (Collected Works of Han Yü). Reprint. Basic Sinological Series.

Ho-nan Ch'eng-shih i-shu (The Literary Legacy of Ch'eng Hao and Ch'eng Yi). In *Erh-Ch'eng ch'üan-shu (Complete Works of the Two Ch'engs)*. Reprint. (*SPPY* ed.).

Ho-nan Ch'eng-shih wai-shu (Additional Works of Ch'eng Hao and Ch'eng Yi). In *Erh-Ch'eng ch'üan-shu* (Complete Works of the Two Ch'engs). Reprint. (*SPPY* ed.).

Hsiang-shan ch'üan-chi (The Complete Works of Lu Hsiang-shan). Reprint. (*SPPY* ed.).

Hsün Tzu. HYIS. Supplement No. 22. *A Concordance to the Hsün Tzu.* Reprint. Taipei: Ch'eng-wen Publishing Company, 1966.

Huang Tsung-hsi. *Sung Yüan hsüeh-an* (A Critical Account of the Sung and Yüan Dynasties). Reprint. (*SPPY* ed.).

———. *Ming-ju hsüeh-an* (A Critical Account of Confucians in the Ming Dynasty). Reprint. (*SPPY* ed.).

Kim Kir-hwan. *Han'guk Yangmy'onghak y'on'gu* Studies in Korean Wang Yang-ming Learning). Seoul: Ilchisa, 1984.

Liu-tsu ta-shih fa-pao t'an-ching. (*TSD* ed.). 2008:353b.

Lun-yü Ho-shih teng chi-chieh (Collected Explanations on the Analects by Master Ho and Others). Reprint. (*SPPY* ed.).

Mishima Yukio. *Kakumei tetsugaku to shite no Yōmeigaku* (Wang Yang-ming Learning as a Philosophy of Revolution). *Shokun.* (Sept. 1970): 22-45.

Mencius. HYIS. Supplement No. 17. *A Concordance to the Meng Tzu.* Reprint. Taipei: Ch'eng-wen Publishing Company, 1973.

Mo Tzu. HYIS. Supplement No. 21. *A Concordance to the Mo Tzu.* Reprint. Taipei: Ch'eng-wen Publishing Company, 1974.

Mou Tsung-san. "Wang-hsüeh te fen-hua yü fa-chan" (The Dissemination and Development of Wang Yang-ming Learning). *Hsin-ya shu-yüan hsüeh-shu nien-k'an.* Vol. 14. (1972).

P'ang Yün chü-shih yü-lu (The Sayings of Layman P'ang Yün). In *Hsü-tsang ching* (The Chinese Tripitika). Reprint Hong Kong, 1967.

Shih Pang-yao, *Yang-ming hsien-sheng chi-yao* (The Essential Works of Master Wang Yang-ming). Reprint. (*SPTK* ed.).

Wang Yang-ming. *Ch'u-k'o Ch'uan-hsi lu* (Original Edition of *A Record for Practice*). Compiled by Hsüeh K'an (d. 1545). Nan Kan: 1518.

———. *Ch'uan-hsi hsü-lu (Further Records for Practice). Compiled by Ch'ien Te-hung (1496-1574). Ning-kuo: 1555.*

———. *Hsü-k'o Ch'uan-hsi lu* (Supplement to *A Record for Practice*). Compiled by Nan Ta-chi (1487-1541). The original edition, printed somewhere in Chekiang in 1524, is now lost. The edition that is today known by this name is an amended version, printed in Te-an Fu in 1544.

————. *Wang Wen-ch'eng-kung ch'üan-shu* (The Complete Works of Wang Yang-ming). Compiled by Hsieh T'ing-chieh (*fl.* 1572). Reprint. (*SPTK* ed.).

————. *Yang-ming ch'üan-shu* (The Complete Works of Wang Yang-ming). (Same as the *WWCKCS*. It appears under this name in the *SPPY* ed.).

————. *Yang-ming hsien-sheng chi-yao* (The Essential Works of Master Wang Yang-ming). Compiled by Shih Pang-yao (1585-1644). Reprint. (*SPTK* ed.).

————. *Yang-ming hsien-sheng wen-lu* (The Literary Works of Master Wang Yang-ming). Compiled by Ch'ien Te-hung. Reprint. (*SPTK* ed.).

Yamashita Ryūji. *Yōmeigaku no kenkyu* (A Study of Wang Yang-ming Learning). Tokyo, 1971. 2 Vols.

Yun, Nam-han. *Chos'on sidae ui Yangmy'onghak y'ongu* (Studies in the Korean Phase of Wang Yang-ming Learning). (Seoul, Chimmundang, 1982).

Index